I AM NOBODY'S SLAVE

Lee Hawkins

I AM NOBODY'S SLAVE

HOW UNCOVERING MY FAMILY'S HISTORY SET ME FREE

AMISTAD

An Imprint of HarperCollinsPublishers

This is a work of nonfiction. The events and experiences detailed herein are all true and have been faithfully rendered as I have remembered them, to the best of my ability. Some names, identities, and circumstances have been changed in order to protect the integrity and/or anonymity of the various individuals involved. Though conversations come from my keen recollection of them, many are not written to represent word-for-word documentation; rather, I've retold them in a way that evokes the real feeling and meaning of what was said, in keeping with the true essence of the mood and spirit of the event. Some of the conversations are direct quotes from recorded interviews and interactions.

HarperCollins books may be purchased for educational, business, or sales promotional use. For information, please email the Special Markets Department at SPsales@harpercollins.com

FIRST EDITION

Library of Congress Cataloging-in-Publication Data has been applied for.

ISBN 978-0-06-282316-8

24 25 26 27 28 LBC 5 4 3 2 1

This book is dedicated to my father, Lee Roy Hawkins Sr., and all the other Black American survivors of Jim Crow apartheid and their descendants, especially the children.

Go back to where you started, or as far back as you can, examine all of it, travel your road again and tell the truth about it. Sing or shout or testify or keep it to yourself: but know whence you came.

—JAMES BALDWIN, *Go Tell It on the Mountain* (1953)

CONTENTS

A NOTE ON LANGUAGE AND TERMINOLOGY

As I share the story of my family, tracing our history back to my great-great-great-grandmother and those who came before and after her, I want to address the language used in this book. Many of my ancestors were Black and endured the horrors of enslavement. For them, I prefer to use the term "enslaved" because it reflects that slavery was something forced upon them—not something that defined them. This distinction is important to me, as it honors the strength, resilience, and dignity of those who came before me, ensuring that their legacy is seen for the courage and greatness it truly represents.

In accordance with Amistad's policy, we will be using "enslavement" instead of "slavery" wherever possible. Initially, I intended to put the word "slave" in quotes to reflect my discomfort with the term. However, after thoughtful discussions with my editor and editorial team, we agreed that while "enslaved" is the more accurate and respectful term, there are moments when using "slave" may be more practical for the flow of the narrative. This decision was made with deep respect for my ancestors and the horrific and complex history they lived through.

On a related note, I want to explain my choice of terminology when referring to the Muscogee people. After consulting with experts who have studied the history and culture for decades, I will be using the term "Creek" in this book, as it has been traditionally recognized and is still acknowledged by many members of the community. However, in some instances, I will also use "First Nations" and "Indigenous" to honor their status as the original inhabitants of this land. My preference for these terms reflects my deep respect for the Muscogee as a people, and I have striven to tell the story of their involvement with my family with the utmost sensitivity and love.

As you read this book, please know that every word was chosen with care, with an unwavering commitment to honoring the history, strength, and enduring legacy of my family and the communities connected to it. Thank you for joining me on this deeply personal journey through our shared history.

I AM NOBODY'S SLAVE

PART 1

Black Boy in Maplewood, USA

Hawkins

was raised to revere being a Hawkins.

It exemplifies our Black power and pride—an inheritance for those blessed to bear this name.

From the day my legs were too short to touch the footrest of the chair at Mr. Harper's Barbershop in the heart of St. Paul's historic Rondo neighborhood, that message was drummed into me. This haven for Black men was a hub of stories that seemed to reverberate through every soul waiting for a trim. And even fifteen years later, it still resounded in my brain when I heard the words "Lee Roy Hawkins Jr." boom through the loudspeaker as I walked out in my long-tail tuxedo, marking the pinnacle of my senior year Beautillion gala in 1989.

The Beautillion, a male version of a debutante ball, introduced young men transitioning into the Black men we were groomed to become.

At every stage, my father, my grandfathers, and every other Black man I looked up to—from the barbers who perfected my flattop at Mr. Harper's to the ninety-year-old church deacons who took communion to sick and shut-in congregants every first Sunday—reinforced this theme: a Black man's name was a gift from his ancestors. The Hawkins name, they said, was to be celebrated and protected, always with an eye toward advancing the bloodline for future generations.

"Lee-Lee," they told me, "always take pride in your family, because your name is all you have. Uplift it and protect it."

These World War II and Vietnam veterans, Pullman porters, doctors, autoworkers, custodians, bricklayers, preachers, city councilmen, school principals, lawyers, and human resources executives bombarded me with so many mantras about Black male dignity that failure wasn't an option.

"Keep your head up, Black man. You come from greatness, Black man," I heard, again and again. "We hail from African kings and queens. We are strong, proud Black men, and we carry our names with dignity, honor, and excellence."

Most of these role models, with their steam-cleaned three-piece suits on Sundays, firm handshakes, one-arm hugs, and declarations of "I can do all things through Christ," had similar stories. They had left places like Mississippi, Alabama, Tennessee, and Louisiana in pursuit of better opportunities in a faraway northern Promised Land called Minnesota.

They stood upright and kept mahogany cigar cutters and gold-plated pocket watches in their suit vests, with American flag pins on their lapels and Masonic rings on their pinky fingers. Their reading glasses hung from gold chains, down over their cherry-red silk power ties. These elders spoke with a powerful, sometimes intimidating regality, a commanding confidence that, from the time I was a little boy, I came to associate with being a Black man. The belief that I was representing and embodying the Black community every single day meant I had to look the part. As I grew older, my father's patience for seeing me in gym shoes waned, unless I was headed to the gym or playing outdoors. For him, "tennis shoes" were reserved for sports. Dress shoes, always well-polished, were for business and school—and to him, school was serious business.

When I was six, my father gifted me a handcrafted wooden shoeshine box and taught me the art of spit-shining to perfection, so that my shoes proclaimed "Lee Hawkins Jr." to the world. I grew fond of brogue shoes, or wingtips as they're called in America. These shoes, distinguished by their unique perforated patterns resembling bird wings, trace their origins back to sixteenth- and seventeenth-century Scotland and Ireland. Although we thought our heritage wasn't at all European, their shoes filled our closets, seamlessly blending into our family story.

Names, like the polished shoes I wore, carry histories that beckon us to probe deeper into their origins. Even if I didn't know much about the Hawkins name and where it came from, my father, whom I idolized, made me proud to carry it. The name on my birth certificate is Lee Roy Hawkins Jr. When I was growing up, almost no one ever called me Lee Roy, because that's what my father's friends and family and my mom called him. As an elementary school student, the only exception came on the Sundays when I had to get up in front of the whole congregation of four hundred people and welcome the visitors to our church, Mount Olivet Missionary Baptist. On those days, my name always appeared in the church bulletin as "Lee Roy Hawkins Jr.—Welcome of Visitors."

I performed this task at the request of my beloved Sunday school teacher, Deaconess Verda Williams. Known for her fanciful, fabulous hats, white gloves, and color-coordinated outfits, the deaconess always gave me a week's notice. But I can't remember a time after she called that I didn't end up spending Saturday night in front of the bathroom mirror, practicing my delivery as hard as I could. Mount Olivet's youth knew that the elders in our congregation expected us to make them proud. My biggest fear was flubbing my lines, embarrassing myself, and disappointing my family in front of hundreds of Black folks.

My greatest loyalty and sense of duty were to my father. He coached my older sister Tammi's softball team and was the musical director of our seven-piece Soul/R&B group, the Jack and Jill Kids. Additionally, he led the Mount Olivet Youth Ensemble, a teen contemporary gospel group in which I served as the drummer and lead singer. Our group also featured a flutist and even a conga player. Every third Saturday, I accompanied Dad and my mother's dad, Grandpa Buddy, to the Brotherhood Breakfast, where we ate and talked sports, politics, and Christianity with other Black men and their sons and grandsons. We spent two nights a week playing hoops and working out at local gyms, mainly the YMCA. During summers and on Saturdays during the school year, I fished for sunnies and croppies with Dad, Grandpa Buddy, and Great-Grandpa Sam Davis (my mother's grandfather). We fished everywhere, from Lake Minnetonka—where, in the movie *Purple Rain*, the Minnesota legend Prince famously tells his girlfriend to purify herself—to the lake in front of Great-Grandpa Sam's vacation cabin just across the Wisconsin border.

At the time, I didn't think twice about having three generations of patriarchs around me, probably because most of the Black boys I knew also had theirs. It was only when I was older that I realized my upbring-ing ran counter to the pervasive and false belief that Black men rarely play a part in their children's lives. A 2013 survey conducted by the Cen-ters for Disease Control and Prevention revealed that Black fathers are more likely than their white and Hispanic counterparts to eat with, feed, diaper, bathe, play with, dress, and read to their children daily.

The fathers I knew in the church and around the Rondo commu-nity invested everything in their kids.

It seemed that, like me, five or six out of every ten Black boys I knew at church were named after their fathers. So many of us were called Ju-nior or Tre. I didn't know a single Black kid named Jim, Mike, or Rick. In the 1970s and 1980s, Black boys with those names were James, Michael, or Richard. We were being trained to excel past the previous generations, so our names needed to be as formal as possible. Being a namesake added an extra layer of gravity to the notion that a "Black man's name is every-thing." Singing and playing drums with a father who was a gospel singer and guitarist didn't exactly lessen the pressure. But singing in churches, I met a lot of preachers' kids. And believe me, they carried an even heavier weight when it came to their names.

In my father's case, the significance of a Black male's name stands out in an inverted way. For reasons it took me years to figure out, the white people at Dad's job called him Leo instead of Lee Roy, the name his parents gave him. In every business setting, the name that the white people used was the one that stood. Similarly, I was known as Lee-Lee by my family and the members of our all-Black church. But in Maplewood, the 99 percent white suburb where my parents had moved when I turned four and where we lived, the teachers and white kids at school called me Lee Hawkins. And that name, in every formal or business setting, is the one that stands.

On some days, while riding my orange Skyhawk bicycle through the winding dirt trails near our house or looking for the flattest rock to skip over the muddy-green pond just a few blocks away, I'd ponder the name Hawkins.

Where, and whom, did it come from? Certainly, none of the Afri-can kings and queens we supposedly descended from carried our family names—Hawkins, Pugh, Blakey, and Davis—though you wouldn't have known that from the way my dad and grandfathers comported themselves at church. Clearly, the Lee-Lee version of Lee Hawkins Jr. didn't know anything about the origins of the Hawkins and Pugh names on my father's side of the family, or the Blakey and Davis names on my mother's side. All I knew was that the paternal names came from somewhere in Alabama and the maternal names from Yankton, South Dakota, and either Kansas or Missouri.

The Blakeys were the family of my mom's father, Zackarious "Buddy" Blakey. Since the Blakeys were widely hailed as one of the first Black families to move to South Dakota from the South in the early 1900s, I knew a lot about them.

Grandpa Buddy's first cousin Ted Blakey still lived in Yankton, the town the Blakeys settled in back then—on the Missouri River, just north of the Nebraska border. When I was growing up in the seventies and eighties, the family still had farms and acreage in the area, so every few summers we'd convene in Yankton for big family reunions. Cousin Ted had an accent like the one in the movie *Fargo* and an encyclopedic knowledge of Black history, especially concerning our family and Black settlement in South Dakota. He was also the state's official "Black historian" and founded South Dakota's branch of the NAACP, which impressed me as much as a kid could be impressed.

The Minnesota contingent—in all, about forty men, women, and children, from Grandpa Buddy and his eleven siblings down to babies-in-arms—would pile into a caravan of Cadillacs and Lincoln Continentals and roll west to Yankton. We could always count on Mom and my grandfather's wife, my cherished Aunt Loyce—who was much younger than he—(she was nobody's aunt, but she was too young for us to call her our step-grandmother), to pack ice-cold fried chicken in a paper bag and sodas in a cooler in the trunk.

Grandpa Buddy loved road tripping and using his booming bass voice to provide more bottom to the best gospel sound an eight-track could produce, from Rev. Clay Evans and James Cleveland to the Mighty Clouds of Joy and the Five Blind Boys of Alabama, all the way down I-90.

The minute we reached Yankton, we'd be greeted by the flickering sign of the local Holiday Inn: "Welcome Blakey, Blakely, White Family Reunion." My sisters and I usually hit the pool on the first night. The next day, we'd run through the fields on the family farm with cousins who made us feel we were looking into a mirror, always keeping a healthy distance from the wild turkeys and farm-raised chickens squawking around the barn. In the evening, we'd head back to the hotel to yawn through Cousin Ted's slide presentations on family history. Back then, I was more interested in playing hide-and-seek behind bales of hay and on farming tractors than I was in studying a family tree that traced "back to the slave days." In truth, I barely listened to any of it. All I knew was that "some of our people from way back in the 1800s were slaves, and the Blakey family was one of the first Black families to settle in South Dakota."

To be fair, I'd already heard the highlights of this history from Grandpa Buddy. In those days, he was more open about his family history than Dad was about his.

Because Dad talked so little about Alabama, on the rare occasions that he did, I paid attention. Once a year or so, as we cast rods and watched bobbers on the banks of one of Minnesota's "10,000 lakes," he'd reminisce about the all-Black barbershops and soda fountains back in Alabama, or the thrill of playing Little League baseball in the afternoon on the same field that Negro League great Satchel Paige played on at night. Brief as Dad's musings were, I found just one of them far more intriguing than a dozen of Grandpa Buddy's yarns about farm life "in the olden days."

The most head-scratching detail about the Blakey family was our three names. How could the descendants of the same siblings from one family end up with three different last names? I was always told that it had to do with enslavement. Back then, I was satisfied with that answer, especially since it seemed like the "whole enslavement thing" had happened a million years ago and had nothing to do with me.

Still, for a boy with a reputation for asking too many questions and occasionally sticking his nose too far into "grown folks' business," my lack of interest surprised even me.

Regardless, I upheld tradition by taking pride in my family names— all of them. Questioning the wisdom of my elders was blasphemy in my family.

The Bleeding Tongue

S omewhere, packed away in a closet, drawer, or dusty attic, there's a book with a canary-yellow binding that chronicles my life, up to my enrollment in preschool. I remember holding that "baby book" with my young mother as she sat with four-year-old me on our black Chesterfield sofa and read aloud her joyous descriptions of her wildly energetic, playful baby boy.

"Every day, Lee-Lee gets stronger and stronger," she wrote. "He doesn't know his strength. We gave him a new nickname: Bamm-Bamm"—the super-strong adopted son of Barney and Betty Rubble, the next-door neighbors of Fred and Wilma Flintstone in my favorite cartoon show. Hearing that, along with my mother's tinkling laughter as she read, told me that she loved and valued me.

These sessions with the baby book—which chronicled the antics of a fast-footed early walker-turned-explorer known for opening forbidden cabinets and darting around the house at dizzying speeds—became less and less frequent as time passed, and they disappeared entirely about a year before I entered first grade. My attention shifted to a book Grandpa Buddy bought me about John Henry, a Black folk hero who was so fast, so strong, and so powerful that he could drill a hole through a rock faster than a steam drill could.

I became enthralled by this Black man. He reminded me of my grandfathers Buddy and Sam and their seemingly boundless strength. Reading that book, I became impatient, eager to grow muscles, get massive, and be the fastest, strongest, most industrious man ever to sling a sledgehammer. Even so, I still liked to page through the baby book between bouts of bug-collecting and ball-throwing. But I no longer did it with my mother, and only when she wasn't around.

I'm not sure when or why my mother's enthusiasm about her high-spirited, gregarious little boy began to wane. But somewhere along the line, her joy with regard to me, and the magical bond we forged while poring over those pages, vanished. Looking back, I believe that my mother was being overtaken by flashes of grief that she and my dad had to stop coddling their Black son and start preparing him for the stringent rules of the racist society that awaited him in adolescence and beyond. I could sense both, in their individual ways, pushing me swiftly through the various boyhood rites of passage.

At the time, I didn't mourn the maternal distancing. I didn't even note the absence of the baby book. But I do remember why, even as a preschooler, I cherished its contents, which included my mother's account of moving back to Minnesota in 1973 after my father completed his air force duty. Then twenty-three, my parents rented the spacious top floor of a brown-brick duplex on Dale Street in the Rondo neighborhood. Tammi was three; I was almost one.

My baby book is firsthand proof that my parents once encouraged me to be free: to meander and explore, to question and break rules, and to speak my mind, even if I had just begun to find the language to express my thoughts and wants. I was happy and relieved to discover Mom's gleeful entries, as my own earliest memory is dramatically different.

My first fully formed memory is that of my dad chasing me around the duplex as I darted across a hardwood floor, seized by terror. I don't remember what I'd done, but I knew I'd better run for my life. My father's anger was almost as intense as my fear, and as he chased me, his tongue hung out of his mouth. Once he caught me, he folded his tongue and started biting down on it, just as he began whacking me, repeatedly, as hard as he could.

From that point onward, whenever I felt rage coming on, I unconsciously mimicked my father, folding my tongue between my teeth and biting down on it. Sure, I remember moments of childhood joy as I rode my Big Wheel in never-ending circles around the patio or shaped and threw glow-in-the-dark slime and Play-Doh with my sisters and neighborhood playmates. And even minutes after being slapped around at age three, I could always find something to smile about. But my parents' example was chillingly powerful: I, too, exploded quickly into rage, hitting back at toddlers who bullied me, and bullying others whom I pounced on as scapegoats for my free-floating animosity. With every meltdown, I folded and bit my tongue; even today, no matter how hard I try to suppress the urge, anger triggers me to fold my tongue. The habit is so deeply entrenched in my subconscious that I doubt I will ever be rid of it.

Me and my two sisters, Tammi and Tiffany, at various times attended the Martin Luther King Center, a nursery school in St. Paul. On the days we weren't at the King Center, our parents sent us to a sweet, matronly babysitter we called Granny. A close family friend who lived near my great-grandparents' house back in Rondo, Granny watched a lot of Rondo kids.

Once, when I was in first or second grade, I was playing indoor football in the playroom at Granny's with my cousin. As we were both trying to tackle the other, I folded and bit down on my tongue so hard my teeth punctured it, causing a nasty gash. Blood filled my mouth, dripping all over my shirt and onto the floor. At the doctor's office later, he told us there was no treatment for a tongue puncture; I would just have to wait a few weeks for it to heal.

Maplewood, USA

With the fire of my father's temper burning inside me, I entered the sacred halls of the King Center. For me, the King Center was akin to a church, a place where my identity and perception of myself as a Black boy began to take shape. Even at the tender age of four, I felt enveloped in a panoramic display of Black Americans who instilled in me a profound sense of pride in both my skin color and my heritage. Everything around me in both my church and the King Center whispered that Blackness was synonymous with freedom.

The staff at the King Center brought in a variety of notable Black celebrities to address us, including Rod Carew, the baseball star from the Minnesota Twins, and Alan Page, the defensive tackle for the Minnesota Vikings who would later serve as an associate justice on the Minnesota Supreme Court. I vividly recall encountering Dr. King's widow, Coretta Scott King, who gave a speech there, just a stone's throw away from where I once played ball as a child.

Every classroom wall was adorned with vibrant depictions of Black history's luminaries: Harriet Tubman, Crispus Attucks, Sojourner Truth, Louis Armstrong, Jackie Robinson, and Malcolm X. Each day, our teachers would take down a different colorful illustration and regale us with the story of the Black hero portrayed, sparking classroom discussions about our glorious history.

It might seem incredible that preschool children would possess the aptitude, interest, or inclination to comprehend the significance of Crispus Attucks, a Black man who was the first casualty of the Revolutionary War. Yet, on the day our teacher unveiled his portrait and told us about his accomplishments, I caught a glimpse of myself and the other Black children around me in the image of that Afro-wearing Black man fashioned in colonial attire. We all grasped the reality that our ancestors were among the first to lay the foundations of freedom for the country we called home, even if we didn't understand all the implications. The King Center, with deliberate intention, molded my early identity, bolstering my self-esteem and providing me with my own personal definition of what it meant to be Black, even before I stepped foot in a kindergarten classroom. Every day, I departed brimming with pride, embodying the epitome of Blackness and Black excellence. To me, this meant being free to be my true self: an attentive Black boy, eager to learn, and dedicated to giving my utmost to my teachers.

Little did I know that these lessons and my unwavering, positive beliefs about my beautiful, free-spirited people, their brilliance, and their rightful place in American history were about to face an almost insuperable challenge.

In 1975, my parents bought their first house. For them, this two-toned, orange-and-black three-bedroom colonial starter on Hazel Street in the lily-white suburb of Maplewood represented their grasp of a small sliver of the American dream.

I was four and a half years old and growing up way too fast, but I was oblivious to the magnitude of the war that was about to erupt, both within and around me. Thankfully, even after we moved, I still had the King Center, Mount Olivet, and my whole Rondo "village" metaphorically shielding me from the missiles and shrapnel of everything that Maplewood kicked up: the negative stereotypes about my culture that I was expected to accept and internalize, the assault on my freedom to be my true self, my self-esteem, and my confusion about my own racial identity.

I was in no way prepared to enter this battle, despite my constant assertions to anyone who would listen, "I'm a big boy now."

My mom never told me whether my yellow baby book survived the move from St. Paul to Maplewood, but I wouldn't have cared either way. I had put babyhood firmly behind me. The problem was that I had no understanding of what "big boy" status would mean for a Black boy in Maplewood.

I was hardly shy about letting grown-ups know that I had graduated from my pedal-powered original red Big Wheel tricycle with the oversize front wheel to the faster action of my two-wheel All-Pro Skyhawk bike. I took special pride in the fact that the colors of my orange-and-brown Skyhawk—equipped with a banana seat that had a fierce-looking hawk sprawled across it—were a near-match with those of my family's new house.

My parents had plenty of reasons to be proud. It hadn't taken me long to graduate to the two-wheeler and to start recognizing the words on the pages of my John Henry book. Even more impressive, they had closed on a house a whole three years shy of age thirty. At the time, I didn't realize how special it was for my parents to own a home so young, because my great-grandparents had two homes, and plots of land in Minnesota and Wisconsin, and probably beyond. Though they were divorced by then, my two living grandparents, Grandpa Buddy and Grandma Loretta, affectionately known as Nanny, also had homes in Maplewood. These maternal grandparents, my aunts and uncles, and most extended family members had nice homes with yards in the suburbs, in Rondo, and all over Minnesota. On sizzling summer days, my sisters and I had more than our share of sprinklers to run through.

Our home unveiled two undeniable truths. First, we were still connected to Rondo. Our old neighborhood was a mere thirty-minute drive away, facilitated by the seven-year-old interstate. Every time we merged onto I-94, it was a celebratory moment with Dad. Riding in his light-blue 1968 Mustang, I felt as swift as my favorite cartoon character, the Road Runner, dashing across the television screen.

The second, more uncomfortable truth was that while Maplewood was a short joyride away from Rondo, it existed in another universe. As far as I could see, none of our neighbors in Maplewood—not one—was Black. Pedaling my Skyhawk past all the ranch, rambler, and colonial-style homes up and down Hazel Street was like sailing on a gusty, Caucasian Sea. Everywhere I biked, I saw boatloads of white faces, from octogenarians rushing to their mailboxes to check for Publishers Clearing House forms, to assemblages of cackling eighth-graders drinking from garden hoses and then putting their thumbs over the spigot to spray their dogs and one another with bullets of water.

As a neophyte bike rider, I should have been sternly focused on the road in front of me, not the white people. With the smell of freshly laid tar filling my nose, I stared at the pale, pink, and tanned strangers. And they surveyed every standing stride I took on my cruising Skyhawk. Neither of us waved or smiled. But neither did we frown. Not yet anyway. In the earliest days of settling into our new American paradise I just kept pedaling and wondering about them, as they surely wondered about me.

It dawned on me that these were white people—the mysterious fair-skinned and light-eyed strangers we often saw at Sears and Montgomery Ward. During my half-decade on the planet, I'd had extraordinarily little contact with these Nordic types. Now, suddenly, they were everywhere.

On Sundays, I was back on familiar ground, attending services with my family at Mount Olivet. I was still too young to understand the sermons of our pastor, the Reverend Dr. James W. Battle. But I registered, with terror and alarm, their impact on other congregants. As big a boy as I considered myself to be, I would fight off tears every time the big old ladies wearing hats would hear something Rev. Battle said and start screaming: "Owww! Thank ya Jesus!"

These screams turned my stomach into a tumbling mat for what felt like frogs somersaulting through my body, which would suddenly be suffused with heat.

Sometimes, these stout church matriarchs would leap randomly from their portable red cushions on the church pews into the aisles. Instantly, they would be encircled by four white-gloved ushers who'd join hands to, I assume, prevent broken bones, concussions, and bloody-nosed four-year-olds who were slow to get out of the way. The grown folks called these raucous outbursts "getting happy": the women were hollering to the rafters because of their joy at all that Jesus had done for them. As I sat cowering in my pew, I wondered why these sisters couldn't be happy about Jesus without scaring us children. Sunday school had taught me a million reasons to be happy about Jesus, but calmly.

Rev. Battle did plenty of screaming and whooping himself, though he built up to it slowly. In the early part of the sermon, the call and response between him and the congregation was as rhythmic as the bonnet-style grandfather clock in Grandpa Buddy's rec room.

"Sometimes I think my life has been a soap opera," Rev. Battle would call out, prompting an "Oh Lord!" from the deacons and trustees in the second row, and sudden grunts of approval from the older deacons who'd been roused from their sleep. "Without all the negativity and drama! Because I know that He has taken and rescued me . . . all the *Days of My Life*."

"Well!" the congregants classically responded.

"You see, your mama may have to check in to *General Hospital*."

"Well!"

"But if she's a prayin' woman [more "wells!" and whoops] . . . she'll get on her knees on the side of the hospital bed! And she'll say, 'Lawd, I need you to take care . . . of *All My Children*. And even if I die, I know I have more than *One Life to Live*. And even though, I am *Young and Restless*, I can send praises up to *Another World* . . . and He will send down a *Guiding Light*!"

Every week, Rev. Battle's sermons unfolded in the same way.

Sometimes, Rev. Battle would step down from the pulpit and start walking down the aisle. "When I think about where I came from in that little ol' town in Alabama . . ."

"Well!"

"And my momma and daddy worked all day in the hot sun until that sun went down."

"Say that!"

"We didn't have a lotta money, and we still had to work the fields!"

"Uh huh!"

"But somehow, some way . . ."

"Preach!"

". . . we made it through, and we supported our community."

"Well!"

"We didn't run out to go live by the white man. The old folks used to say, 'I don't know how I made it over.' Well, that's how—supporting each other! The community and the businesses in that community. You know, sometimes Black folks forget where they come from."

Any newcomer who was aware that my parents and other family members had relocated to Maplewood would have sworn that Rev. Battle was talking directly to them. Later, I learned to recognize the guilt it stirred up in my parents and the hundreds of other Black families who eventually left Rondo in the 1960s and 1970s for Twin Cities suburbs.

After we'd gathered with friends and family for after-church meals at Red Lobster or the Old Country Buffet, Dad always felt the need to explain why we moved away. He shared stories about Blood Alley, the infamous backstreet not far from Marshall Junior High, where he went to school. Not everyone in Rondo was a Gordon Parks taking photos, an August Wilson writing plays, or a Black husband-and-wife team practicing medicine at an affiliate of the Mayo Clinic. There were people who had it rough, living in Rondo's toughest areas. And often, skirmishes with other kids revealed the underside of the "Black man, be proud of your name" message that my church hammered into me. The streets of Rondo were home to hundreds of families, some of which were known as "brand names"—symbols of top-notch fighters, hustlers, dealers, and even killers. For some, incarceration was a proud rite of passage. Often, picking a fight with one meant you were picking a fight with all of them. Blood Alley was where families or anyone involved in a feud settled their scores. As my dad put it, anyone who'd "gotten into some mess" couldn't chicken out. The tensest disputes had to be resolved by fighting there after school.

My parents never forgot the intensity of Blood Alley. Neither of them was ever stomped on or beaten down there, but the threat was ever-present. And that was enough, once they started a family, to send them out to the 'burbs to look at houses.

In the mid-1970s, crime in St. Paul was rising. And Rondo, which was 80 percent Black by the late 1960s, had just experienced a trauma that rippled through the neighborhood for decades: the government built a highway straight through the middle of this historic Black neighborhood. Many Black families and business owners got pushed out, and the neighborhood was impacted greatly by this bisection that took a dozen years to complete.

The construction of Interstate 94 broke the bustling neighborhood apart, causing the destruction of approximately seven hundred family homes and the closure or demolition of more than three hundred businesses. Most affected families received compensation that fell short of their actual losses. My family, like many others, relocated to the suburbs in search of a fresh start. Grandpa Buddy constructed one of the first Black-owned homes in Maplewood while the asphalt of I-94 was still fresh.

In 1975, when Tammi was six and before Tiffany was born, we moved to a house situated roughly four miles from Grandpa Buddy's and just a three-minute drive from Nanny's. They had divorced and both remarried, and Mom relished having her parents nearby. Their homes felt like extensions of our own. The Hawkins family seemed on track to emulate a Black rendition of the *Leave It to Beaver* dynamic. Our move to Maplewood placed my sisters and me in what I call the "integration generation"—Black children entering mainly white schools and areas between 1965 and 1985. However, soon after finalizing the house purchase, my parents began sensing that Maplewood might not be as inviting or secure as they had hoped.

Becoming Buckwheat

n 1976, when I entered kindergarten at Webster Elementary in Maplewood, I quickly learned that my schoolmates were far more interested in the color of my skin than of my slightly gray tooth, and in touching the short Afro I sported. Every morning, Mom styled my hair with a black hair pick with metal teeth and a handle in the shape of a Black man's fist, all balled up like he was about to punch somebody. Dad said that fist was the Black Power sign.

On that first day, I needed all the Black power I could get, because I walked into the playroom, and the other kids rushed over to run their hands all over my head.

"Your hair doesn't move! Why doesn't it move?"

Then, one boy started rubbing my head really hard and fast. "Ewwwwww, what is that?" he yelled, pulling his hand away as if he'd touched a hot stove. "What's this grease on my hands? Ick!"

I bit my tongue, and pop!—I punched that white boy right in the arm, turning the laughs of the three or four kids around me to tears. They promptly tattled on me to Mrs. Hansen.

She scolded me and said I should keep my hands to myself, but I felt that white boy deserved what he got. I had seen him around Maplewood before, riding bikes, and he had never asked me about my hair then. He waited until he got around all those other white boys to clown me in front of them. Because of my favorite TV shows, mainly *Sanford and Son* and *Good Times*, I thought to myself, "So, *this* is what 'honkies' are."

And they kept at it. Every day, those kids reached for my head like I was an animal in a petting zoo or the "midget in a cage" I had seen for a dollar at the Minnesota State Fair. The Arabic-looking "pygmy" was about my height with an adult man's face and a muscular build. He was locked in a large, chicken-wire cage, with a sign on the lower left corner that read: "Please Keep Your Hands Away from the Cage. He Bites!" At that age, I believed that man was from another species. That's how some of my classmates saw me.

I'd arrive at school in the morning with a smile on my face, only to hear kids start to snicker, calling out, "Good morning, Buckwheat!"

I hated that name because I had seen *The Little Rascals*. And I knew that Buckwheat was viewed by everyone around me as a nappy-headed, bug-eyed little Black boy who was usually the butt of the joke.

Every day, my mom used her strong hands and that ten-toothed hair pick made of steel to keep me from looking like Buckwheat. "Boy, you need to comb this hair, it is nappy!" she always said, prompting me to sit down on a kitchen chair so she could help me "get my hair right."

I knew if it didn't have enough chemical-smelling spray, cream, or pomade in it, the kids back in St. Paul would start "cappin'" on me, which was the term my generation of Black kids in the Twin Cities used for what people my parents' age called "playin' the dozens." "Cappin'" was a match of verbal warfare in which we'd humorously insult one another until someone gave up or was ready to fight. Every time I'd get around the older kids at church or in the neighborhoods of family members who lived in Rondo, somebody was always cappin' on somebody for their hair being "so nappy that . . ." or their skin being "so Black that . . ."

"Your head is so nappy that the barber has to pull out a chainsaw!" or "You're Mama's so Black, when she goes outside, the streetlights turn on!" and so on and so forth.

I listened as closely as I could, to refine my cappin' skills. It was becoming clear that Buckwheat's hair was the barometer for how nappy a kid's hair should never get, and his skin was also a measuring stick. Kids whose skin was as dark as or close to Buckwheat's shade were like sitting ducks in the cappin' game. Being smack dab in the middle of light-skinned and dark-skinned, I knew that "so Black" jokes didn't apply to me. But my coarse hair made me a sitting duck for "nappy-headed" jokes.

Like so many other messages I got about my Blackness, those in the cappin' sessions were at once clear and terribly confusing. Yes, we should be proud to be Black, but, according to many of the Black people around me, being Buckwheat Black was shameful. That declaration never felt right. I didn't know which was worse—the Black kids who teased me when my hair was "too nappy" or the white kids who felt disgusted by the grease coating their palms after they'd touched my hair.

The product Mom used was called TCB Hair & Scalp Conditioner. It was a thick grease, like Vaseline, and it smelled remarkably similar, except more pungent. She put globs of that into my hair and then massaged it in.

As I grew older, Mom started putting a lye-containing relaxer in my hair every few months. She'd scrub it all in, and then I'd have to tell her when it started to burn. The older I got, the longer I waited to tell her. The longer the relaxer was in, the straighter, curlier, and wavier it made my hair, depending on the effect I was going for. Anything but nappy.

A few times, I waited so long that my head had scabs for a few days after the treatment. That's how desperate I was for "good" hair like Cab Calloway's and the dudes from the movie *The Cotton Club*. The pomade I used—Murray's—came in an old can from the 1930s. I also tried Sportin' Waves, which helped especially after "Ronnie, Bobby, Ricky, and Mike" of New Edition came along with their sought-after wavy cuts. During the mid-seventies, my Rondo friends and I battled constantly over who had "the best shag," and then in the mid-eighties over who had "the smoothest waves" or the flyest Jheri Curl. Thank God, my parents never let me get a Jheri Curl.

From the city to the suburbs, Black men had to take extraordinary measures to maintain their hairstyles. On Brotherhood Breakfast Saturdays, Dad and I would rise early to visit Mr. Harper's barbershop before heading to the pancake house. This meant waking up at 7 a.m. and embarking on a thirty-minute drive to St. Paul to secure our place in line. With Mr. Harper being one of the few Black barbers in Minnesota, patrons would line up with their cars, and the early birds would get served first. Anyone arriving after 9 a.m. could expect to spend their entire day waiting.

Mr. Harper's shop was more than just a barbershop; it was a sanctuary for Black men. It was among the rare establishments in Minnesota skilled in crafting styles like the flattop or "box" haircuts, shags, Jheri Curls, waves, and perms. To be "fly," those of us with coarser, tightly coiled hair had to let it burn. All this came later, of course. But even before kindergarten, I'd learned to despise the nappy-headed Afro that was my hair's uncombed, natural condition.

I had moved into Maplewood carrying the pride of the King Center and everything I'd been taught there about Black being beautiful. Now, I was Buckwheat. And nobody, anywhere, saw beauty in him.

One axiom that's often trotted out is that children come into the world pure, innocent, and colorblind and thus cannot possibly be racist. Anyone who believes that never met my classmates and teachers in kindergarten. Not a day went by without someone, often a teacher, having something to say about my brown skin or black hair, which was studied and dissected like holy writ. My name changed according to the day; it might be "Blacky" or "the Brown kid," and all-too-often, "nigger." Many kids, along with bus drivers and teachers, would high-five me or say, "Gimme five, bro." All of it made me want to hit them—but not as much as I wanted them to like me.

Finally, on the bus ride home from school one day, I had the opportunity to make a friend. A white boy on the bus was carrying a nicely wrapped birthday gift. I wanted to see what was inside, thinking it might be a G.I. Joe.

"Hey, happy birthday," I told him. "Why haven't you opened your gift?"

"Oh, it's not my birthday. It's Patrick's. He's having a birthday party, with games and everything. You wanna come?"

I was thrilled that this white kid was inviting me to a party where everybody was going to be. But would this Patrick kid be okay with a Black kid coming?

"That sounds cool, but I wasn't invited. Won't he be mad if I come?" I asked. "Don't I need one of those invitation cards that moms send out?"

"No, you don't need that. Just come with me. It's just a few stops."

And sure enough, instead of waiting to get off at my stop and going home, I got off at that white boy's stop, and we walked right into that party. Patrick's mom opened the door. Seeing me, she got red-faced and confused.

"Hi! Can I help—"

Before she could say anything else, the other kid told her that I was on his bus and that he said I could come. I told her my name and apologized for not having a gift, since I hadn't known I was coming.

"Okay," she said, smiling. "Do you live around here? And do your parents know that you came to the party?"

"I live over on Hazel Street, but I wanted to come here and have ice cream."

She laughed, and other mothers came over, trying to figure out exactly who I was. She grabbed the massive Northwestern Bell phone book off a shelf and told me to join the other children.

She pointed to a dark-wood-paneled living room off the kitchen, where a pin-the-tail-on-the-donkey game was going on. I met the other kids, and they seemed cool, even though everybody knew I hadn't been invited.

I had just finished my turn on the donkey game when I heard his mother on the phone, talking to my mom. "Oh, he just came right in and made himself at home. He's all excited for the ice cream. He's welcome to stay. We can make an extra spot—"

There was a pause, then, "Okay, well, I'll have him ready to go. He's right here with the kids."

Then it hit me. My mom was coming to get me instead of waiting until the party was over. I had made a big mistake. As the kid's mom talked, my body heat soared, my heart rate increased, and I felt a surge of what seemed to be a hot liquid spilling into my upper chest and up to my brain. I couldn't lash out or flee, so I just froze and let the liquid flow like a stream through my head and every organ. Today, I know that what I perceived as liquids were "fight-or-flight" hormones flooding my body. Back then, I just called them poisons.

Mom walked in with a huge smile, introducing herself as Roberta Hawkins, not Bobby, as she was known in our family and by most Black people. Hearing her use her official "white people name," I knew I was in trouble.

"I am *so* sorry that he invited himself to your son's party," Mom said, her mouth still stretched into a broad smile. "He knows better. I hope he hasn't caused you too much trouble."

"Oh no-o-o," the white ladies said in unison, and Patrick's mom said, "We love having him, but I figured you'd want to know where your kindergartner was, and now that I know you were wondering, I'm so glad I called."

Mom looked over at me, rendering her best June Cleaver impersonation. "Lee-Lee, why did you come here? You know better than to invite yourself to somebody's party. Say you're sorry."

I was so filled with dread that I could barely squeak out an apology.

Not a second after the car door slammed, she leaned in less than an inch from my face and pinched and twisted my skin. My baptism in "Black boy" fire had officially commenced, burning much fiercer than the spark of the whacking I'd gotten at the Rondo duplex when I was three.

"Boy, don't you EVER embarrass our family like that again! Don't you know these white people don't want you in their homes?" she said, speaking so sternly that some of her spit flew into my eye. "That boy didn't invite you to that party! He doesn't even know you, and you go waltzing in there like these white people want you there? And you had the nerve to ask those white people for ice cream? What are they going to think about us, with you begging for food? We have food! They're going to spread this all over the neighborhood! Those white women are going to say, 'Those niggers didn't have food'! Don't you *know* you're a nigger to them? Are you stupid or something? You're an embarrassment to this family, boy! Wait until I get you home!"

Then she slapped me, hard, across the face.

But I knew that was just the opening act. The main event was yet to come. Dad would be biting his tongue for sure.

But when he got home, he didn't pull out his belt immediately. He grabbed me and shook me, hard, then put both hands on my shoulders, pressing down, with his thumbs digging into my neck. He launched into a screaming lecture, adding frightening dimensions that Mom hadn't even brought up.

Then he unbuckled his belt and brought it down on my back. *Hard.*
"Boy! Don't you ever disappear like that!"
Whap! Whap! Whap!
"Don't you know that you can disappear and never be seen again?
They'll KILL you!"
Whap! Whap! Whap! Whap!
"Don't [*Whap!*] you [*Whap! Whap!*] know that some of these white
people [*Whap! Whap! Whap! Whap!*] will KILL you if you go into their
homes! And then I won't have a son! You're not a kid!!!! [*Whap!*] You
can't be a kid!!!! [*Whap! Whap!*] Stop acting like a kid!!! [*Whap! Whap!
Whap!*] You're not a white kid! You're Black, boy! Don't you know you're
Black? You're Black! And don't you ever forget it!" [*Whap! Whap! Whap!
Whap! Whap! Whap! Whap! Whap! Whap! Whap! Whap! Whap! Whap!
Whap! Whap! Whap! Whap! Whap!*]
I was five years old.

He literally beat the child out of me. From that day forward, I
would never be anybody's baby, least of all my parents'.

Slowly, it began to register that being Black rarely meant freedom;
instead, it meant there were strict rules to follow and my parents would
belt-whip me every time I broke them. My job was to learn those
Black-boy rules and be exceedingly careful, and if I stepped left or right
instead of exactly on the line, a beating would ensue, and that beating
would be all my fault, and deserved. I learned that day that my parents'
job was to whip me, to scare me into being afraid to ever go to another
party without asking permission. I never doubted back then that they
loved me, but I blamed myself for not being mature and wise enough
to know better than to attend that party.

The severity of that birthday party beating and the derangement it
unleashed in my parents was my first inkling of both subtle and major
differences between my family and the white families in Maplewood.
Scores of white families left their front doors unlocked, even while they
slept, but my parents went ballistic if me and my sisters failed to lock
ours behind us the minute we walked in the house. If we had ever left
the door open, it wouldn't have been white people killing us—it would
have been our parents.

But I didn't understand why Dad said I could have gotten kid-napped or killed at that birthday party. Yes, the kid's mom was white like the scrunchy-faced women I'd seen on TV screaming at Dr. Martin Luther King and his fellow marchers from the side of the roads, but she seemed nice. All the mothers did, and they didn't seem to mind if I wanted ice cream. Mom kept screaming that nobody wanted me there, but it had felt like they did. No one seemed like they wanted to kidnap or kill me. But my parents reacted as if I'd come *this* close to disappearing forever or getting stabbed forty times in the neck by a white soccer mom who would then throw my body into a dumpster.

I longed to live in a world where I would be invited to a party, where I wouldn't have to just show up, and the mothers wouldn't have to think twice about whether I lived in the neighborhood. A world where I could just call my mom and say, "I'm going to this party at this friend's house, and I'll be home soon," and live just as freely as that white boy who'd invited me to the party without a formal invitation. I longed for a mom who *wanted* me to go to a birthday party and have a joy-filled time. But that day marked the beginning of my assumption that such an event would never happen.

I went back to being Buckwheat, the odd kid out, the one the moms saw and immediately knew didn't fit in. And in the tradition of my father, I hid my anger in public and established my public persona as the happy, giggling Lee-Lee who found the good in even the worst situations. It wasn't hard to find the good on that day: first, a white kid from school had invited me to a party, and second, nobody there had touched my hair.

Nazi Land

Most of our working-class suburban Hazel Street neighbors kept what I'd call an uncomfortable comfortable distance. I say that because the discomfort arising from the fact that everyone, including my parents, felt more comfortable being apart was . . . deeply uncomfortable. There were few friendly waves when we'd drive by one another's houses. Sometimes, I'd wave at neighbors, only to get sullen stares in return. Some of them appeared to be running auto shops out of their homes, with muscle cars on blocks and white teenagers standing around pickup trucks with the hood popped. I'd walk by kicking a soccer ball on my way home and they'd look up from the carburetors or replacement hoses they were installing just to glare at me.

After about a year at our first house in Maplewood, my parents heard about another part of Maplewood about a mile away where several Black families lived near one another, including Nanny and her husband, my mom's stepfather, Papa Elmer, and my mom's three younger half-siblings. It was no Rondo, but even 0.05 percent like Rondo was better than where we were living. Plus, the houses were bigger and close to John Glenn Middle School, where we would eventually go to school.

My parents had grown tired of living around so many people whose faces would flush into the color of pink champagne every time I brought over a piece of misdelivered mail or returned a Frisbee that had gone astray into our yard. It wasn't that they were mean—most weren't. But, like me, my parents made very few friends in that part of Maplewood.

My parents wanted to upsize their American dream—to move to a bigger house they could eventually build equity in and sell for another profit. So, fewer than two years after relocating to Maplewood from

Rondo, my parents bought a house in what I call "Black Maplewood." For some reason, about six or seven Black families lived on our block. It was easy to tell where the Black people lived; their houses were the most immaculate, with carefully manicured lawns, the greenest grass, and fancy sprinklers flickering in circles.

My parents bought their new house from a Black family, and they sold our old brown-and-orange house to another Black family. I immediately fell in love with this house. I still had my own room, a concrete future basketball court that was raised three feet off the ground, and a recreation room in the basement that stretched the length of the house.

When we moved in, just in time for the new school year, Tammi and I thought that moving to a more integrated section of Maplewood would go a long way toward retiring the N-word from our day-to-day lives.

Since we lived only four blocks from our new school, Weaver Elementary, Tammi and I walked to school every day. On most days, we were joined by our friend Sharon, a Black girl who was in the same third-grade class as Tammi and who lived with her grandparents a few houses from ours.

It didn't take long before I made another stupid, childlike blunder that reawakened my parents' fears that someone would kill the whole family. This time, the trigger was something I said during my walk home from school up Sandhurst Avenue.

A few days earlier, my father and I had been in the kitchen tinkering with the rabbit ears on our old black-and-white TV. He was watching a documentary on public television, with grainy black-and-white footage playing from the late 1930s.

"Who's that guy?" I asked Dad, pointing to the mustached, brown-haired white man on the screen speaking to thousands of people, all lined up in orderly, single-file lines. The people were all dressed alike, and as the man spoke, sometimes yelling and gesturing wildly with his arms, they gave him their full attention. I couldn't understand the language he was speaking, but he looked powerful.

As the people clapped, Dad shook his head in repulsion. He explained who Adolf Hitler was and what he and his regime had done to several groups, particularly Jewish people.

"The Jews. A lot of them are not like the white people out here, son. Some of them marched with us down South—right there with Dr. King," he told me. "Some of the people who got killed in King's movement were Jewish. And if there were six million Black people in Germany to kill, he would have had us all killed, too."

He then told me about all the men in my family, at Mount Olivet and around Rondo, who had served in World War II in part to help save the Jews, from my dad's elder sister Aunt Corene's husband, L.C., to Papa Elmer. I was happy to hear that so many men I knew had stepped up.

I went to bed that night and had nightmares about Hitler. The next day, as we all walked home from school, I shared my dream and the fact that Hitler had murdered our Jewish friends with Tammi, Sharon, and the other kids walking with us. And then I yelled, "I hate Hitler! I hate Hitler! I hate Hitler!"

That day, when Mom and Dad got home, Tammi said, laughing, "Lee was walking up Sandhurst yelling, 'I-I-I-I-I-I-I Ha-a-a-a-a-te Hitler-r-r-r-r-r!'"

Dad grabbed me and started shaking me, hard, just like he had the day I went to the birthday party.

He was obviously livid, but surprisingly, he didn't start whipping me. Instead, for the first time ever, he performed the classic Lee Roy Hawkins Sr. squeeze: He'd stand over me, put both his hands on top of my shoulders, and squeeze them with what felt like a vise exerting a thousand pounds of pressure. Then, he'd shake me a few times, sending my body back into that familiar fight-or-flight tailspin in which I understood that neither fight nor flight was an option for me. So, as always, I froze, the poisons streaming and trickling into my brain and upper chest area, which seemed barely able to contain my pounding prepubescent heart.

"Boy, what do you think you're doing? Do you know where you are?" he bellowed. "Don't you know Nazis live all around us in this neighborhood and all over this country! You can't be running your mouth about that! They're watching us! Every single one of them knows who we are! Whether we want to be our not, we are public figures, because we're some of the only Black folks out here! They know us, and everything about us! And they will come and blow our brains out and burn our house to the ground while we're sleeping!"

Then Mom stormed into the living room and proceeded to scream some sense into my bumbling brain. And then, in unison, my parents belted out what eventually would become the number-one song on the Hawkins family playlist: "You're going to get us all killed! Boy, these white people will come and kill us all!"

Looking into the whites of my hysterical parents' eyes, I braced myself on the edge of the couch, poised to spring into a standing position if necessary. My biggest fear, bar none, was that somehow, I wouldn't close my eyes fast enough to prevent the leather belt from tearing into and scarring my eyeball, leaving me blind and disfigured. I never stopped worrying about my eyes whenever my parents went into their rages.

I couldn't stop thinking about how deranged my father was. I couldn't understand why he would scream that the very people who hated or harmed the Jews were living all around us, by the hundreds if not thousands. All that had happened in Europe, not in America, and the grainy black-and-white footage of Hitler and his soldiers seemed like something that had happened hundreds of years ago. How could my father possibly believe there were Nazis in America now—particularly in Minnesota, of all places?

6

The Living Room Plantation

One Sunday afternoon after church, when I was in second grade, I walked into the kitchen. "Hey, Dad! I scored another touchdown," I said, holding up my handheld video football game. I loved that game, which had been endorsed by the Pittsburgh Steelers's "Mean" Joe Greene, one of my favorite players. It was a gift from my father, which is another reason I loved it so much.

"Do it on the field!" he yelled. And then he body-slammed me to the floor.

All my beatings, at least from my parents' perspective, resulted from my misbehavior. In their minds—and in mine too—I deserved to be "spanked," as they called it, for disobedience: talking back to my mother, appearing as if I wanted to talk back, failing to complete my daily chores to their satisfaction, leaving my brand-new pigskin in the backyard where it got stolen, or skipping school band rehearsals.

Usually, I knew why I had welts up and down my arms and legs and took full responsibility. It was my own damn fault: if a Black kid breaks the rules, he needs to be welted up. I understood that. But over playing a handheld football game too much?

One of my most vivid memories dates to 1977, when I watched the *Roots* miniseries on our large, wood-cabinet RCA television. This was a family affair, and the anticipation and hysteria around this adaptation of Alex Haley's bestselling book about his family history dating back to enslavement were so intense that it felt like the Black people's Super Bowl.

Sitting on our couch in the basement rec room, my parents and I and my sister watched as Kunta Kinte grew from a child born in Gambia, West Africa, in 1750 into a brave teenager who scared off a leopard with just a slingshot, and who then passed a range of "manhood training" rituals his elders designed to develop Kunta and his peers into strong, proud, African men. At six, I felt a swelling pride as I witnessed young Kunta grow, and was shaken scenes later, when he was captured by white *and Black* slave traders and sold to English slave traders. I was confused. My child's mind couldn't process the notion of fellow Blacks wanting to see Kunta Kinte enslaved.

We watched as he fought to stay free, to escape the shackles and the horrific life that awaited him in the United States, where English colonist John Reynolds purchased Kunta and took him to his plantation. Reynolds launched a campaign to break Kunta of his free mind, his dignity, and his connection to his rich past and family name, and to replace those points of pride with self-hatred in the deepest recesses of that proud Black boy's soul.

In the series's most iconic scene, Kunta doubled down on his refusal to shed his native African name for his assigned "slave name," Toby. I dropped to the rug and scooted forward to get closer to the TV screen, gaping at Kunta Kinte, this clear revolutionary, with astonishment and joy.

Kunta was not a jive talkin,' dancin', and smilin' young J.J., Rerun, or Arnold Jackson. Back then, popular culture deprived American kids of all races of any Black characters who showed the pride and depth of character of young Kunta Kinte. Seeing him onscreen raised questions for me that I could not even contemplate with any bit of certainty or evidence, let alone answer, until well into my forties.

In the scene, Kunta is beaten with a bullwhip, a weapon of cruel efficiency far removed from the belt my parents used. This whip, with its long, tapered leather lash, ended in a vicious cracker designed to inflict maximum pain. Its handle, sturdy and designed for a firm grip, allowed each strike to resonate with a terrifying snap, echoing the whip's lethal intent.

The more they whipped Kunta, the more he refused to capitulate. I lay sprawled across the floor in my Superman pajamas, my eyes locked on the screen as Kunta was strung up and beaten mercilessly in front of all the other enslaved people, who had been ordered to gather 'round.

I felt more hot poison trickle into my stomach, my chest, and my brain—the same sinking sensation I always felt just before my parents whipped me. In the darkened room, illuminated only by the glowing screen of the TV, I glanced up at my parents to see my father's arm around my mother as they sat there, unaware of the panic overtaking their son.

The whip tore into Kunta Kinte's flesh, as everyone on the plantation—and my family—looked on.

"What's your name?" the white man demanded. "When the master gives you something, you take it. He gave you a name. It's Toby, and it's going to be yours until the day you die! I want to hear you say it!"

I winced as the leather of the whip penetrated deeper into the flesh of Kunta's back. With every lash, I thought, "Just say it, Kunta, so you can live," but a big part of me also wanted him to refuse and remain Kunta Kinte. I wanted the next scene to show Kunta standing over the overseer's dead body. Failing that best-case scenario, I hoped to see Kunta's burial, with his name and pride intact.

I wanted to see a Black boy, for the first time in my six-year-old life, win against the "Do as they say or die" rules being drilled and spoken and beaten into him every day by everyone and everything around him.

But as more blood oozed out of his stinging flesh, Kunta Kinte finally succumbed: "T-T-Toby. My name is Toby."

"Aye. That's a good nigger. Cut him down." Groaning and whimpering, Kunta dropped to the ground.

I looked up again at my parents, who seemingly saw no connection between that whipping scene and their "spankings."

I left our basement for bed that night making a silent pledge that, as far as I was concerned, Kunta Kinte would always be his name.

From that scene, I got the sense that Kunta Kinte had never been viciously whipped by his own people in West Africa. In fact, it was while watching *Roots* that I first contemplated the idea that my parents' use of the belt as a form of discipline might be a lingering echo of the era of enslavement. From my parents and so many others around me, especially other Black kids, I had learned that whipping was "a Black custom" that Black Americans originated.

Just as Kunta Kinte had his West African culture, we had what I believed to be our Black American culture. By the time I turned seven, my average whipping count was up to about two or three a month, not including the several-times-a-month across-the-face slaps, pushes, pinch twists, and other more spur-of-the-moment assaults my parents unleashed, usually Mom. As they acclimated me to the reality of life in Black male skin, my entire world began to revolve around parental violence imposed to keep me in line with all the rules for being a Black American boy. Yet, every time I felt certain my parents despised me, perhaps even wishing I'd never been born, I found myself drawn back by the deep-seated belief, ingrained through relentless conditioning, that violence and Blackness were intertwined. I, too, came to view violence as a necessary part of life, not as abuse. It would be over my parents' dead bodies if they ever caught me—a damned Black child—in any act of what they considered disrespect. In the strict hierarchy of the nuclear Hawkins family, a kid was on the lowest rung of the ladder—an entity to be seen, not heard, and subject to the absolute authority of every adult.

Any challenge to that pecking order was an affront to my parents' personhood.

While hitting me, they appeared to experience a fleeting emotional wellness—a momentary escape from the mysterious source of their chronic stress and pain, and the myriad fears they harbored over what the world had in store for their growing Black son. My awareness—and that of many of my friends—of our place in the Black American family meant that we'd better carry ourselves like soldiers, and never even think about "showin' out," as the grown people loved to say. In Rondo and especially in Maplewood, I rarely saw Black kids running free or even talking loud in public the way all the white kids did.

I understood that I was the property of my parents, the Black elders in Rondo, and the white teachers at school. Any of those people had the right to smack me upside my head if they had a notion to. In fact, my mother always told me that she'd given the white teachers at school permission to "spank" me if I was ever to misbehave. That was how it used to be when she and my dad and everyone they knew were kids. Black kids, they said, were community property.

"When I was kid, if you acted up at church or in the town, the storeowner or whoever it was could spank you," Mom would say. "And then they'd take you home and tell your parents and you'd get spanked by them too. You better not ever embarrass us, because everybody has permission to beat your little Black behind!"

This "community property" law was ingrained.

In church, when it wasn't the turn of the teenage and children's choirs to sing, we'd settle into the back-most pew. From that vantage point, we'd discreetly pass notes, sneakily chew gum, and share hushed conversations throughout the service. However, before engaging in any mischief, I'd instinctively glance toward the choir stand, ensuring my mom wasn't looking our way. This was a ritual for all of us kids. If our parents caught us, they might rush down the aisles, drag the offending child out, and beat them silly, either in the bathroom or behind the church. Even more daunting, they might send a note to Rev. Battle, requesting that their kid stand and apologize before the entire congregation.

"Marcus, I have a note here from your mother," Rev. Battle would say, to rousing applause. "Stand up young man! Because nothing you could possibly talk about during the service is more important than the Lawd!"

"Amens!" all over the sanctuary.

That was never the time to get nervous and stutter. "I would like to a-a-a-polo—"

"Speak up, young man! You were talkin' fine a couple of minutes ago, and now you can't talk? You need to *respect* the service and apologize!" Applause from every corner of the church.

Thank God that never happened to me. My parents literally would have killed me.

Across all US demographics, normalized violence directed at children is most prevalent by far in the Black community. According to 2022 data from the Pew Research Center, Black parents are about twice as likely as white and Latino families to use corporal punishment on their children.

When my elders witnessed white kids "actin' up," they would start with "Mmmmmm" and modulate their tone upward. I thought of it as a form of lip-smacking, as if they were looking at a plate of Grandmother's sweet potato pie with excitement and anticipation. Dreaming about beating a white kid.

And then, they'd start chattering, with me anticipating their every word. Even at seven, I had heard that script too many times to count. They'd say, "Mmmm," modulate, and then: "Somebody needs to grab that white boy by his little narrow behind and take him out of here and tear his ass up! In fact, let me do it!" as the whole table laughed. But for all the times I heard Black folks go into that ever-so-nostalgic script of euphoria and excitement about beating a white kid, I never actually saw a single Black person ever lay one hand on one. And that remains true to this day.

Mom had that bravado every Sunday. Before going into any restaurant, she told us exactly what she would do to us if we misbehaved. "If you do anything to embarrass this family, I'll half kill you!" or "I'll rip the tonsils out of your throat!" she'd say. "I'll slap your mouth off and have you picking up your mouth off the floor." I wasn't sure what "half kill" meant, but when she beat us, she beat us so vigorously that I honestly believed she might die trying.

My father, on the other hand, was mostly action, not talk. If he was warning me of what he might do, chances were the attack was under way. His threat of choice was, "I'll break your neck." That was my signal that welts were coming.

Every time a whipping happened, I'd chalk it up to just part of being Black. I forced myself to get up off the floor and find reasons to smile—stuffing my face with candy, ice cream, and anything else I could find that was sweet; shooting baskets or playing catch with Dad; trading a Luke Skywalker or Reggie Jackson card; playing with a Super Ball, or the pet turtles, crayfish, and spiders I loved to collect.

And even in the scene of Kunta Kinte being whipped, as bleak and brutal as it was, I was inspired that, unlike me, he held out for so long; he endured a walloping to preserve his pride. That, I believed, forced "the white slave master" to respect him.

But for about forty years, all the way until I started researching my family's enslaved past, my memory of that scene and its circumstances had a flaw. For more than three decades, my brain edited out one small detail that I now consider to be crucial, if not colossal.

Almost every time I referred to the scene, I said, "Where the slave master whips Kunta Kinte." It was decades before I realized that I had made a grave error in my recollection of *Roots*. Rewatching the scene years later, I saw the white overseer of the enslaved people hand the whip to a *Black* man and command *him* to do the whipping. In his relentless pursuit to strip the proud Black boy of his confident sense of freedom in his Black identity, the white man never even had to touch Kunta Kinte. The enslaved Black man obeyed his order and did the white man's dirty work for him.

7

Dichotomy

Somewhere, packed away in a closet or cabinet in my parents' house, there may still be a brown pleather half-filled diary, small enough to fit into the pocket of the khaki chinos I often wore to school.

The genteel stitched pattern on the front of that old Victorian-style book would have been a perfect complement to the antique wood-carved bedside tables in my great-grandmother Roberta's house. And in fact, that diary was a gift from Great-Grandmother Roberta, her first step in planting the idea in my young mind of becoming a writer or journalist.

I'd sit on the plastic that kept her antique couch pristine, and she'd tell me about writers, especially her former tenant, journalist Carl Rowan, then a master's degree student at the University of Minnesota. "That young man wrote furiously, into the night, and sometimes into the early morning," she told me. "Writing allows you to express what's in your brain. And that's power."

She also mentioned Gordon Parks, whom she knew as a contemporary from Rondo and who, like her, had also spent some of his formative years in Kansas.

I was eight years old in 1979, less than a decade after Parks directed and released the iconic 1971 movie *Shaft*, which Dad and I loved to watch and rewatch through the years, as well as the 1972 *Super Fly*, directed by Gordon Parks Jr. And because both of us loved everything Isaac Hayes and Curtis Mayfield, we played the soundtracks to both movies nearly every day.

But my socialite great-grandmother focused instead on the photos Parks took for *Life* and the other work that sealed his reputation as one of the groundbreaking photographers of the twentieth century. But at that stage in my life, I didn't care about that. *Shaft* defined him.

With most of the R-rated blaxploitation movies Dad reluctantly allowed me to watch—from *Shaft* to *Super Fly* to Rudy Ray Moore's *Dolemite*—he made me close my eyes and put my hands over my face at the parts he deemed "for adults." But in *Super Fly*, when I saw Priest lying back in a bubble-filled Jacuzzi, tongue kissing the stunning, brown-skinned woman with whom he would eventually retire into happiness, I had to peek through my fingers. How could I resist?

And in *Shaft*, I was captivated by the soulful vibe of Isaac Hayes's theme song and idolized the brash bravado of the smooth-talking ladies' man Detective John Shaft. The shiny leather coats and the seventies-era turtlenecks, along with the pimps, the pushers, and the numbers runners in all those movies sparked new life into old conceptions of Black manhood in my developing third-grade mind. Those movies formed my earliest vision of a "real nigga": a streetwise, debonair Black man—always dressed clean—who could stay cool and calm but could also morph in a split second into a profane ass-kicker over any nigga or bitch, just like my dad. I rounded out my definition of what made a nigga "real" with my interpretation of Mad Dog, a lead gang member in *Good Times*, my favorite sitcom. I saw myself in Mad Dog, and that third-grade year, he became my alter ego.

I see now why Mad Dog edged out the polished drug pusher Priest and the ball-busting Detective Shaft as my number-one hero. Mad Dog was a lost Black boy—too proud to admit wanting to be found—who gained power by transforming himself into the kind of "real nigga" who would stomp the heart out of anybody who dared to mess with him. The other definition of the model Black man was a "square"—educated, professional, and brainy. But my great-grandmother's admiration of Parks showed me that a square could also have swagger, and that filmmaking, journalism, and authoring books were compatible with coolness. Rowan and Parks had walked the same ground that I had, and that was evidence that my dreams of playing for the Minnesota Twins or drumming for Prince could perhaps take a back seat to a career as a scribe. According to Great-Grandmother Roberta, all I had to do was start writing.

Maybe this grand idea is why she never seemed annoyed with or "disrespected" by my constant questions. She seemed to see a kind of beauty and promise in the youthful curiosity and self-assuredness that unsettled my parents and so many other adults.

Great-Grandmother Roberta reminds me of a cross between Maya Angelou and Ella Collins, the erudite older half-sister of Malcolm X, who took him in when he was twelve. Upon watching Ms. Collins's interviews recently, I felt as if I were watching my precious great-grandmother discuss how to nurture Black male confidence.

"Malcolm was an aggressive young boy," she said. "I admired it. I stimulated it. I felt that a young Black man, over the period of four hundred years in America, had been deprived of any aggressive thoughts. Even if you show aggressive thoughts before the white man, he would erase you, set you apart from the others as a villain. I felt that it was my duty to stimulate his arrogance, stimulate his impulsiveness, let him feel that the life that God gave him, belonged to him. He didn't have to pay homage to anyone. This is how I guided him."

Ms. Collins, born in 1914, and Great-Grandmother Roberta were born only four years apart. It was from my great-grandmother that I learned that Black excellence is synonymous with freedom and audacity to be our authentic selves. I suppose that was why Great-Grandmother Roberta would just chuckle and answer my questions. Her encouragement of my thirst for knowledge was diametrically opposed to my parents' staunch refusal to indulge "nosy" children.

In the Hawkins household, there were a thousand missteps that could provoke a painful whipping. However, the Seven Deadly Sins were consistently clear: (1) disobeying or disrespecting my mother, (2) disobeying or disrespecting my father, (3) asking questions, (4) receiving a behavior-related note or call from school, (5) upsetting any white person my parents were wary of, (6) not finishing chores perfectly, and (7) "embarrassing" my mother.

Great-Grandmother Roberta was always patient with me. In third grade, I mustered the courage to ask about her missing right hand. Having never seen her with two hands, I was unfazed by its absence, but asking about it was another matter. I expected a reprimand from the nearby adults, but none came. She simply smiled, placed my hand on the end of her arm, and said, "I had an accident." Because of her saddened expression and hesitant tone, I didn't push.

Great-Grandmother Roberta shared a unique connection with all her grandchildren and great-grandchildren, as if she knew each of us before we came into the world. "Keep writing your questions and feelings down, Lee-Lee," she told me. "And build your vocabulary. Paint a picture of your world with words."

And because she encouraged me to write, I wrote in that precious diary, with its gold-edged pages and Roman-style lettering that spelled out "Diary."

I don't recall most of the entries, but one of them is unforgettable: In third grade, I unknowingly fell into what I term "nigger traps" or "Black boy 'real nigga' traps," or simply, traps. These traps are deeply ingrained racial stereotypes. When these stereotypes are both projected onto and internalized by young Black boys or men, they can distort our self-image and behavior. This distortion raises the likelihood of committing missteps toward incarceration or increases vulnerability to having a negative paper trail created around us—bad marks or grades, misdemeanors, and felonies—which can later be used to prevent or derail our opportunities. These "Made in the USA" stereotypes portray Black males as inherently criminal, violently aggressive, and academically inferior.

The perceptions of us imply an innate unruliness, likening us to pain-immune undomesticated creatures that can be tamed only through force. The presumption is that our minds aren't as capable as the minds of white people, so reasoning with us isn't an option. Stereotypes paint us as being persistently poor, fatherless, and hypersexual from kindergarten on, as well as being much older than we actually are. They suggest we're destined for the limelight in only sports or entertainment, rather than leadership in politics, business, or the sciences. Moreover, we're expected to suppress our feelings and remain mute about any racial discrimination we face, all in hopes of ingratiating ourselves with the white people around us, who should be viewed as authority figures. One form of trap is the "principal's office–to–prison pipeline."

My diary was filled with accounts of my struggles with stepping into these traps. This constant tension and identity crisis coursed toxins through my body. I was torn: Should I be true to my inquisitive, bright, and free-spirited nature? Or should I conform to the "real nigga" stereotype, a persona frequently portrayed on TV and expected of me by many?

This internal conflict fueled the anxieties my mother felt for her only son—but expressed in a frightening way. "If you keep this up, you're going straight to prison when you grow up," she would caution me daily, her eyes wide for emphasis. "You'll either be in prison or dead."

Much of my reactive behavior was in self-defense. As a spirited kid, it was natural for me to stand up for myself. However, retaliating often landed me in trouble—being sent to the principal's office by my teacher Mrs. Blumer, leading to a call home—while the white kid next to me went unpunished. In deciding who'd be up first in kickball or hide-and-seek, I'd be constantly triggered and enraged by the chant "Eenie meenie miney moe, catch a nigger by the toe" or the shrieks of white kids who'd scream "Black germs!" if I inadvertently touched them.

Yet not all my aggressive outbursts were reactions to racism. Embodying a "real nigga" persona, I sometimes lashed out at weaker peers, mirroring how my parents often treated me. Those moments of rebellion were my exhale. I was caught in a whirlwind of societal expectations, my potential overlooked, my faults magnified.

Completing classroom reading assignments ahead of others often left me bored, causing my chattiness with the friends I did have. Yet nobody connected the dots. Instead of understanding, my parents—chiefly my stern mother—viewed my restlessness as inherent misbehavior, assuming it could be remedied only with the belt.

I was caught in a perplexing dichotomy, treated as both subhuman and superhuman. My parents upped the frequency of whippings, believing that I, a child, could endure a dozen beatings a month with no negative consequences for my mind, body, and spirit, in the short or long term. In my parents' Black boy boot camp, I was being trained to withstand intense pain, avoid all possible errors, and manage without assistance or empathy from the white people at school. "Don't think you can get away with anything out here—or anywhere—but especially here in Maplewood," my parents yelled. "No matter what you do or where you go, you can bet that somebody's always watching you!"

I was taught that the legal system wasn't there to "protect and serve" me but to incarcerate me. And Mom often reminded me that the Maplewood police would never rescue me. As a result, I eventually thought, "I'm gonna end up in prison. I'm gonna end up dead."

Still, I retained a sliver of hope, thanks to Great-Grandmother Roberta. Her encouragement helped me become one of the fastest readers and best spellers in my class. Under the Mad Dog persona, diaries and top grades seemed reserved for boys deemed less "real niggas." Yet, my fondness for Tootsie Pops and other treats that resulted from my spelling bee triumphs in Mrs. Blumer's class outweighed my desire to fit in. So, away from the white boys of Maplewood and "real niggas" of Rondo, I secretly continued my reading and writing at home.

This secret dedication paid off. I won more class spelling bees, keeping my Six Million Dollar Man lunchbox stuffed with candy. Even though Mrs. Blumer didn't seem to see the potential in these victories, with every win, a thought would nonetheless grow in the recesses of my mind: *maybe I am smart.* This thought had room to grow during the times I finished my reading before the rest of the class.

Inside, I was battling between two identities: the rambunctious, free-wheeling, and confident Black boy who ran afoul of his parents' calls for passivity in favor of audacity and curiosity, and my alter ego, the "real nigga" wannabe, Mad Dog. But even when I favored my Attucks and King influences, Mrs. Blumer didn't support me.

Every year, for Dr. King's birthday, Mom gave us a note to take to our teachers: "Our family will be missing school and work tomorrow to march in recognition of Dr. Martin Luther King Jr.'s birthday, until Congress passes legislation to make it a federal holiday." We would join all the Black families from across Rondo's community and churches in skipping school to march by the thousands from our church to the state capitol, in protest. When I handed Mrs. Blumer my note, her face turned red and she said, "Okay," with a sigh. "But you'll have to make up the work."

Mrs. Blumer perceived me as a problem. Once, when a friend and I were playing, we—perhaps more accurately, I—knocked over and broke Mrs. Blumer's fan. She burst into tears, exclaiming, "My husband is going to be terribly upset that you broke our fan! What am I going to tell him?" Subsequently, she isolated my desk in the corner of the room, enclosing it with a three-panel, foldable wooden partition that felt like being in a cage away from my classmates for the rest of the day.

Even when I engaged in skirmishes with classmates that involved racist slurs, she would send me to the principal's office rather than recognize the racism I faced. She used a mocking nursery rhyme to indoctrinate me with the understanding that, as a Black boy in America, I'd need to learn to accept racial epithets without protest: "Sticks and stones may break my bones, but words will never hurt me."

For my constant failure to avoid the traps, I got reported for "poor behavior," my mom would be called, and I'd have to endure whipping after whipping. Mom assured me that the world isn't fair; while those white kids spewing hatred were shielded, my reactions prompted another trip to the principal's office and led to a whipping. All of this intensified the damning echo of Mom's warning: "Prison or dead. Prison or dead."

In particular, I struggled with math and needed extra attention that Mrs. Blumer didn't spare. Every call to my mom about my math issues disrupted her day, pulling her away from her work as the health coordinator at an assisted living complex. "If your teacher calls again, I'm going to come to your school and spank you in front of your whole class," she'd threaten, "and then your dad will take over when we're home."

Although my mom had given Mrs. Blumer permission to beat me for any reason, she never laid a hand on me. By simply picking up the phone, she effectively handed the belt to my parents.

Fearing the impending punishment on days marked by red-inked math papers, I'd stealthily take the phone off the hook to prevent calls with a busy signal. Then I'd run back upstairs and put on two pairs of long john underwear and sometimes as many as three long-sleeved shirts, plus a sweater over that, hoping to cushion the blows. Even on the hottest days, I'd skip short-sleeved shirts and shorts in favor of long sleeves and pants or jeans. I was desperate to hide the stinging, raised, reddish-brown welts all over my arms and legs. If one of the other kids had seen them, I would have died of humiliation.

But hiding was tough. Even if Mrs. Blumer never glimpsed a welt or bruise, she saw me with my elbows on the desk, head buried in my arms, refusing to look her in the eye. On the days I struggled with my math assignments, my silence and fatigued look of defeat were proof that my industrious Black parents had delivered perfectly on her "assignment" to them.

None of this is to suggest that Mrs. Blumer didn't find plenty of ways to punish me herself. When she announced another spelling bee, for example, she decided to block me from the one small achievement that had the potential to vanquish the Mad Dog within me: "Lee, because you could not keep your hands to yourself this morning during your disagreement with Christopher, you will not be allowed to participate in today's spelling bee."

I'd stepped into another trap.

But even as I tried to avoid casting myself as a victim, I saw that I wasn't the only Black kid Mrs. Blumer picked on. Two years earlier, she'd given Sharon, the Black neighbor who walked to school with Tammi and me, what seemed like a thirty-years-to-life sentence in that wooden cage behind the three-panel partition.

In Mrs. Blumer's classroom, being isolated behind that partition felt like a precursor to the life of imprisonment my mother feared for me. My life was already scripted. The biography of Lee Hawkins could be written without my living another day. I was a wild animal—a walking, breathing Black stereotype, never too small for handcuffs or that orange prison jump suit. That partition that Mrs. Blumer wrapped around me against the corner walls was the paradigm of all the traps set for Black boys like me in Maplewood and throughout the USA. Our inmate numbers were being processed at birth.

In fairness to my parents, I don't think they ever knew that Mrs. Blumer sentenced me to that wooden cage. Out of fear of more severe whippings, I kept it a secret from them, and for her own reasons, so did Mrs. Blumer. That was the only positive aspect to being marooned in that cage. Every single time Mrs. Blumer called my home—two or three times a week during that third-grade year—I received a whipping. But on my days in the cage, Mrs. Blumer never called.

Memories of that cage still sting to this day. I'd feel Mrs. Blumer's hand descend heavily on my little shoulder, shoving it forward into that corner. During those perp walks to the cage, I'd tense every muscle and recite my go-to mantra: "Don't cry, don't get mad." But mainly, "Don't cry."

This cycle was my future as a criminal playing out in real time, and it was all my fault. Mrs. Blumer feared me probably as much as my unrelenting mother feared *for* me.

And every time I'd go home and write in the diary I kept hidden in my drawer, I'd be doubly aware of that tension, even though "real niggas" didn't write in diaries about their feelings. I can't count the times I considered cramming that diary into one of the trash bags Dad taught me to prepare for Wednesday morning pickup. But that diary was a gift from a great-grandmother who loved and believed in me. I couldn't bear to throw it away.

8

Pink Slips and Whips

couldn't figure out my life.

Still, there were moments of brightness. Somewhere along the line, my love for reading landed me in an elementary school reading program called Junior Great Books. It centered around higher-level books, critical thinking, and discussion. While this extra reading helped me expand my vocabulary and quell some of my boredom at school, it wasn't enough. The main problem: I still couldn't master math.

I wanted to be as perfect as the mom I loved so much. Strict as she was, I genuinely believed that improving my behavior and math scores and continuing to excel in reading and writing might stop Mrs. Blumer's constant calls. Then, rather than whipping me as she or my dad usually did after those calls, Mom would treat me with the warmth and kindness she was famously known for outside of our home. Everyone, kids and adults alike, experienced her graciousness. So why was it different for her third-grader behind closed doors?

Unlike me, she never caused trouble for her elders. For instance, at Great-Grandmother Roberta's house, Mom cheerfully helped with her medicine and gently guided her to her walker. On the drive home, she'd always stress that "senior citizens"—a term she insisted we use when referring to older people—need us to listen with patience. She told us to touch their arms or hands when talking with them, and to offer help whenever possible.

My great-grandmother clearly brought out Mom's patient side. She'd sit with her for hours, smiling and laughing as they watched Lawrence Welk's band on TV playing polkas in polyester V-neck sweaters, blazers, and cascading, ruffled skirts. There, she seemed transformed.

Mom shared the name "Roberta" with my great-grandmother and had lived with her and Great-Grandpa Sam during her teens. She never explained to me why she left her mother, Loretta, and stepfather, Papa Elmer, but from the way she screamed about her childhood while beating me, I knew it had been bad.

"This is NOTHING compared to what I got from my stepfather!" she'd bellow, standing over me as I cowered on the floor, wielding the belt. "Stop crying! When I was a kid, I was locked in the basement, cleaning up dog shit from his hunting dogs!" Mom rarely swore, but when she did, she'd morph into what seemed to be her own Badass Ghetto Diva alter ego, like my Mad Dog.

She radiated a calm and gentle warmth when she interacted with children at church or, notably, with the white kids in Maplewood. If a child scraped their knee or faced an issue, our mom's compassionate side shone through. "What did you say, sweetie?" she'd ask, or offer a comforting "Oh, bless your heart," embracing them tenderly. She reserved her stern, no-mercy scolds and reproaches for me, the Black boy she was tasked with raising in a world she often cautioned was horrifically racist.

Both Great-Grandmother Roberta and my mom had a love for opera-style singing and the song "His Eye Is on the Sparrow." By the time I was born, Great-Grandmother Roberta—who had sung opera before many audiences in her life—was no longer giving public performances, but I envision her bearing a resemblance, in aura and voice, to Mahalia Jackson. Mom never danced or twirled us around with glee, but during her episodes of despair with Dad and us, she'd recount how she once had danced with one of the country's premier modern dance companies in her youth. With tears in her eyes, she'd mourn leaving behind the success and fame that had been within her reach to marry Dad and raise us. Her words often cast a weight of guilt, especially on Dad. "Well, Bobby, I truly am sorry that we held you back. I truly am," he'd say.

For myself, hearing her voice such regret, consistently pointing to her marriage and children as the cause, taught me a clear lesson: for the sake of happiness and inner peace, don't get married, don't have kids, and never forsake my dreams for anyone else.

Dad's apologies to her were infused with a Southern twang, and in our house, there was an unspoken understanding that Mom was Northern and Dad was Southern, from what he jokingly called "the wrong side of the tracks." I sensed this difference made Mom self-conscious in some of our family's social circles. But Mom had Dad on such a short leash that he knew exactly when to turn off the free-wheeling Southern charm and tone down his accent.

Dad regaled us with funny stories and had us laughing with tongue-twisters like "I saw a saw from Arkansas" and "Study long, you study wrong" during our spirited checkers games. At times, he'd lift my giggling sisters, squeezing them like cherished Strawberry Shortcake dolls, and then playfully rub his rough five o'clock shadow against their baby-soft faces. Our collective laughter would grow louder, drawing playful glances from Mom.

"Lee Roy? Are you hard of hearing?" she'd say.

"Well, baby, you know me, I'm just a country boy," he'd respond. If we were in the car, he'd turn his head toward the back seat and say, "Kids, I'm sorry, you know I get hyper."

Dad's "hyper" side made him more fun. His radiant personality, combined with Southern wit, felt like a weighted blanket of joy draped over me. Knowing that my sociable nature and the "talks too much" comments on my report cards were inherited from Big Lee, I needed to figure out how to keep my own vibrant spirit and budding talent for networking and making friends from irritating my authoritarian mom.

I tried to observe and mimic Dad's skill at calibrating his energy and personality around Mom. I always failed.

Dad never used his down-South lingo or street talk around folks from Mount Olivet or the Black organizations we belonged to, such as Jack and Jill of America, where he was the volunteer director of our J.J. Kids band and everybody's favorite dad. Through Jack and Jill, a membership organization of Black mothers with children ages two to nineteen that focused on nurturing future leaders with volunteer service and other activities, my sisters and I attended monthly events and parties with Black kids from all over the Twin Cities, but mostly the suburbs.

Mom would've been mortified if Dad had sworn around their Jack and Jill friends, given that some in Rondo viewed them as "bougie" or "upper-crust Blacks." I never saw them that way. To me, they were just friends. We grew up together, through events like the Debutante Cotillions and Beautillions in our senior year, and I sensed no elitism around me.

Dad, too, believed that the old-fashioned social rules and regulations Mom insisted on served a positive purpose. To her credit, every day was a master class in etiquette. Breaches like not saying "thank you" or not dressing appropriately for the occasion were "tacky" missteps exhibited by "uncouth" whites, who were either too poor to know any better or too privileged to feel they needed to care. Mom, thanks largely to Great-Grandmother Roberta, taught us that exhibiting good manners was part of our heritage. And somewhere underneath her self-consciousness about being unfairly judged or looked down upon by white people, she also seemed to recognize, albeit with a nuanced understanding, that many of them weren't raised in homes like her grandmother's, with plastic-covered furniture and imported china, wearing long white gloves up to their elbows and designer shawls to Saturday night galas or afternoon meetings with the girls and ladies for tea and crumpets. As elementary schoolers, we children each had our own set of thank-you cards, always made eye contact, and called adults "sir" and "ma'am." And if we forgot to send a card, it was considered "an embarrassment" or just plain uncivil. The punishment would be tougher than military school could ever be—especially if we talked back in the process of explaining why we hadn't sent it.

"Do you think you're white or something? You're not white, you're Black!" Mom would scream as she walloped. "And don't you ever forget it! You're Black!"

Whap! Whap! Whap! Whap!

It would continue for several minutes, until Mom tired out, leaning against a dining-room chair to catch her breath. Then, she'd pick up her purse from the dining-room table, walk down the long hallway toward her bedroom, turn around, and issue a grim final warning: "And you better not even *think* of hitting zero on that telephone to call the operator! Your cousin tried that, and the police didn't even care. They gave her right back to your aunt. If you touch that dial and the police come, you're going to get your butt torn up even more after they leave!"

From my parents' perspective, they had successfully followed the blueprint of success that was preached from many Black pulpits across the United States: "We have to start whupping them in the highchair, so they don't end up in the electric chair."

Mom wasn't always a drill sergeant. She was invariably there for me when my allergies flared up, compassionately taking me to doctors and caring for me. I often wondered why she couldn't be that tender when doctors weren't involved. But even in my fragile state at nine, I appreciated her kindness.

Our status-conscious mother had a complicated relationship with whipping. Unlike the scores of Black parents who didn't hesitate to take a belt to their kids' behinds any time, anywhere, our mother was careful never to act so uncultivated as to beat us in public. The violence that permeated our household was the biggest part of our "family's business" that we had damn well never discuss with outsiders—or, for that matter, even among ourselves.

She saved the in-the-face screaming and the welt-inducing belt walloping for when we were back home, behind the airtight, shuttered windows that she rushed to close throughout the house before projecting her fortissimo-level operatic force against us.

My parents' dual nature mirrored the very contradictions that tormented me. To the world, they epitomized ideal, nonviolent, model Black parents, effortlessly debunking the pervasive stereotypes about Black American families. They were pillars in our suburb and our church and held respectable jobs. We lived comfortably, our needs always met and then some. They owned a home with a meticulously maintained yard; we were strangers to government assistance, "Baby Mama Drama," or stereotypes associated with it. When Maplewood whites saw us walking sharply dressed alongside our father, they naturally assumed our upbringing was exemplary. And in most aspects, it was.

My parents' method of disciplining me, severe beatings disguised as "spankings," was not seen as abuse and further cemented their image as excellent parents, especially among those who believed Black boys required taming. Mom always made sure the community knew that her strict parenting kept her potentially dangerous Black son in line. In Maplewood, among the sparse number of Black kids, I knew I wasn't the only one getting my ass beat. I witnessed it firsthand in department store bathrooms and at church, amid the ignored screams and cries of terror-stricken Black children.

One muscle-bound family friend visiting from out of town even asked to use Tammi and Tiffany's room to "discipline" his eight-year-old daughter. He took her in there and belt-whipped her like a drum in a storm, while all the adults nonchalantly continued their conversation about Diana Ross, seemingly oblivious to her anguished cries ricocheting down the hallway.

Some Black parents even took pride in their "spankings," openly discussing and laughing about them afterward with friends. Dad never told anyone he beat us, but occasionally, I'd catch snippets of Mom's conversations with her Rondo friends. She never shared these stories with the Jack and Jill mothers, but she'd switch to an awkwardly delivered "street" accent and chuckle about her Bill Cosby–like warnings to me: "Girl, I told that boy, 'I brought you into this world and I can take you out.'" Her thunderous laughter, which seemed to bolster her acceptance among the moms in the hood, was unmistakable.

Some of the kids bragged about beatings too. Imagine my astonishment when a Black brother and sister from down the street seemed to almost howl with joy when recounting the lashings their dad would administer with an extension cord to their bare asses. "He makes us lie across the bed, and he keeps hitting us over and over," the girl told me, high-fiving her brother as if she'd begun to like it. "It bleeds so much we can't even sit down!"

Having been hit "only" with an open hand and a belt and pinched and choked, I considered their father abusive and extreme, and my parents moderate and rational. I soon realized that kids with parents who'd spent time in Mississippi seemed more likely to get extension cords and braided branches. I joined their laughter, relishing the rare feeling of being accepted in that moment as a "real nigga."

But as we laughed, I was secretly consumed by self-loathing. I felt disconnected, like what one might call a "sellout," for my inability to celebrate and love the whippings. To be genuinely "Black enough," I believed I had to not only accept the belt's sting but also find humor and a sense of belonging in it. These were my mother's critiques, not mine: she saw me as the "too arrogant," smug Black boy, "spoiled" by his father and grandfathers, who, in her eyes, mistakenly and arrogantly believed he was equal to or even better or smarter than the white kids at school, and therefore "too good" for "spankings." With every strike, her intention was to grind me back to "Blackness," to remind me that I wasn't privileged, entitled, or set for life like my white friends, and that I needed to curb that Black boy joy and finally accept that life wasn't a crystal stair.

She believed she needed to beat heightened maturity into me, to whip the naively self-assured smile off my face. Yet, I had never seen her, my father, or any other adult get viciously beaten with a belt. Reflecting on it, maybe I was the strong one. However, such a realization escaped me each time my dad's belt descended, and I fought back tears, almost hyperventilating. I wondered: If I was indeed the stronger one for regularly surviving what adults around me didn't have to face, why did each whipping bring me to the brink of tears? Mom perceived my tears as a sign of frailty, impressing upon Dad that any Black father worthy of his title needed to be constantly whipping his son. Whenever my father saw a minor misstep of mine—like forgetting the trash or not clearing the driveway sufficiently of snow—as meriting just a stern reprimand rather than a full-blown whipping, I'd often breathe a sigh of relief prematurely. He'd step into the bedroom with Mom and five minutes later explode out of their door and burst through mine, swinging his belt like the 1977 Mr. October version of Reggie Jackson.

Sometimes, they'd both bust in, with my 250-pound dad doing the beating as Mom screamed in my face between whips. I still remember the sound of Dad flicking on my glow-in-the-dark Superman light so suddenly that it was like an alarm going off. He'd snatch me out of bed with one hand and lift my small body up into the air by my long john shirt, like an emergency red alert with no siren. The sting of my shirt scraping against the side of my neck would trigger that panicky sense of being in a burning car, with only seconds to escape before the whole vehicle exploded into a roaring black cloud. Seeing Mom and Dad racing toward me, with all their vastness, their seemingly limit-less strength, was, to my nine-year-old frame and brain, equivalent to being pounced on by a growling pack of the German shepherds and Dobermans that people kept back then for "security." I was that gutted, incessantly blinking little boy in the middle—jumpy, jittery, helpless to fight or flee, and just plain scared. Enduring this agony multiple times a week completely messed up my system. There was no way I could deliver on Mom's demands that I be less "hyper." With my body always primed to go into overdrive, I was perpetually nervous or exhausted and I could never sleep deeply or remain calm.

I was sinking. My efforts to be older and tougher were a disaster; I was still that pathetic third-grader who whimpered on the floor after ev-ery beating. I still played with my Tonka trucks and my handheld football games. And I still thought longingly about that missing baby book and the times when Mom read it with me on the couch at our old place on Hazel Street. Alone in my room at night, I would pull out my diary and, following Great-Grandmother Roberta's advice, write down my feelings.

The biggest cloud hovering over everything continued to be my abysmal performance in math. Whether at my desk or in Mrs. Blum-er's wooden cage, I could rarely calm down enough at school to follow every step of the math process. And I couldn't find the language to ex-plain to my parents that I was giving it my best, and that whipping was probably not the best way to help me improve. (Back then, of course, I had no idea what these near-daily beatings were doing to my body, specifically to my brain and the "fight, flight, or freeze" circuitry of my entire central and autonomic nervous systems.) I couldn't tell them that I needed more time, and more explanation, and that I was too nervous and fidgety to concentrate. My parents swore I was "being bad" and simply wasn't trying hard enough, so they kept whipping. The worse I did, the harder and more frequently they whipped.

"No son of mine needs improvement in math," Dad would scream. *Whap! Whap! Whap!* "You're playing around in class, trying to be cool!" *Whap! Whap! Whap! Whap! Whap!*

"Yeah, you're showing out for the white kids," Mom would interject amidst Dad's strikes. "What you don't understand is that those white kids' parents are doctors and lawyers, and they can afford to play around. Their parents are setting them up for life, and if you don't get your math right, you're gonna end up working for them!"

Unsurprisingly, my math performance declined even more. *I'm stupid in math, like all those white kids in my class who read so slow and don't know words,* I thought. My nerves were constantly firing. Some nights, I stayed on edge through the night, trying to slow my mind and stop worrying. It was impossible. Because I always seemed to be in trouble for something, I was consumed by fear of my parents' ever-changing moods and was constantly primed for a whipping.

Eventually, my math troubles prompted the dreaded "Needs Improvement" warning letter, which I was to take home to be signed by one of my parents. In the after-school hours before our parents got home, I pulled the pink sheet of paper out of my book bag and stared at it: a decree of my summary execution by belt. Desperate to stave off that fate, I searched frantically for a temporary stay. It occurred to me that, though my math was bad, my cursive writing was stellar.

Lacking all rational judgment, I pulled out a pen and carefully crafted the signature "R. Hawkins." I knew that, despite the identical match to Mom's expert penmanship, Mrs. Blumer would eventually call, or worse, Mom and Dad would hear about the letter at the parent-teacher conferences scheduled for just weeks later. But at least writing Mom's "signature" would delay the butt-kicking.

The next several weeks were torture. Not only did I lie awake in a cold sweat every night fearing the phone would ring and picturing the clobbering I would get for signing Mom's name, but my self-esteem plummeted to an all-time low. I fell deeper into bouts of all-night tummy-turns and sleeplessness. The dread gnawed at me ceaselessly. Even when I found a way to divert my attention long enough to enjoy an episode of *Tom and Jerry* or a Minnesota North Stars hockey game on TV, my knotted stomach and the awareness of a ticking bomb waiting to explode all over the house never went away.

Mom and Dad finally attended the parent-teacher conferences and were hit with a "Needs Improvement" in math on my report card. Mrs. Blumer pulled out the signed pink slip, which Mom was seeing for the first time.

At home, I prepared carefully, dressing myself in my two layers of long johns, my dark blue "Toughskin" jeans, and three sweaters. When I heard the front door open, I was already in bed, fully clothed and sweating through all that padding. My thoughts pinballed between my fear that Mom would tattle on me to my beloved great-grandmother Roberta and my Sunday school teacher Deaconess Williams and the horror of the death that conceivably awaited me. My poor decision kept replaying in my head. I tried to rationalize it, noting that I had done it only because Mom and Dad refused to accept that I was genuinely struggling with math. Meanwhile, the voice of Mad Dog kept interrupting those thoughts to set me straight, to remind me that "real nigga" criminality was my nature. I tried to convince myself that what I'd done wasn't dishonest—but I knew better. And for that, God would punish me, too.

Mom barged into my room, shouting uncharacteristic profanities. Looking up at my mother's darkly animated, disgusted face as she verbally pummeled me, I yearned for some alternative reality where my mom would hug me and say, "Son, it's okay. You're not stupid—you just need help with math. I was wrong. You're not perfect, but you're not a criminal. You have nothing to be ashamed of. We'll help you with your math. I'm sorry, and I love you."

But that was some Brady Bunch treatment reserved for a white kid. There would be no such tenderness from Roberta Hawkins, only her trademark military glare.

With my heart hammering and my mind racing—*how soon before Dad appears?*—I tried to explain to Mom that I couldn't concentrate during math lessons and that I often felt sleepy because I was up all night worrying about my messed-up life. When she responded with more cursing, I pinned my hopes on Dad. Maybe, by some miracle, he would choose picking me up and hugging me over the stealthlike assault that I knew was coming. I had seen him studying math for one of his college courses—he was working on a degree at night—and he, of all people, would understand that missing even one step during a lesson was enough to confuse any student. In fact, Dad was already committed to getting his master's degree after that—a feat he eventually accomplished years later. He knew that sometimes certain classes could be tough. Perhaps this time he would refrain from leaving reddish-brown marks up and down my arms and legs.

He did neither. I had a big one coming—not only had I embarrassed my mother in front of a white woman, but Mrs. Blumer had also given *them* an assignment to turn in the next day—and my father beat me to a bruised pulp, my multiple layers of padding notwithstanding.

After dragging me across the red carpet of my room, down the hallway, and into the living room, Dad walked away, exasperated, then stomped back to tower over my small body writhing on the floor. "Forgery? *Forgery*, Lee?" he roared. "That's a felony!"

I didn't comprehend what "forgery" was all about, but clearly what I had done was a thousand times more serious than misrepresentation. The "poisons" pumped from my heart into my veins, producing the familiar hot, stinging burn.

The poisons soon settled in my mind and began to sink in what seemed like a bottomless pit of fog, confusion, and misery. "I'm so tired," I kept saying to myself. "I'm so tired of this life." I wanted nothing more than to go to sleep, right there on the floor. The weight in my chest felt too heavy for me to get up. My parents had gone into their bedroom and slammed the door, but I knew if my father were to come back, it would not be to help me up. Based on the force with which he'd thrown me down, I feared that this time he wanted me dead for real.

"I'll break your neck!" continued to be one of his signature warnings, and Mom still wanted me half dead.

Between this violent language and the horrific attacks themselves, my parents stole half my happiness. I fought hard to hold on to the rest. Because at the end of the day, I was still a young child who craved nothing more than to be loved by my parents and be my free, authentic self—basically, a typical, unapologetically happy American boy who loved reading and writing, kept a diary, enjoyed competing in sports and playing with handheld video games, was eager to explore the world as freely as possible, and who felt the full range of human emotions, including anger, sadness, curiosity, and wonderment. But my parents, perhaps unconsciously, seemed to equate those simple desires with "trying to be white."

I was still too young to comprehend the severity of my situation: my impressionable mind couldn't reconcile dueling definitions of Blackness.

Oddly, my parents' belief that violence was part of who we were as Black people may have buttressed me in one sense. It gave me the warped but affirming feeling that my parents weren't beating me out of hatred, but out of love, and violence was just fundamental to being Black in America.

To say that all this was deeply demoralizing to a child in the third grade doesn't begin to do justice to the confusion and despair I felt much of the time. But somehow, I managed to project optimism and happiness and a smile that glowed to the outside world even at times when my insides were burning up. I turned to faith, believing the lesson Deaconess Williams taught in Sunday school, which was that all children who die go to heaven. Matthew 19:14, she said, was proof: "But Jesus said, 'Let the little children come to me and do not hinder them, for to such belongs the kingdom of heaven.'"

That night after the parent-teacher conference, as I lay crumpled on the floor, my last shred of optimism was gone and all I wanted was to die and go to heaven. "God loves me," I thought, "even if Mom and Dad don't." That night, I started to negotiate with myself. *Should I continue to lie here, or should I go back to my room and kill myself? How would I even do that? But I can't go on living like this. I'm better off dead.*

In truth, this wasn't the first time I'd thought about death by suicide. My pain ran so deep that, in the calm after the beatings, I often wrote dark, suicidal messages in my diary. Slowly, I pushed myself off the floor, walked back to my room, and pulled that diary out again.

I don't want to be here anymore, I wrote. *I should kill myself and go to heaven. Mom and Dad don't love me. They spank me all the time. I can't take it anymore. I want to die and go be with Jesus.*

As I had before, I left the diary open on my nightstand, above the orange nightlight, in the hope that Mom, who came in my room every night to tell me when to go to bed and turn off the lights, would read those words, find some compassion and empathy somewhere inside, and tell Dad that they should stop whipping me so frequently and severely. But the next morning, as it had been the other times, the suicide diary was closed. Mom never spoke a word about what she saw there in that open diary. She just closed it and never even acknowledged it. I didn't know if she even told Dad about it. But the whole scenario, reinforced the crystal-clear message: "We don't care if you kill yourself."

Shortly thereafter, the diary disappeared.

9

The Separation

Forgery is a felony! You're gonna grow up and go straight to prison, boy! You're either gonna be in prison or you're gonna go out there and get killed in the streets! You're a failure in math and an embarrassment to this family!"

It was probably the millionth time my mom told me that I could end up incarcerated or in an early casket, but this time was slightly different. She didn't qualify her statement with the standard preface, "If you don't get your act together." This time, she stated outright that I was basically a pathetic, Black class dunce who would *definitely* end up working on some chain gang somewhere. Or I'd be dead.

I looked down at the baked chicken and potatoes on my dinner plate and took slow bites. Tammi and Tiffany had already obediently eaten theirs and were back in their bedroom. I wished I could go to my room, too, but Mom wasn't finished with me. I kept eating, so I could focus on the baked chicken, and not her face.

"And when you get there, don't call us," she continued, "because we won't come to bail you out!"

I was surprised to see Dad dart up from his seat. "Now Bobby, don't tell my son that! He needed the belt, but now you're going too far!"

My mother looked taken aback, but Dad kept going. "My son ain't going to no jail! Stop telling him that! And don't put his life in it. Don't say he's gonna get shot! Don't go wishing death on my son! That's too much! He's a good, smart kid who has everything it takes to be successful! He's just playing around too much!"

"You think this son of yours is so smart, but kids who are going to be successful and avoid prison don't fail math, Lee Roy, and they don't forge signatures! He's failing, and I'm sick of him! If you're so confident in him," Mom replied, changing my "Needs Improvement" to a "Fail." "If you think he's so great, then *you* raise him! I'll raise the girls! You raise him!"

"Okay then! I will," Dad shot back.

And that was that. Mom and Dad struck the parenting arrangement that lasted until I was a grown man.

Mom's declaration that I was officially a lost cause brought me face-to-face with my alter ego Mad Dog, who was fast becoming my primary identity. A scene from an unforgettable 1974 episode of *Good Times* offered me a snapshot of what my life, according to my terrified mom, would look like when I was seventeen, Mad Dog's age on the show.

In that episode, Mad Dog is sentenced for shooting the show's main character, J. J. Evans, causing a superficial wound. Because Chicago County's juvenile reform school and jails are full, the judge gives Mad Dog three years' probation.

After Mad Dog leaves the courtroom with his mother, he tries to reassure her.

Sitting at that table, between my parents, I wanted to tell Mom not to worry, that I could work hard to quickly raise my math score, stop acting like a kid, and quickly become a man. But I couldn't find the courage. All I could think about was the argument Mad Dog and his mother had in that scene.

After they left the courtroom, Mad Dog told his mother not to worry. But she responded: "Don't you talk to me, boy. Don't you ever talk to me again. There ain't nothin' can be done for you, Cleon. You're no good. Lord knows I have done my best, but you're just plain no good."

"Is that any way to talk to your beloved son?" Mad Dog asks, but his mother's disgust intensifies.

"You were beloved once, a long time ago, but no more. And I give up on you. Cleon, I pray to God every night that none of my other kids turn out like you." Finally, she said, "I never thought I could feel this way about my own child, but I hate you. Sometimes I wish you were never born!"

Then, his mother slapped him across the face like my mother

sometimes slapped me. When I saw it, I intuited that I would someday reenact that scene in my own life. Now my fears were materializing, a lot earlier than expected. I had begun to believe in my heart that my mother despised me.

My parents had disappeared into their bedroom, and I could hear them yelling at each other. I strained my ears to hear what they were saying. Then, I tuned them out and just sat and picked over that baked chicken, alone with my racing thoughts.

I was surprised that Dad had stuck up for me. I wondered why, until I realized something: although I had heard Mom's predictions of my future incarceration or early death dozens of times, she'd never made them in front of Dad—not in this biting, curselike version, anyway. Her venom released a spine-chilling energy into the kitchen that my father couldn't stand to have lurking around us.

Of course, I knew Dad was disappointed in me, too, but I realized that Mom often saved her most biting critiques for when he wasn't home. While I was squandering my educational opportunities in a wooden cage in the corner, he, at age thirty-one, was working doubly hard every night to make up for the fact that his stint in the air force had forestalled his hopes for a four-year degree.

Still, with Dad, I felt he had some kind of residual love and even, sometimes, a certain regret about taking the belt to me. As strong-minded as he might seem, Mom cast an almost magical spell over him. When it came to fulfilling her demands that he "discipline" his Black son with the relentlessness of a striking cobra, Dad was more obedient to Mom than I was. And when she'd haul off and slap me, he never stepped in to stop it. For him, the line between "spanking" and "abuse" was never crossed unless blood was drawn. Anything up to that point was fair game.

During my childhood, Dad never explained why he got so nervous when he witnessed any pummeling that drew blood. But when we watched Muhammad Ali's fights, I noted the same clamminess that he exhibited during gory movies. At the sight of blood, he'd clamp down on his teeth and grind them together.

Technically, my parents' whippings never drew blood, though I often saw lines of blood along the edges of the welts on my arms and legs that I always hid from my parents and the world. Still, I was grateful that I wasn't one of the kids who got the extension cord. My welts usually went away in a day or two, but the extension cords caused bloodied gashes and long-term Kunta Kinte–caliber scarring.

Dad may have wanted to beat me into manhood, but he didn't want to see welts or scars. Within a day of every whipping, he'd joke around and ask me to come with him to McDonald's or to go fishing at Keller Lake in Maplewood.

In the car, our awkward silence would quickly turn to talks about everything from "that new kid from Minneapolis called Prince" to the punishing left jab of Larry Holmes to what I wanted to be when I grew up. The walloping I'd received just hours earlier would always go unmentioned. In those moments, Dad was all smiles and laughs. He always talked about the fact that God had taken him "a mighty long way," all the way to Minnesota from "L.A."—lower Alabama. He was always encouraging everybody around him to use their gifts. Even to me, he'd often say out of the blue, "Like the song says, let your light shine, boy. Let it shine, shine, shine. And keep up all that readin' and writin'. You can literally write your way to your future!"

I knew Dad harbored secrets that fueled his anger, but in spite of the turbulence, Lee Roy Hawkins Sr. always believed in me. I never questioned his inherent goodness. When Mom feared I'd either end up "in jail or dead," Dad's resolve to guide me only intensified. He was determined to not only ease her worries, but prove her wrong, a sentiment I didn't feel as deeply. All I wanted was to distance myself from Mom's putdowns and, most of all, her energy, as much as possible within the confines of our shared home.

In fact, I found relief in the new arrangement, recognizing that my father and my grandfathers would guide the rest of my life.

My collaboration with Dad ignited a gradual transformation that started the moment I stepped out of Mrs. Blumer's classroom.

Grateful to the numerous Black women from Rondo who were teachers, principals, and professors, I started a weekly math tutoring program at the church. With their dedicated one-on-one guidance, not only did my understanding of fourth-grade math solidify, but both my scores and my schoolteachers' assessment of my potential and my behavior significantly improved.

Dad often gave me pep talks, urging me to recognize the little successes and use them as a foundation for bigger achievements.

As I continued to grow taller and stronger, I became even crazier about basketball, sprinting, and everything else sports related. I spent hours outside, usually hooping on our raised backyard basketball court, or playing kickball, padless full-tackle football, soccer, and street hockey with friends.

Dad, a former star high-school basketball player, loved to tour the backyard court and challenge us all to games of Horse, always wowing us with his assassin-level outside shots. In actual gyms, he shot effortlessly from the NBA regulation three-point territory. His shot, combined with his trash talking and incredible finesse for a man his size, made our house a popular gathering spot for the cluster of athletic kids who made up my growing, mostly white, social circle.

As my pickup games became faster and started to attract more kids, Dad suggested that we all head over to Friday Night Open Gym at John Glenn Junior High across the street. Every Friday, there were always two full-court games going at once, the men on one side and the boys on the other.

Sometimes, I'd take a break from my own games to go over and watch Dad and his friends school the dudes from Maplewood with no-look passes, flawless dribbling, and high-intensity defense. Despite the potbelly he'd acquired from all those after-church buffets, Dad's outside shot was a thing of beauty. He'd bring the ball down to the top of the key, with that spare tire bouncing, and launch bomb after bomb. When he did that, it was often lights out. Swoosh.

Dad came over to watch me as well, teaching me and my friends how to take the ball to the hole, the importance of assists, faking, and awareness and how to "box out."

As I watched him teach, I couldn't help but recognize that not everybody had a father who spent his Friday nights playing basketball with his son and teaching other kids. At Open Gym, in our backyard, and in just about every other venue where my father mentored me, he helped the other kids around me just as much, especially those whose fathers rarely came around.

"Follow your shot!" he'd yell from the other side of the court. Or if someone fell, Dad always ran over to pull them up and say, "Okay buddy, shake it off. Now you're sure you're okay, right? If you need to sit out for a while, take a break."

Most vividly, I remember the positive reinforcement he gave me and every kid who responded to it.

I'm assuming that these encouraging words and moments of father-son bonding are what qualified as "spoiling" for Mom. Whatever the case, I was caught in the middle between Mom's insistence that Dad be even more violent with me and his attempts to normalize our relationship with glimmers of kindness after whipping me or throwing me around the room.

10

Soul Food and Sugar

n my grandparents' kitchen I never tasted a collard green without also devouring the scrumptious, squiggly textured pork they boiled into every pot: ham hocks, pig snout, pig ears. Whatever random part of the pig they added to the melt-in-the-mouth greens that day, I'd chow down with gusto. Consequently, I've never been able to enjoy greens without the "seasoning" of textured fatbacks, strips of bacon, or whatever lard they'd throw in. That steaming hot, soft-textured mix seemed to moonwalk into my stomach with a soulful jiggle.

At home, too, pork and lard were such staples of the delicious soul food Mom cooked that I probably had my first bite before I even had teeth. Mom, with her background as a nurse, would vow to cut down on our pork consumption. "We can't always do this," was her mantra, trying to stress the importance of moderation. "But today is a special treat." Soon, however, her plan to serve pork only a few days a year ballooned to several days in a month. And her evangelism for healthy eating was no match for the euphoria throughout our large extended family whenever potentially deadly foods were on the table. Indeed, for a family like ours in the '70s and '80s, pork was about as common as a hot comb or a worn-down copy of the James Brown's album *Live at the Apollo*.

My penchant for these "heart attacks on a plate"—gargantuan portions of soul food cooked with pork, sugar, white flour, and salt—lasted for decades before I developed any awareness that eating this way was responsible for the considerable number of aunts, uncles, and cousins walking around saying, "My sugar is high today." Even as I came to recognize that comment to mean "I have type-2 diabetes," I failed to see its dangerous implications. I perceived type-2 diabetes more as a nuisance than a potentially fatal condition. The same misconception existed for me regarding high blood pressure, which I never associated with fatal heart attacks, strokes, or diet. Yet, a surprising number of peers from my childhood mourned their Black fathers who passed away in their forties and fifties.

Almost every instance of such early deaths was met with my mother's hauntingly consistent explanation: "He died in his sleep." Growing up, I began to interpret this sentence as a veiled truth. These men hadn't merely died without cause; they had in fact succumbed to heart attacks or strokes. But I regarded such tragedies as mere unfortunate events that wouldn't touch me or my family.

In 1979, Nanny, my maternal grandmother, was abruptly hospitalized after collapsing. She was around fifty years old and worked at the Gould battery company. I never linked Nanny's heart attack to her grueling factory shifts or any aspect of her lifestyle. In my eyes, people in their fifties were old, and given how prevalent heart attacks seemed within that age group, I deemed it a typical age for dying. Thank God, Nanny survived.

I recognized the rarity and blessing of having great-grandparents in my life. At sixty-eight, Great-Grandmother Roberta struggled, but sixty-nine-year-old Great-Grandpa Sam often displayed more vitality than my parents, who were some forty years his junior. The pork he ate didn't seem to have negative health effects. I attribute this to Great-Grandpa's consistent pairing of those hearty meats with fresh vegetables like green beans, okra, onions, and cucumber from his extensive backyard garden. He never sported a potbelly, seemingly practicing organic eating before it became a buzzword. While he and other elder acquaintances might not have attributed their longevity and vigor to their garden-fresh diets, Great-Grandpa Sam always prioritized natural food sources.

But for my peers and me, brands like McDonald's and Burger King and sugary cereals like Cap'n Crunch and Cocoa Pebbles were the pinnacle of gastronomy. Though Mom, being ahead of her time in scrutinizing food labels, tried to steer us toward healthier options like oatmeal and Cheerios, I'd sneak in heaps of sugar and butter to my oatmeal for my comforting sugar rush.

In the rare moments of breath-catching that followed my parents' whippings, I'd scrape together coins and dollars that my grandpa had given me and ride my bike to McDonald's to freeze out the humiliation with a vanilla shake. And if I couldn't escape, I'd sneak into the kitchen, pull out the ice cream and milk, pour in soda or a heaping tablespoon of Nestle's Quik, and mix it all together. All of this for that burst of sugar, which would soon flood my body with a sense of peace.

Today, I recognize that sugar was and is my high, my drug of choice for calming my nerves and easing my pain. And while the source of that pain was my own family, my most energetic pushers came from the same ranks.

My grandpa Buddy was known to the kids at church as the Candy Man. Every Sunday, less than a second after Rev. Battle had spoken the last words of the benediction, the race to Grandpa was on. Kids in the choir stand, in the back row—kids everywhere—walked toward the sanctuary as fast as they could without being scolded, hoping to reach him first.

And for Dad and me, the Super America gas station was our crack house. That was our pit stop from relentlessly chasing that constant fix.

"Lee Roy! And Lee!" the cashiers yelled as soon as we set the bell off on the all-glass front door on Friday nights after Open Gym. "How was the gym? Good games?"

"Yeah, man, we shot them out of that gym tonight!" my dad would say. "And Lee took the kids to the hoop, too! We had a good ol' time down there, man. You need to come and play sometime."

"I know. I'm hoping to get a Friday night off on the schedule so I can join you."

"Aw man, you sure you're ready? Lee, I don't think he's ready for us."

With all of us laughing, Dad and I would plop last week's empty bottles up on the counter, primed to apply the deposit refund to our next eight-pack purchase. Then, we'd head to the back and start mixing up our eight-packs with every 1970s staple brand from orange and grape to root beer and cola.

Once we got it, I'd get in the car and guzzle a whole bottle, stopping only long enough to keep the fizz from burning the back of my dry throat. With the salt from my dried sweat still on my upper lip, I'd follow up my slam of a half-bottle of Orange Crush with a Twinkie and whatever chocolate Dad had bought me that night.

The love for the Pepsi-Coke taste tests and those craving-filling pop runs were part of the father-son glue that united us. Neither of us ever stopped to think that we were gulping down the calorie equivalent of a full meal, all after running at near-full speed off and on for two or three straight hours. And since I was unaware of the nutritional differences between soda and water, I doubt there was ever a time during my childhood that I opened the refrigerator and grabbed our water pitcher instead of a can of pop. If both are liquids, I thought, why not choose the one that tastes better?

Thanks to my rapid metabolism and my passion for hoops, skateboarding, playing on fields, roller-skating, and even the daring act of tunneling through towering Minnesota snow mounds, I burned calories off quickly and was never a candidate for childhood diabetes. Yet, I often wonder whether Dad would have maintained a healthier weight without our shared sugar cravings. That sweet indulgence was a cornerstone of our father-son relationship, as beautiful and unwavering as it was intricate and challenging. Back then, I was unaware that my sugar addiction would be a lifelong struggle.

But it wasn't sugar alone that could sweep our family from gloom into euphoria; it was piles and piles of food. Food was our narcotic, antidepressant, and family unifier—a way to lighten and inject joy into an otherwise dismal day. On any Sunday after church, we could go to a restaurant in St. Paul or Minneapolis—especially the buffets—and find large Black families spiffed up and dressed to the teeth, eating together. Momma, Daddy, Granny, Grandpa, and all the cousins. Eating was a family affair.

One of our favorite spots was Old Country Buffet, known for its after-church "all-you-can-eat" spread. The buffet featured big soft serve machines like the ones at the Minnesota State Fair: you just pull a lever and delicious ice cream would flow straight into your bowl. That was after the main food, which could be anything from prime rib to baked ham to fried chicken.

Dad and I always hit the buffet at least three times, often four or five.

Thank God all the buffet food never bore the stench of the chitlins my parents made us clean and eat during special holidays, like Christmas and Thanksgiving. My mom told us that chitlins, or chitterlings, as they were labeled at grocery stores, were "a delicacy." For a long time, I didn't know exactly what they were, just that they were from some part of a pig. Then she showed me how to clean them.

"You see that clear film on it? Pull all of that off and take off any of that black dirt that you see," Mom said. "Do it right, because if you miss something, we could all get food poisoning and die."

I always had a hard time processing the notion that these were so great that they were potentially worth dying for. They looked like the squiggly part of the brain, and they stretched out like an accordion of flesh. Eventually, I found out that chitlins are pig intestines, that the clear film is the membrane, and that the black stuff could be dirt or even pig feces. But by then, I had already learned to love these slimy pieces of pig guts as a vestige of enslavement that we should all embrace with pride.

Mom explained that chitlins were "part of our Blackness," our very identity, and that's why we should eat them on special holidays. Mom said that "the slave masters took all the good parts of the pig"—the pork loin and the finest ribs—for themselves and threw the chitlins, the pig snout, the pigs' feet, and the ears to the enslaved. "And we found a way to make them our own," Mom told us. "We add spices and all the right ingredients to make them special."

It never crossed my mind to inquire of my parents or Great-Grandpa Sam about our ancestors' diet before enslavement. I was aware we hailed from a proud lineage somewhere in Africa, but I never asked, "Did our ancestors eat chitlins in Africa?" Judging by how my parents and others praised chitlins, one might think African royals dined on them daily. During the Christmas season, grocery stores around Rondo stocked large containers of frozen chitlins. As the New

Year's Eve feast approached, my family and I would gather around the kitchen table, separating the stinking membrane from the octopus-like intestines. The festive atmosphere led Tiffany and me to believe that the joy chitlins brought justified the assault on our nostrils. Once the chitlins were cleaned, we'd fill a huge pot with chilly water and boil them. Mom used many different seasonings, but I have no idea which ones. All I know is that within several hours, I was shoveling those hog intestines into my own intestines.

Guilt about having fled a Black community for the suburbs may have fueled some of my parents' enthusiastic embrace of these "Black" food traditions. I know my mom loved to boast about making chitlins, as if to say, "We moved to the suburbs, but we're not trying to be white. We still relate to our own because we eat 'Black' food." (Oddly, many family members who came to gatherings at which chitlins were served claimed to be disgusted by them—yet, somehow, at the end of the night, the chitlin pots were always bare.)

But through eating chitlins, we reestablished our connection to what we believed to be our heritage. Through eating chitlins, we were automatically Black enough.

11

The John Henry Within Us

My mom's stepfather was "Papa Elmer" instead of "Grandpa." He married Nanny after she divorced Grandpa Buddy. Papa Elmer had green eyes and ginger hair, hinting at some Irish roots, combined with his caramel-toned African heritage. Though he had a limp, he was a hard-working roofer, contributing to Minnesota's tallest building, the IDS Center, and Maplewood Mall, where my sister Tammi had her birthday party with her church friend Kimberly Coleman.

Our lack of blood connection never fazed me.

Though Mom and Aunt Connie were Grandpa Buddy's children, they never used the term "half" for their three younger siblings. Yet Mom's vague references to Papa Elmer's harsh treatment of her as a child were clear, and sad. Even though he never mistreated me, I often wondered, Why couldn't he have treated Mom better? God knows my innocent young mother suffered, and our household paid the price for that. She deserved so much more. Was I wrong to admire Papa?

Papa was one of the few adults who let me be a child. Once, while walking on my great-grandparents' land with him, he mentioned, "John Henry worked here, Lee-Lee." Just then, I spotted some rusty chains on the ground. "Papa," I asked, "did John Henry leave this?" He examined them and said, "He sure did. That John Henry was a hard-working Black man. No task too big for him!"

Grandpa Buddy had introduced me to John Henry's story. Through Papa's tales, John Henry felt more real to me than Santa Claus or Peter Pan. His story mirrored the superior work ethic and resilience of the men in our family.

John Henry's famous declaration "Before I let this steam drill beat me down, I'll die with my hammer in my hand" became our family's mantra. He outpaced steam-powered machines, hammering spikes to save his fellow workers from automation. "I worked them two jobs for a long time, Lee-Lee," Grandpa Buddy once shared, as we floated down Highway 36 in his brand-new, tan-on-brown Cadillac Fleetwood. "And I'm nearing my end. I've explored much of the world, but there's still more out there! Two pensions! Yes indeed, I've paid my dues!"

He worked at the Burlington Northern Railroad by day, was a janitor at Montgomery Ward by night, and was among the first of the few Blacks in Maplewood in the 1960s, where he built a spacious colonial home.

Hard work defined the Hawkins, Blakey, Pugh, and Davis families. Though Dad's father, Columbus "Lum" Hawkins, died when I was three, Dad shared stories about him. Papa Lum built their Alabama home by hand and worked for more than thirty years at the railroad and the lumberyard in Greenville, Alabama. Every grandfather of mine had more than three decades of union labor. Even with pensions, two took on side jobs like painting or invested in real estate.

Great-Grandpa Sam, born in 1909, juggled jobs at a meatpacking plant, Montgomery Ward, and the St. Paul Science Museum. He also repaired radios, earning well. The community often sought his services. He assisted at Brooks Funeral Home, too. Great-Grandmother Roberta worked at the St. Paul YWCA and served on the board of the Hallie Q. Brown Community Center.

I cherished visits to their Wisconsin lake cottage. But Great-Grandpa Sam insisted on chores first. He'd instruct me in tasks like moving oak tables, yelling, "Boy, you better not drop my table!" Visits occasionally left my hands calloused.

"Those old-timers have rough hands from factories and sharecropping," Dad reminded me. "When they shake your hand, feel their roughness. They have rough hands so yours can be smooth." Lots of them, in fact, were missing fingers. Dad told me they were chopped off in sawmills and packing plants.

"You know why Rev. Battle makes everybody who makes the honor roll or gets their master's degree stand up and announce their achievement to the whole church?" he asked. "Because a lot of them—especially from down South—couldn't go to school. They want you to be able to do what they couldn't. When you grow up, you'll be earning what your grandpas make in your one job, probably way more."

I was raised firmly in the belief of American capitalism. My family's 1980s success model was clear: secure a corporate job, buy house, buy land, invest in stocks, stay at that job for years, rent out your real estate, and retire at a reasonable age. Guided by the "work twice as hard as the white man" principle, they believed success was attainable in one generation, even with half the opportunities. They, who built or bought houses fresh out of or well before Jim Crow without G.I. Bills and against the grain of redlining and racial covenants, were living proof.

For them, working twice as hard often meant working two or more jobs, like Great-Grandpa Sam. Dad worked at Northwestern Bell during the day and played lead guitar with groups like the Sounds of Blackness in Minneapolis by night. We'd sing gospel in various churches across the Twin Cities on Sundays. Yet he prioritized family and chose not to tour outside of Minnesota, no matter how successful a band became.

Although Dad never seemed content with his blue-collar job, often coming home agitated, he instilled in me that all work was honorable. However, he made it clear he wouldn't want me in a role like his. We were comfortable, with three sources of income: his two and Mom's. After working as a health coordinator, she transitioned to being a human resources consultant. Inspired by Mom and the many adults at our church who pursued higher education, from BAs to PhDs, Dad chipped away at his night classes, taking advantage of the phone company's tuition reimbursement program. Early on, he set his sights on a master's degree.

On barbershop trips, Dad would show me an injury, saying, "Look at this, son. A wire sliced into my hand on Friday. Study hard. Aim for an office job. You don't want to be out in this freezing Minnesota cold! The wind up on those poles can be deadly!" Though I never experienced a telephone pole's height, I took his advice to heart. Because of all the nonstop lawn-mowing and landscaping, snow-shoveling, and painting I did, I had a sense of how grueling the labor sector could be.

Dad knew from his air force days that a union job with the Communications Workers of America would benefit a Black man like him. Despite Black World War II veterans often being denied the benefits of the G.I. Bill, many landed union jobs at major companies. While many wives pursued education at Black colleges, numerous men served in the military and then went to work, aided by the presence of several Fortune 500 companies in Minnesota.

Yet Dad never counted on any company. The possibility of a labor strike was ever-present, especially in the 1970s when potential telecom work offshoring weakened union influence. Starting at Northwestern Bell in 1974, he landed jobs that hadn't been available to millions of people in the Black generations before the Civil Rights Act of 1964.

"Before the civil rights bill and affirmative action, these companies didn't have to even look at a brotha," Dad told me. "I got the job, right on time, but me and every other brotha have to go through a helluva lotta stuff to stay there. And if anything racist happens, I can sue, but even if I were to win, I'd never be able to find work again."

Grandpa Buddy put more trust in the union and the Democrats than Dad. He was politically vocal and deeply patriotic. He generally favored Democrats but had a Republican exception: his cousin Ted Blakey, a GOP convention delegate for South Dakota and our family historian. Cousin Ted demonstrated that a Black man could succeed in white circles, maintain conservative beliefs, and still champion Black rights. He cast his delegate vote for Richard Nixon in 1972 and, later, Ronald Reagan. Despite Reagan's silence on Black issues, Cousin Ted and the convention's Black caucus were hopeful. "Inflation probably hits Black people the hardest," he told the Associated Press. "They're often the last hired and the first fired."

Grandpa Buddy and Cousin Ted, while close, had quarreling beliefs. Grandpa supported unions, while Cousin Ted leaned toward business. Grandpa would say, "Ted mentions our ancestors were Republicans, but that was a different party back then."

Grandpa Buddy pushed me to expand my reading beyond stories

of John Henry. He promoted critical thinking, and I found my views to often align with the family's: fiscal and moral conservatism paired with social progressivism. I remained receptive to voices from both political spectrums. Despite some relatives labeling our business-owning Cousin Ted an "Uncle Tom" for his GOP ties, my patriarchs taught me that every Black American deserved ideological and political freedom and that the Democratic Party—not just the GOP—could be very racist. We tuned into *Firing Line* and *Tony Brown's Journal*, spurring my interest in diverse media content. The *Wall Street Journal*, with its in-depth page one stories, became my favorite.

Dad perceived the allure of Reagan's campaign messages among his white colleagues. "Even though he's against their interests, some of them will vote for Reagan," Dad observed. "The prejudiced ones just want someone to hold the Black man down." Reagan's slogan, "Let's Make America Great Again," deeply upset Dad. With a shiver, Dad said Reagan's slogan was code for wanting to "put Black folks back more than fifteen years, like it was in Alabama for us."

His reaction hinted that Jim Crow's realities were possibly graver than school lessons suggested, that they went beyond just Rosa Parks and segregation into a more terrifying experience. He told me: "Son, a lot of white folks see jobs like mine—where you can work overtime and make as much as an executive—as their American dream. That's why I'm in night school. What a lot of white folks down at my job don't understand is that, probably in less than ten years, all these high-paying labor jobs in telecommunications are gonna be gone. And just like Black folks were the last hired, when these layoffs hit, we'll be the first fired. But they'll be next."

"Let's Make America Great Again" was a hit, because "from 1965, going back centuries, America was great for white folks," Dad said, because the country's laws gave them supreme status in terms of jobs, housing, education, military benefits, land grants, and every aspect of American life. "And believe me, if Reagan can find a way to put us back in chains, he will," Dad continued, getting increasingly upset. "He's telling all those white people out there that America is their country. Those racists are thinking, 'If it's up to me, a Black

won't even have a vote, let alone a well-paying job.' But always remember what Curtis said, son." And then he started singing Curtis
Mayfield's song "This Is My Country":

> *We've survived a hard blow and I want you to know . . .*
> *This is my country.*

That year, Dad voted for incumbent President Jimmy Carter, the
fifth election since Blacks gained full voting rights.

However, I initially believed Dad's concerns about Reagan were
exaggerated. It wasn't until 2019 that a White House tape exposed
Reagan's racist comments. In 1971, he told Nixon, "To see those mon-
keys from those African countries—damn them, they're still uncomfortable wearing shoes!" Nixon laughed in response.

A year into Reagan's term, he officially announced the National
Air Traffic Controllers Association's refusal of a $40 million raise, af-
ter their $600 million request. By standing firm, Reagan marked the
decline of labor unions in the United States. Even as a ten-year-old, I
sensed Dad's concerns about the declining industrial economy and the
risk to his job and those of unsuspecting parents of the working-class
kids at school.

Dad prepared me to break into a white-collar world that, fewer
than twenty years earlier, had no legal requirement to accept us.

"That's the power of your generation," Grandpa Buddy told me.
"You can be whatever you want, Lee-Lee. Yes indeed, even president!
We'll have a Black president one day! I really believe it!"

My family and community—my "village"—nurtured both me and
other Black boys I knew, teaching us to see ourselves as victors, not
victims. By the time I entered junior high, the haunting thoughts of
suicide, prison, or early, violent death were long gone from my anxious
mind. I knew I needed to strive to be like John Henry, but I couldn't
afford to think about the metaphorical implications of John Henry's
story—the fact that in the end, he died of exhaustion.

12

Chest Pains

On September 17, 1982, we had just returned from school when Uncle Ronnie urgently told us to get in his car. I had always admired Uncle Ronnie. He was a respected military officer and a jovial prankster. That day, however, Uncle Ronnie was out of jokes. The eerie quiet in the car as we hit Highway 36 to my great-grandparents' house should have clued me in, but I had no idea what awaited. As soon as we walked through the door of the big white house, I ran over to Great-Grandmother Roberta's chair, planning to give her a hug and kiss on my way to the kitchen to see what Great-Grandpa Sam had cooking. But I encountered a room so full of relatives that it might have been Christmas. Cousins of all kinds, my grandmother, Mom, and various friends sat around Great-Grandmother's empty chair in tears.

I knew Great-Grandmother Roberta—the woman who spoke life into her inquisitive, writerly grandson—was gone.

Mom took us upstairs to break the news officially.

Mrs. Moore, who lived a few houses up from us in Maplewood, had been styling Great-Grandmother's hair, when she told Mrs. Moore that she felt weak and went to her bedroom to lie down. I was grateful that Mom didn't give us the whole backstory but was thoughtful enough to reassure us that our great-grandmother died in peace.

I marvel today at the fact that her heart gave out at only age seventy-two. She seemed a million years old to me then. And with so many of my elders suffering from stress-compounded "high sugar" or blood pressure problems, many seemed older than their chronological ages.

Mom, who was extraordinarily kind to me that whole week as I grieved, turned to me at the funeral and sweetly gave me a rare hug and affirming squeeze in front of the flower-flanked pink-and-burgundy casket. The serenity of that day had the strongest impact on Mom. In the car, she and Dad talked about how Great-Grandmother had "rescued" Mom, but once we arrived at the church and greeted other family members, all such talk subsided. I would have loved to hear more about that rescue, but Mom brought it up only when she was whaling on me. In the welcomed harmony of those somber days, I wondered whether Great-Grandmother Roberta's death might inspire a permanent turnabout in Mom.

Alas, it was not to be, as I learned in no uncertain terms the day after the funeral. I was on the phone with Rochelle, a Black girl I had a crush on at school. Back then, I wasn't allowed to talk on the phone to girls—white, mostly, but also Black. I did it anyway, but always on the sly.

Still reeling from the funeral, Mom picked up the extension line in the bedroom, realized I was talking to a girl, and instantly yelped, "Lee! Get! Off! This! Phone! GET OFF NO-O-O-O-O-W-W-W!"

Without speaking, I hung up on Rochelle.

Mom and Dad were notorious for a psychological reaction that I learned about that year in my health class: displacement. Broadly speaking, displacement is defined as "a psychological defense mechanism in which a person redirects a negative emotion from its original source to a less threatening recipient."

That term opened a world of understanding for eleven-year-old me. It explained all those times my parents seemed to be making *me* pay for all *their* traumas and tragedies, or would seem to come home looking for a child to scold or hit. It helped me understand that my parents didn't hate me, but my role in those moments was to be their target. And targets can't talk back.

I'd gesture or speak with a tone Mom didn't like, and with a snap, she'd catapult me into a land of misery. Today, Tiffany and I humorously liken those memories to an image of Fred Sanford from *Sanford and Son*, grabbing at his heart and calling out "Elizabeth!" to his beloved widow. Since our mom, "Fredericka Sanford," survived, we can joke about it now. But back then, no one was laughing.

"Lee Roy, I'm having chest pains!" she'd yell at my father, grabbing her chest and sometimes swooning against the kitchen counter. Breathing heavily, she'd stagger to a chair, and wait for our frightened Dad to rush to pull it out for her, all the while moaning, "I need to sit down. These kids are going to kill me. My heart! My heart!"

Whenever this happened—dozens of times over the next decade—Dad would frantically run around grabbing my mom's coat, purse, and whatever else she told him she needed. Then he'd yell, "Y'all get in the damn car! We need to take your momma in now! Hurry the hell up!"

We'd drop whatever we were doing and rush to the car so Dad could whisk us all to the ER. Every time this happened, I'd sit in the facility's family waiting area and pray desperately for Mom's heart to keep beating. And I'd pray even harder that Tiffany or I—whichever of us would be blamed that day (Tammi never did anything to trigger Mom's "chest pains")—would survive the beatdown that our father would inevitably unleash on us later.

Our Dad was psychologically and genetically possessed by fear that he or one of us kids would cause my mother's heart to give out. In response to this threat on her life, he regularly promised to beat us within an inch of ours, and even take us out.

"If anything happens to my wife, I'll kill you," he'd scream at Tiffany and me, pushing or slapping us while herding us out the door to get Mom to urgent care. If only I could have said the same for Tiffany and me.

When we were old enough to become latchkey kids, Mom taught Tammi how to operate the crockpot and taught all three of us to sweep, mop, and vacuum. She called regularly from work to check on our progress with chores. Tammi did a fantastic job with all these tasks, and Tiffany and I were grateful—but also guilty that, like Mom, she carried the burden of being the oldest child.

I expressed my guilt to God relentlessly. Every time I sat in one of those ER waiting rooms, I'd pray to him for forgiveness for disrupting Mom's dreams of being a dancer, and for being responsible for her bad moods, her apparently weak heart, and a boatload of embarrassment and trouble. Tiff and I both accepted and carried that blame.

I would estimate that 80 percent of the whippings Tiffany and I received from our dad—on top of Mom's—had to do with our upsetting Mom, and 90 percent of the beatings from Dad were ordered by her. Whenever that happened, the raging bull attacked.

When Mom grabbed her chest, it was as if she electrified and plugged an emotional cord directly into Dad's heart, in the chamber right under the one that held the death of his mother when he was only twelve years old. With a single gesture, Mom had the power to produce an instant meltdown throughout our household.

"Heart problems" were the most recent addition to the ever-growing list of health issues plaguing Mom and almost worrying Dad into an early grave. She'd already been diagnosed with an underactive thyroid, which was said to run on her side of the family, though no one ever looked into why. It was a matter of legend that my mom's great-grandmother—the daughter of enslaved people—had a thyroid mass the size of a golf ball on the side of her neck and simply lived with it. Mom was also stricken with fibromyalgia, a chronic condition that caused her to hurt all over. In our home, it was a given that stress, illness, or anything bad that ever happened was the fault of Tiffany, me, or both of us.

Mom's life and gatherings with her side of the family took up so much of the oxygen in our household that we kids rarely had a chance to ask about Dad's upbringing and family down South. And when we did, Mom shut us down with a sternly whispered, "He doesn't want to talk about that."

I knew Grandma Opie, Dad's mom, had died when he was twelve in 1961, and his father, Papa Lum, had died in 1974. I was curious about Grandma Opie's death and how Dad ended up in Minnesota. But without directly asking him, I waited for scraps of information to dribble out.

The only time Dad spoke with emotion about losing his mother so young was when he was walloping me with his belt. "You talked back to your momma!" he'd bellow while beating me. "Let me tell you something. If I could have five minutes with my momma, I would treat her like a QUEEN! [*Whap!*] Five minutes! [*Whap!*] My momma loved me!

I spent all my time with my momma! [*Whap! Whap!*] I was the baby! I never disrespected her! [*Whap! Whap! Whap!*] She took me with her everywhere! Even when she went to do work at the white folks' houses! [*Whap! Whap! Whap!*] I went with her! [*Whap! Whap! Whap! Whap!*] If I could have five minutes with her, I wouldn't ever do anything to make her unhappy! [*Whap! Whap! Whap! Whap! Whap! Whap!*] I would have taken her out of Alabama! I would have taken care of her for the rest of her life! Boy, I would give anything to have my momma back! [*Whap! Whap!*] I'm gonna tear your rump up for disrespecting your momma! I really miss my momma! I really miss my momma! IF YOU EVER DISRESPECT YOUR MOMMA AGAIN, I'LL BREAK YOUR NECK!! [*Whap! Whap!*]"

From there, the "spankings" would only intensify.

His mother's premature death fed Dad's fears that Mom could die, too—all because of the stress piled on her by her ill-behaved son or daughter.

More than a hundred times, as I crouched on the floor with Dad pummel-whipping me all over my back and arms, I asked myself the same questions: What happened to my daddy? What happened to his daddy? And what happened to his mom?

Above all, what happened in Alabama? What the *hell* happened in Alabama?

13

White Girls and Their Fathers

My school district made a budgetary decision to expand the John Glenn Junior High school to include sixth-graders. I was twelve. Entering middle school thrust me into an academic and social climate that brought together under one roof sixth-graders from all over Maplewood—aka, a bunch of awkward, insecure preteens longing and hankering to prove themselves and find acceptance among a circle of "cool" friends.

At the beginning of that year, all of us, of every race, tested each other. We constantly assessed each other with taunts and punches to the chest and arms. If a boy didn't stay primed to fight back and instill fear, he would be bullied day after day. And it seemed like every time I would step outside my persona of the fast-talking, cappin', mother-fuckin' "real nigga," I'd be tested. But whenever I brought that persona out, I was a superstar, and not to be messed with. I strived so hard to fit in that I tucked away any *A*s I received on English assignments and flaunted my shaky math scores. I didn't want to be accused of "acting white."

I stood at a pivotal moment in my life. Though I'd embraced the persona of a stereotypical "real nigga," there were times when I couldn't hide my upbringing in etiquette, usually around teachers and administrators. Deep down, a nagging sense reminded me of the need to get serious about life. The choices I'd make in the coming years, influenced by my father, my faith, and key mentors, would see me either donning an orange prison jump suit or walking free in my trademark navy blazer, Polo Oxford, and penny loafers or wingtips.

For a time, my "real nigga"/inner pimp side won the battle for my self-worth, thanks in part to the street-lit author Iceberg Slim. On the bottom shelf of a bookcase in our rec room, I found an old, tattered copy of his book *Pimp: The Story of My Life*. Tantalized, I snuck it into my room, and within a week, I had read it cover to cover. I was fascinated by Iceberg's depictions of courtship and dogged, dazzling womanizing, without understanding how they would shape my thinking. Iceberg's worldview was one that emphasized burying your emotions and refusing to reveal any vulnerability to anyone. The book made me take a closer look at my "square" father's obedience to my mother's whipping commands, and I started to see "catching feelings" like a "square" or "simp"—making bad decisions at the behest of women—as a weakness. I naively ascribed wisdom to the pimps, the players, and the hoe-slayers and the game they broke down.

That book instilled the "real nigga" belief that trust was a luxury I couldn't afford—not in friends, "whores," or especially my parents. In my eyes, genuine intelligence was gauged not just by academic prowess but by the grit to survive in the real world. Iceberg's narrative had such a grip on me that at times, it echoed the grimiest, most negative stereotypes prevalent in certain rap music today, making it harder for me to see past his portrayal of Black men. He illuminated a controversial truth: some Black men felt compelled to embrace pimping and crime, seeing them as the only avenues to success in an otherwise exclusionary world.

My confusion was compounded by my failure to recognize that the book had been published in 1967, when options for Black men were fewer than in 1983. I developed empathy and interpreted the archetypal Black pimp as a heroic figure who was what I so desperately wanted to be: *free*. Iceberg was outhustling a system that for too long had hustled Black men by subjecting them to the same relentless brutality that had been used on their enslaved forebears for centuries.

"[The book of pimping] was written in the skulls of proud slick Niggers freed from the slaver," Iceberg wrote. "They wasn't lazy. They was puking sick of picking white man's cotton and kissing his nasty ass. The slave days stuck in their skulls. They went to the cities. They got hip fast."

Iceberg wrote that he wanted to pimp his way to "some real white type living."

I felt powerful knowing I had the verbal power and secondhand street wisdom and swag to captivate and, if necessary, scare off my peers. That year, my whole social circle of Rondo-influenced "real niggas," preppy white boys, and jocks were fascinated and seduced by the profane yet smooth game I brought to school: especially my daily personification of the pimp and hustler definition of what it meant to be Black. Iceberg stressed the importance of having people love me but also fear me.

Instead of internalizing Mom's vision of me as a negative, I spun my new outlook into a positive. I'd adopt the "pimp" mindset, but then, instead of prison, I'd find a legal hustle or get rich as a "real nigga" pro basketball player or an entertainer. Captivated by the culture of '80s celebrities and luxury cars and goods, I believed that sports and entertainment were possibly my best options for success.

Neither me nor any of my Black friends realized that the self-aggrandizing, narcissistic, white supremacist view of Blackness we'd adopted was just self-hatred in a different form. I hadn't yet realized that pimpin' was not freedom, because it denigrated women and also stood to land us exactly where racists wanted us: in prison.

Then, one day, all my pimpin' ways and talk backfired on me. Some dudes from my class were cappin' on each other. One of my crushes, who I'll refer to as Ashley, entered into one of our cappin' conversations, and I decided to cap on her. A striking white girl, she had flowing, blondish-brown hair and a knack for hilarious, quick-witted comebacks. As a twelve-year-old who had yet to kiss a girl, I was besotted with and terrified of Ashley in equal measure.

Most of the time Ashley and I joked around and were friendly. I loved how she saw through my façade, always pushing me, in her subtle way, to be the Black excellence-inspired Lee Hawkins who was so much more than the "real nigga" persona I was projecting. Some days, we bickered like an old married couple. But on that day, I took things too far with name-calling while cappin', and I didn't spare her or her mother. I replaced "Ashley" with "bitch" and "hoe" and other colorful names that were more suited to a Richard Pryor standup act than a middle-school playground. Of course, I threw in the recycled line about seeing her mother on the corner of Selby and Dale—famous at the time as a corner for prostitution and hustlin'.

To her credit, Ashley wasn't having any of it. Our fathers knew each other from co-coaching Tammi's softball team, and that relationship only made it easier for her dad to call my dad.

And he did just that.

Ashley's father told my dad that I had called his daughter an assortment of names, most offensively, a whore. All the way to my bedroom, I could actually feel my father's anger rippling through his body and releasing into the air. Even more palpable was the fear in my dad's voice of "that white man" on the other end of the phone. Without hanging up, Dad strode to my room, grabbed me by my shirt, and dragged me to the dining room, where the white man was still on the line. Within seconds, the attack escalated into a full-fledged beatdown. Dad dragged me around the house, delivering punishing belt blows and slaps, making sure that Ashley's dad heard it all.

Dad returned to the phone, whereupon he instantly morphed from the fearlessness of Muhammad Ali to the docility of Stepin Fetchit. Speaking in an Alabama drawl more dramatic and distinct than he'd ever used before, he breathlessly assured Ashley's dad that such an outrage would never happen again. "You be sure to call me, sir, if your daughter ever has any more problems with my son," he said to Ashley's father. "You do that, okay?"

Then he made me apologize. After he finally hung up the phone, the beating continued, along with my mom's screams.

"That white man could come here and kill us all," my mom shrieked, using the same script she'd used a thousand times before. "You're talking to that white man's daughter like that? And a white girl?! That girl and her father have the power to get you killed or destroy your life forever! You better learn to respect her! Don't you know these people out here could be KKK?"

"You're going to get the whole family killed!" my parents yelled in unison. "These white people will kill us! Don't you know that, boy? They will burn our house down and hang you from a tree!"

The scene was pure déjà vu. As usual, Dad did all the whipping, but Mom stood by egging him on. Having both of them in my face always ramped up the intensity a hundred notches or so. It was mayhem. Total mayhem.

My dad's decision to destroy me in hopes of placating that white man on the phone was directly at odds with my parents' previous obsession with whipping us only when they were out of sight of white people, and in places that they knew we would cover with clothing. One might think that my father's decision to let Ashley's father hear the massacre as it was happening was risky. But in that moment, I saw a sense of fear and utter compliance overtake my dad.

Though Ashley's father never once suggested that Dad touch me, Dad evidently felt he needed to beat me so severely that Ashley's dad would let go of any inclination or motivation to hang me. At that point, if that white man had demanded that I moonwalk across the kitchen, my father would have made me do it, Greenville, Alabama–style.

Somehow, Dad knew Ashley's father wouldn't report him. And if he had, the Maplewood police would have rolled up to the front steps of a household led by two gainfully employed, married Black homeowners and probably would have been happy to hear a responsible Black father tell them, "My son called a white girl a whore, so I'm whipping him."

And that, I genuinely believe, would have earned Dad the key to the city.

14

Kareem Abdul-Jabbar

My beloved St. Paul chapter of Jack and Jill of America changed my life forever.

Every month, there was a special event, which could range from going to museums and sporting events to listening to guest speakers, roller-skating, dancing, and attending parties. In February, the club sponsored a Black History Month program.

I preferred the events to the programs because the parents always attended those, which automatically made them "boring." In truth, my lack of enthusiasm for those adult-inclusive events arose mostly from Mom's off-the-charts anxiety level whenever we went to one. Before leaving for any Jack and Jill function, she'd remind us that punctuality was their creed, far more than at church. "These people start promptly," she'd say. "They won't wait around for us."

The tension on the ride there was often so high that even Dad would internalize it and express it once we arrived. Instead of "Lee Roy," he'd go by "Leo," his white-people-at-work name. "Hello Richard, Leo Hawkins," he'd say, overpronouncing every word as if he'd just breezed in from Connecticut. But he couldn't sustain that for long. It just wasn't Dad, though he was a serious man, with a business-world sensibility that emerged when needed. But in our early days in Jack and Jill, he'd sweat from his brow, much to Mom's chagrin. She'd look at him wordlessly, and he'd pull out his handkerchief, go into the bathroom, and come back five minutes later looking like Smokey Robinson on *Motown 25*.

I never understood all that angst. To me, Jack and Jill was a chance to be around a bunch of Black friends I could relate to, most of whom attended private or suburban schools similar to mine. Just like the white kids at school, none of them made me sweat. We were all Black kids, absorbing our parents' expectations, often as the only ones of our kind in predominantly white suburbs or private schools. Yet, thanks in part to each other, we still found plenty of joy.

Once, Mom saw me talking to a girl from Jack and Jill at an event that was held at Chuck E. Cheese. As we chatted, I caught a glimpse of Mom in the distance, staring at me with a dark, potentially punitive look. I glanced down at my zipper; it was fine. My shoes, ditto. Everything was perfect, but I felt as if my shirt was hanging out of my trousers. Then I thought, *Maybe I'm not allowed to talk to girls in person, the way I can't on the phone.* But my mom saw me talking to girls at church every Sunday, so that wasn't it.

On the way home, Mom asked, "What were y'all talking about?"

"I don't remember, really. Just stuff we've talked about before."

"Like what? Don't act like you don't know what you were talking about. What did she say? What did you say? You can't just be saying anything to these people."

For some unknown reason, I momentarily forgot that, if Mom directed him, my father would reach back and pull my Adam's apple out of my throat.

"What do you mean?" I snapped. "Am I supposed to be afraid of her? She's cool and she's just my friend. Why should I be so cautious?"

I looked at Dad's profile behind the wheel, and he started to break into a little smile. But Mom was far from smiling. "I doubt she's worrying too much about whether you say hello to her or not," she said coolly. "Her family is very, very prominent. She performs classical music, and I think she's in modern dance."

I scrunched my face into a squint, trying not to laugh, but Dad's widening grin gave it all away. Within seconds, we were both laughing—not at my friend, but at this idea that I should be carrying a red carpet under my shoulder for any musician who plays classical music or dancer who is in "modern dance."

My words leaped forward without a thought for the potentially violent consequences.

"Modern d-ah-h-h-hnce?" I said, mockingly and intentionally

delivering a poor faux British accent. "Am I supposed to be as intimidated and afraid of these kids as you are of their parents?" I asked. "Well, you may think they're better than you, but I know that nobody is better than me. Nobody is better than anybody."

"Did I say that I'm intimidated or afraid? I'm not afraid of anybody! Do you hear me, boy?" Mom's voice had risen a full pitch.

"Then why are you always acting so insecure, like people are so much better than you? I don't think I'm better than anybody. And nobody is better than me. You're the one who thinks like that."

Mom stayed silent and I figured she would wait for Dad to kill me. My brow started to steam, and I braced myself for an explosion. But I was angry and forged ahead anyway.

"You say that I embarrass *you*, but I'm embarrassed that you're so embarrassed and intimidated by some of the mothers and kids in Jack and Jill. They're great people, but they're just people, just like anybody else."

"What did you say, boy? *I* embarrassed *you*?"

"Yeah, you embarrassed me! You made me take clothes from other kids that I don't wear."

"What? What do you mean?" Dad suddenly interjected.

Then I told them both what Andre, a friend of my cousin Eric, had said to me in front of a bunch of other Jack and Jill kids: "You get all of Eric's clothes, don't you?" I guess he was referring to a time when Eric's mom kindly brought over a bag of clothes that my cousin had outgrown. Mom left them in my room. I'd thought it was a nice-enough gesture on my sweet aunt's part, but I didn't see much of anything in the bag that I would ever wear. I honestly believed my cousin meant no harm by mentioning to Andre that I get his hand-me-downs, and I knew it would seem snooty if I said I never wore them or wanted them. So, I just grinned and let my cousin say, "Yeah, Lee gets all of them."

I planned to say to Mom that maybe it would have been better to give the clothes to Andre, or to another cousin who might appreciate them more than I did. After all, I was a twelve-year-old who read *GQ* religiously and shined the tips of his shoes until they shone like mirrors. Though I would grow up to love vintage and resale clothes, I was young then and extremely sensitive to peer pressure. It hadn't escaped me that the kids I hung out with routinely capped on kids who wore clothes that weren't name brand or were hand-me-downs.

But before I could say anything more, Dad exploded into a tirade. I instantly feared for my life, but this time he laid into Mom. "Leo Hawkins" vanished, replaced by a version of "Lee Roy" that we rarely saw.

"What the fuck did you do?" he screamed at his wife. "You gave my son another little nigga's clothes? Are you fuckin' crazy?" His head was turned so close to her that his eyes were barely on the road.

"Why are you taking clothes from these niggas?" he continued. "You act like we don't have the money to clothe our own kids! What the fuck is wrong with you? Don't you ever take clothes from anybody for my son, do you hear me?"

Mom stayed silent. Dad kept ranting. "I'm not playin' with you, Bobby . . . or any of these niggas! Do you hear me? Do you?!"

"Yes."

"I better never see no raggedy-ass, secondhand clothes on my son. You give those clothes back! Do you hear me? Give 'em THE FUCK back!"

Because he used the same tone with Mom as he did with me right before he would knock me into next week, I felt a brief surge of fear that he might lash out at her too. Thank God, he never did to his high school sweetheart and lifelong love what he didn't hesitate to do to one of his kids. But his point was clear. An immensely proud man, my father was meticulous about his wardrobe, and he passed on that dignity to me. But while I was amused by Andre's remark, it clearly touched a nerve from Dad's concealed Alabama past. And from that day forward, my father went by "Lee Roy Hawkins" at every Jack and Jill event we ever attended.

Not long after, my family attended our first Jack and Jill Black History Month program, which took place on a Sunday at the King Center. Since we had to rush from church, Mom was already uptight about our showing up ten minutes into the program. When we took our seats (with time to spare), I opened the program and saw my name listed as one of several kids who would be speaking. "Lee Hawkins Jr." it read;

"Reflections on Kareem Abdul-Jabbar." Shocked, I looked at Mom, pointed to the program, and shook my head. This was news to me.

Mom glared back, and moments later, one of the other moms came to the edge of the aisle and motioned me over. She asked if I was ready and whether I had any questions. "I didn't know about this," I said, my stomach lurching. "Is there any way I could do it next year?"

The woman told me my name had been volunteered—without specifying who did so—and mentioned that I was supposed to have received a confirmation call to ensure I was ready, a call that, as far as I knew, never came. She asked me what I knew about Kareem Abdul-Jabbar, and I told her that he was of the Muslim faith, had played in college for the UCLA Bruins and then professionally for the Milwaukee Bucks and now the Los Angeles Lakers, and a couple of other factoids.

"Well, that's plenty. If you go up there with confidence and tell everything you know, you'll be great. Just talk about what you know."

I was tempted to back out, but seeing my name on the program and fearing my parents' reaction held me in place. I mentally rehearsed my lines, telling myself that facing the situation now was better than facing consequences later.

My name was called, and as I walked to the podium, the poison rushed through my veins. With every step, my thoughts grew more jumbled and toxic. My mom's voice had taken residence in my brain. *You're an embarrassment to the family. You're gonna end up in prison. You're gonna end up dead.*

When I turned to the crowd of fifty or sixty people, I seemed to be staring out at ten thousand faces. "Black History figure Kareem Abdul-Jabbar is a center for the Los Angeles Lakers," I said just before catching a glimpse of my parents. With that, everything I'd planned to say evaporated from my mind.

"He-he-he's on the LA Lakers," I stammered. "And he played for the Milwaukee Bucks, and he went to UCLA." I struggled to remember the supportive lady's advice. "And that's all I know," I added hastily, prompting an outburst of playful laughter.

I walked back to my seat, heart hammering, poisons flowing. Mom flashed me her signature widened-eye scowl, as if to say, "We are gonna beat the Black off you when you get home." I expected that she would slap me around even before we got to the car, once we were out of sight of the other Jack and Jill parents, who seemed to shrug off my performance with a "kids will be kids" chuckle.

On the way to the car, my cousin Darnell came up and said, "You did a great job, Lee-Lee. That was great."

"Thanks, Darnell. I got nervous because nobody told me I was supposed to make a speech. I knew more stuff about Kareem, but I froze up."

"Aw, cuz, that's okay. It wasn't as bad as you think."

I glanced at Mom and Dad, hoping that at least Dad would double down on Darnell's reassurances.

Not a chance. In the car, an epic verbal whipping commenced, first from Dad: "Boy, how could you get up there and not be prepared?"

Fuming, but resisting my impulse to go off on my parents for not telling me about the speech, or at least for not protecting me when it became clear that no one else had told me, I weakly defended myself: "I-I-I didn't know . . . I tried to remember . . ."

Then Mom yelled: "You didn't try anything! You were mad that you didn't know about it, so you messed it up on purpose to get revenge on us! You went up there and intentionally embarrassed the whole family, once again! You made us look uneducated, like we have no couth. You know you were raised properly, boy! You made us all look dumb!"

I hoped Dad would interject a defense, but he just kept driving.

When we got home, I made a beeline for my room, quickly donned two pairs of long underwear, and steeled myself for swinging leather. But shockingly, Mom didn't go into the bedroom that night and get Dad all riled up. Maybe I have Darnell to thank for that meager mercy.

Still, Mom remained "hurt" by her feeling that I had—yet again—"embarrassed the whole family" that day. She never let me forget that eminently forgettable episode. For years, whenever she'd recite the litany of my myriad flaws, she never failed to bring up Kareem.

15

Kings and Queens

n the same year, I had the good fortune to be taken under the wing of another Great-Grandmother Roberta–caliber matriarch from Mount Olivet. Her name was Anna Lee Jackson, a gospel pianist who was Mount Olivet's minister of music. Like other church sisters who had helped me boost my math score, Sister Jackson saw something in me that I couldn't see myself, and slowly she began to hush the voice inside me that kept insisting I should strive to be a no-good "real nigga," whose only career options were basketball, rappin', or—if life got really rough—pimpin'. But surely, I could never do anything involving delivering or writing speeches.

Sister Jackson was directing Mount Olivet's Black History theatrical production. One Sunday, she pulled me aside and asked me to audition for the part of a child version of Dr. Martin Luther King Jr. She handed me a typewritten copy of the last ten minutes of his "I've Been to the Mountaintop" speech, the last speech he ever gave. He delivered it in Memphis on April 3, 1968, the night before he was murdered.

She gave me a few minutes to page through the speech, and then she asked me to read the first part aloud, as if I were Dr. King. I had barely begun when her eyes lit up. "Boy, you have a gift for this! If you listen to the actual speech, I know you could recite it just like the original."

A gift? I thought. I had a gift, all right—for screwing up speeches and bringing on humiliation, rejection, and condemnation. That was my story. But evidently no one had told it to Sister Jackson. Although Dad had set up a modeling audition for my sisters and me in Minneapolis, leading to gigs for ads and game covers, acting was uncharted territory—something I felt I could disastrously botch.

My first impulse was to worm out of the situation. I thought about going to Mom and appealing to her concerns about our family's image. She'd surely agree that I'd be a disaster in the part and would go to Sister Jackson to quash it before I'd have to.

But Sister Jackson didn't give me a chance to plot an escape route. She handed me a cassette tape of King delivering the speech and said, "Play this tape at home and read along with Dr. King as he speaks. Pay attention to his pauses and the places where he emphasizes certain words. It may feel strange at first, but if you keep at it, you'll get better and better each time. Acting takes practice the same way singing does."

Now, of course, it's crystal clear to me that there's no way I could have refused Sister Jackson. Those Mount Olivet matriarchs had a knack for letting me know that they loved me, even when I didn't love myself. But I did love them. There were two other sisters, a set of twins named Ms. Nickerson and Ms. Shelton, who liked to catch us kids in big bear hugs just after we'd scored our candy from Grandpa Buddy. They'd smile and open their eyes as wide as parting seas as they planted kisses on our foreheads. The twins, then in their seventies, weren't just strong-willed; they were strong, fit women. They squeezed all the kids so hard that we could hardly breathe.

We were Protestants, but I considered Sister Jackson and all of those dignified matriarchs to be Baptist saints. Sometimes I'd look at them, some with their weathered faces, labored steps, missing fingers and limbs, and hunched shoulders, and try to imagine the Black History stories their bodies could tell.

In the front row of our church, the deacons, including Grandpa Buddy, sat on the left, and the deaconesses, including my aunt Loyce, sat on the right. Next to the deaconesses were the mothers, who had their own section in the front row. The median age of those matrons clad in white—Mother Hayes, Mother Milsap, and Mother Milton—was around ninety-seven. That made some of them four decades older than Dr. King, who was born in 1929. It didn't strike me as remarkable at the time that many of the people around me had been born in the mid-1880s, a scant twenty years after President Abraham Lincoln issued the Emancipation Proclamation. Some were not just the grandchildren, but the children, of enslaved people.

When Sister Jackson gave me that speech to practice, I went to the library and read Dr. King's "Letter from Birmingham Jail" and several excerpts from his books. In all those writings, his core values ran directly counter to the Iceberg Slim "nigga pimp" caricature of Blackness that I had fallen for. I was stunned as I dug further into King's work because, although he was one of the few Black figures we studied in history and civics classes, nothing I had read in school prepared me for the brilliance and moral complexity of his worldview. His analyses of Black pride and identity were especially perceptive and filled with messages that I desperately needed to hear at that stage of my life. King introduced me to the concept that, as long as the mind is enslaved, the body can never be free. "Psychological freedom, a firm sense of self-esteem, is the most powerful weapon against the long night of physical slavery," he wrote.

This insight was a perfect distillation of my preteen struggles with the notion that Black people should be free to talk, act, dress, and aspire to and be our authentic selves, without having to resort to "real nigga" stereotypes. At the same time, King articulated my circumstances by declaring that the "double consciousness" that W. E. B. Du Bois identified so many years earlier still afflicts Black people. "Each of us is something of a schizophrenic personality," King said in a sermon published in his 1963 book *Strength to Love*, "tragically divided against ourselves." Reading this, I felt a surge of inspiration. I dedicated hours to perfecting his last speech, trying to emulate King's voice and mannerisms with my youthful pitch. This practice not only improved my delivery but deepened my understanding of the speech's significance.

After a week of preparation, Dad drove me to church for a rehearsal with Sister Jackson. Her presence erased the year's accumulated self-doubt, allowing my true self, Lee Hawkins Jr., to shine.

Yet, she continued to challenge me to reach greater heights. "This is good, but it could be so much better," she told me. "You've got to understand something, young man. Martin Luther King gave this speech the day before he was killed. So I want you to go back to the part where he says, 'I may not get there with you, but I want you to know tonight that we as a people will get to the Promised Land.' You need to say that like a man who knows he's dying and about to go to heaven. That shouldn't be you speaking, Lee Roy. That should be God speaking through you.

That's the only way that you can portray Martin Luther King in this context because he was dying when he said that. And he knew he was dying, and by dying would live forever. So, you have to read that with more conviction."

This brand of coaching—not soft but stern, delivered in the firm yet encouraging voice of a mentor deeply committed to intellectual rigor, who aimed to draw out my best potential and instill belief in my capabilities without resorting to intimidation, humiliation, or force—worked for me.

As I continued to practice, I replayed the tape of King's speech, thinking, "This is a man who knows that he is going to die soon. He doesn't know when, but he knows his day is near. But he still speaks with conviction and trusts the Lord's promise that following him will bring him eternal life."

"He is not afraid, Lee," Sister Jackson had said. "You can't make this speech and be afraid. You must raise your voice with power. You must show that you are ready to tear down any door that blocks our freedom. You must turn yourself into a man who is ready to die for the cause of nonviolence and God's teachings."

My thoughts turned to my father's mother, Grandma Opie. Dad had told me that she was always saying: "That Martin Luther King needs to stop all that talkin' about white folks. He's gonna go out there and get himself killed." That never sat well with me. It's always made me wonder why she couldn't have been a fearless activist like Rosa Parks or Fannie Lou Hamer, and why my family always seemed so paranoid about Black people being murdered.

I couldn't help but wonder: Why was Grandma Opie against a Black leader fighting for our rights? Why did the idea of us being free seem so risky? Why did my parents react with anxiety or anger when I confronted the racist comments other kids made and criticized some of my teachers for their inaction? And why weren't my parents suing the school district over any of this? Why did Mom and Dad appear so frightened when Ashley's father called? Why were they so intent on instilling in me a fear of that white man and his daughter? It made me feel ashamed. I could never let any white kid or person sense even a hint of fear in me—the fear that they could kill me or harm me and get away with it, or that they held any power or societal authority over me, unlike my parents and so many others from the previous generations.

On the day of the speech, I was surprised when the adults told me to deliver it from the pastor's pulpit. I could barely see over the podium, but I suppose that added to the appeal of having a twelve-year-old with an Afro portray Dr. King. When I looked out, my eyes had to adjust to the bright spotlight, but I could tell that the sanctuary was packed. In that moment, I lost any lingering desire to be a "real nigga." With the spotlight on me, I transformed myself into the version of Dr. King we had discussed in practice.

I opened the speech with, "Let us rise up tonight, with greater readiness," and the people in the sanctuary started to cheer. Then I began to channel and build upon all the positive energy that Dr. King sparked in me. When the words "free at last" left my lips in the darkened sanctuary, lit only by the glow of a spotlight that shone down the center aisle, I saw on the white walls the shadows of bodies standing in a frenzy and heard the roar of the applause.

I found purpose that day. When, as Dr. King, I delivered that speech reaffirming his commitment to nonviolence and social change even as he faced down premonitions of his own death, I got the same spiritual rush that I got from singing gospel songs.

Speaking out and using my voice to raise questions and seek answers—especially about the scourge of violence—was where I discovered the love, and ultimately the self-love, that the welt-covered little Black boy cowering on the kitchen floor had been missing. Understanding that I could put all of this toward something bigger, I slayed the "real nigga" voice within me and gave myself permission to be the excellence-driven, freedom-seeking Black boy I really was.

This is what Mount Olivet Baptist Church and its kindhearted deacons and deaconesses, and its loving and supportive congregation, did for me. They showed me that I could turn my life around. I could position myself to one day leave Minnesota and put all the violence and dysfunction behind me. They showed me I could be a (lowercase) king.

16

Girls

Despite my progress, Dad still felt I needed to learn many more lessons as a Black man.

Every Saturday, we'd rent a movie to watch on our Betamax VCR. We sampled every genre, from comedy and action thrillers (I devoured the *Dirty Harry* franchise) to films about the mob, pimps, and pushers. But on one Saturday, as we looked through the choices at our local video store, I was shocked to see him grab one from the shelf with the R-rated titles.

On the cover was a picture of a hulking, muscular Black former heavyweight boxer, Ken Norton, holding a white woman, next to another showing a white man holding a Black woman, clearly in the antebellum South. The film's title, *Mandingo*, was spelled out in bold, red capital letters.

"I think it's about time you see this movie," Dad said, as the cashier rang us up. "This will teach you how a lot of these white people see us—the stereotypical characters that some of them want us to play. And how dangerous and powerful white women can be. This movie is based on the slave days, but a lot of it applies today."

Mandingo is set on a run-down plantation owned by the widower Warren Maxwell and run by his son, Hammond. Under pressure from his father to carry on the family name, Hammond marries his blond cousin, Blanche. On the way back from their honeymoon, he purchases two slaves, a woman named Ellen and a prizefighter named Mede, the "Mandingo" played by Norton.

Hammond takes Mede all over the South to fight other enslaved Black men whose owners have organized a circuit for boxing and betting. Mede's victories earn his owner piles of money, but Hammond still treats Mede like an animal, using him as a "breeder" with enslaved women he owns and keeping Ellen as his personal sex slave. Additionally, as part of his brutal regimen, he forces Mede to soak in a cauldron of hot, salty water to toughen his skin.

Through it all, however, Mede is steadfast in his loyalty to his owners. In one heart-stopping sequence, he sprints into the woods with bloodhounds and a group of crazed white slave hunters to capture my hero, Cicero, a fugitive slave who's taught fellow slaves to read and to rise up against their enslavers. Mede tackles Cicero, pins him to the ground, and waits for the white men to catch up. "What you think you is, a hound dog?" Cicero says to Mede, as the white men arrive, ropes in hand. "Peckerwood say go fetch, you fetch. You see me hang, you're gonna know you killed a Black brother!" Those lines have stayed with me to this day.

As he is being put on the platform for lynching, Cicero defiantly says to the white crowd: "I'd rather die than be a slave. You peckerwoods! That's right! You peckerwoods was oppressed in your own land! We was free, and then you brought us here, in chains. But now we're here, you just better know this is just as much our land as it is yours. And after you hang me, kiss my ass!"

Mede says nothing. He just watches Cicero drop.

Back on the plantation, Hammond's neglected wife, Blanche, had become a bitter, slovenly alcoholic. While Hammond is away on business, Blanche discovers that Ellen is pregnant with Hammond's child. Determined to kill the "mulatto" child, Blanche violently beats Ellen, leading to her falling down stairs and miscarrying. While Hammond is away on another business trip, taking Ellen with him, a drunken Blanche calls Mede to her bedroom. The other slaves try to stop him, but Mede follows her orders. She commands Mede to have sex with her, threatening to say he has raped her if he refuses.

The next scene shows Mede thrusting inside Blanche as she moans in pleasure while she rapes Mede. She then rapes him several more times during her husband's trip. I was in shock and uncertain whether

I was supposed to close my eyes, as my parents always made me do in movie theaters during "adult" scenes.

Not this time. Dad saw this as a critical rite of passage for me. "This is what you're up against, Lee," he said. "I know you'd always be a gentleman and would especially never assault a woman, but if a woman, especially a white one, says you raped her, you raped her. A successful Black man is a threat, because white people think you're taking power that belongs to them. Be careful. Don't ever be alone with a white woman in a situation where any woman could lie and say you raped her. And if she starts drinking, get outta there. Nothing you say can protect you against the allegation of a white woman. Whatever they say is the law. And a lot of them know they have that power, and they will use it—especially the more successful you become.

"Remember" he added, "you don't ever have to be an Uncle Tom like Mandingo was. Don't ever sell your soul for white people. Don't ever be a white man's 'boy,' because there's a price to pay. You have to look at yourself in the mirror every day. Find the way to be respectful to everybody without disrespecting yourself. Most of all, son, always be aware of how they see you."

I just sat there, trying to fit his life lessons into the movie's subplots. I realized that enslavement goes beyond bodily shackles; it can infect the mind. Even so, I couldn't figure out how Dad could tell me, "Never sell your soul for white people" on one hand and turn himself into a Black boy whipper as soon as Ashley's dad called on the other. Even more baffling was Dad and Mom's framing of their whippings of me as "protection"—against what the police state and white men and women in general might do to me. At home, at church, everywhere we went, all-too-many Black children were told by their parents, "If we don't beat you, the police will kill you."

I couldn't imagine Malcolm X, Curtis Mayfield, any of the Last Poets, or any of the unapologetically Black, socially conscious men I idolized beating their son so a white man on the phone could hear it. But there was another dimension to the "we beat you to protect you" rationale. This one made even less sense. According to Dad, the white man wanted my parents to beat me into perfect submission because the fear it instilled kept me away from their daughters. So . . . he was whipping me because the white man wanted him to? And he sat there and told *me* not to sell out to the white man?

Every whipping my dad gave me, probably without even realizing it, was supposed to scare me into being perfect and submissive, just like the brutal lessons learned by Kunta Kinte and Mede. But when he showed me that movie, it was like he was trying to tell me something more, something deeper. He wanted me to see the traps of becoming a "Mandingo" to the white man, but also, maybe, he was showing me a way to fight back, to stand tall. He might have been teaching me to walk through a world filled with the snares of white supremacy armed with the wisdom to dodge them, to be militantly independent in a way he never could be. Maybe, in his own way, he was trying to give me the tools to navigate a path he'd been forced to walk blind, every step shadowed and influenced by his upbringing in Jim Crow Alabama.

God knows, the movie succeeded in scaring me half to death. After Hammond returns, Blanche announces that she is pregnant, but when the baby is born it's clearly biracial. The astonished Hammond snaps into action, slashing the baby and leaving it to bleed to death. The doctor then hands Hammond a deadly poison used on old enslaved people and horses. After pouring it into a hot toddy he's prepared for Blanche, he touches her face as if in forgiveness before giving her the beverage and watching her drink it. Then he goes out to find Mede.

He plans to kill Mede by forcing him into a boiling cauldron of water. Mede tries to explain that he was blackmailed into having sex with Blanche, but Hammond orders him into the boiling water. "No, Massa," Mede says, refusing his master for the first time in his life. Hammond fires two rounds into the helpless Mede, who falls into the water to his death.

I was still shaking when I went to bed that night. I didn't need to ask my dad to clarify anything because I finally understood what he had been saying for months, even years. Dad was trying to tell me that having sex with, or even dating, a white girl was a surefire way to piss off the white fathers, the white dudes at school, the white male teachers, and all the other white men in town. As a Black man, he said, I was perceived as a sexual threat to racist white men who believe that my penis, apparently like Mede's, was larger than theirs and that "their women" would be attracted to me. I needed to be aware of these "penis fears," along with "extinction fears" that drove white supremacist men to hate Black men and see us as hypersexual.

He wanted me to understand all the dynamics I could encounter in my life—every day.

"If you're at a party with these white kids, and the cops show up, they are going to zero in on you and say, 'Well, we know that that Black kid, the Hawkins kid, was doing this or that,' and those white parents will get their kids a lawyer and blame what their kids did on you," he said. "And if you have sex with or even just date a white girl and her father finds out, she could lie and say you raped her, just to keep her daddy from calling her a 'nigger-lover' or from kicking her ass or even killing her."

When white supremacists saw a Black man, Dad said, their immediate fear was the threat of that Black man impregnating all the white women, producing enough "mulatto" babies to eventually drive the white race into extinction. This was years before the release by a favorite group of mine, Public Enemy, of the album *Fear of a Black Planet*. For in the United States, a baby born of a white person and a Black person is BLACK. Dad said racists will be forever haunted by their "one-drop rule," which held that any person with even one ancestor with one drop of Black blood was legally Black. That fear, and the sexual insecurity of many bigoted white males, my father said, was at the heart of a lot of racism.

"You're doing a lot of good things now, son. I can see it unfolding as it happens. You're gonna make it," Dad told me. "What makes me proud is that you're doing a lot of shit that's not usually associated with the Black man, in the eyes of a racist. Sports? That's typical, but you're also doing public speaking, debating, writing, and theater. That's gonna make you dangerous. It makes you more of a threat. You're doing stuff that might make the white girls mistakenly think they can take you home to their father or hold your hand walking down the hallway and think that the white teachers over there won't want to drag you with their pickup trucks. If you make the mistake of gettin' too close to one of these white girls who call the house or that I see you talkin' to up at those school events, you'll never get another *A* again. The white teachers and principals—at least the racist ones—will make sure you never move forward in Maplewood. And that's if they don't hang you and the whole family from a tree first."

Then, he spun his message into the future: "And let me tell you about being a Black man as an adult. Do you think you can just walk into your corporate job and do what you want? Get that out of your head now. When you grow up and you're working in these corporations or in politics, don't think for one minute that the white men, the white women, and the Black women aren't all watching you and trying to monitor your big Black dick. The more successful and better-looking you are, some of the Black women will also be wondering if you're single. And if you're not, do you have a Black woman at home? If they don't see photos of a Black wife and family on your desk, some of them might become an enemy because many of them are in pain, just like we are. You have to carry that awareness everywhere. You'll be in there, minding your business and doing your work, but some folks will be more focused on their primary concern—'Is this Black brother gonna fuck all the white women in the office?'—than they are about the job you've been hired to do. And some of the white women will come at you right away, like you're some kind of Black stallion. But never let anyone sexualize you. You must understand that this will always be a thought and fear in some people's minds. You might be just giving a presentation or interviewing for a job, but you'll still bear the burden of having to always find a way to put everyone at ease."

I wanted to view my parents' concerns as unfounded paranoia and deny that the "fear of the Black man's sexuality" was central to white supremacy, as Dad argued. Yet, between Emmett Till's tragic history and my own Maplewood experiences, I couldn't. By the time Dad voiced these fears, I'd seen the photos of Emmett in his casket, a stark testament to a young man betrayed by a deceitful white woman. He was killed on my birthday, August 28, merely sixteen years before my birth. The traps of his boyhood persisted in mine. And since that movie night, I've been hypercautious.

After I saw *Mandingo*, every time a white girl asked me to a school dance or a movie or just a Coke at the high-school hangouts, I always made up an excuse and respectfully declined. I could never tell them the reason.

17

The Bus

n 1984, I began my journey at North St. Paul Senior High, a mere
three miles east of Maplewood. This school uniquely spanned grades
eight through twelve. Among nearly two thousand students, I was
one of the few Black faces, but I was resolute: standing out was my
bridge from a turbulent childhood to authentic freedom in college.
Unlike some Black classmates who understandably struggled with culture shock and navigating racism, usually because of their later entry
to the district, I knew how to thrive. With years of experience in both
white and Black and brown communities, and a wide circle of friends, I
never felt powerless, intimidated, or isolated—my love for meeting new
people meant I resisted self-segregation. I befriended people in every
social group: jocks, preps, metal heads, geeks, "real niggas," druggies,
burnouts, Goths, and the mold-defying outcasts.

My *GQ*-inspired style evolved: wingtips gave way to black and
brown penny loafers, adorned with dimes. This mirrored the collegiate
looks of Michael Jackson's *Thriller* era, Alex P. Keaton of *Family Ties*,
and *The Cosby Show* cast. Since we were eighties kids, aiming to enter
the corporate world sharply dressed, my closest friends from North
High, Rondo, and beyond and I were labeled "preps."

Music strengthened our bond. Alongside my favorites like East
Coast hip-hop, Chicago and Detroit House, R&B, and the Minneap-
olis sound, I enjoyed American and European alternative, new wave,
and punk. While some "real niggas" and racists accused me of being an
"Oreo" and "acting white" due to my diverse friends and eclectic tastes,
I never felt insecure or out of place among different people. Bands like
Depeche Mode, The English Beat, R.E.M., Kraftwerk, Inner City,

UB40, Fine Young Cannibals, and the Violent Femmes from Milwaukee dominated my playlist.

Sporting a Cameo-inspired flattop, trench coats, and scents like Obsession, Polo, and Benetton Colors, I resented being confined to a box. This sentiment was heightened when such expectations came from some Black kids in Maplewood, who were largely disconnected from and unknown to droves of Black people in St. Paul and Minneapolis. I was "Black enough" across the Twin Cities, so why couldn't I be considered "Black enough" in Maplewood? My joys were performing with the J.J. Kids, The 2 + 2 Crew, being on the basketball and track teams, modeling on game covers and in advertisements, and diving deep into books and dance. Maplewood's boundaries paled in comparison to the excitement of a Twin Cities scene lifted by the melodies of the Minneapolis sound, so I spent most of my time city-side.

Meeting kids from citywide teen clubs and roller rinks, plus my friends from Rondo and North Minneapolis, enhanced my confidence to be authentically me. My close friend since sixth grade, Kyle, a preppy, 100 percent Swedish kid who even ate lutefisk (the Swedish version of chitlins), pop-locked and break-danced, which led us to anoint him an honorary Black man. He rapped, played drums and horns, and even gigged with Dad and me, sometimes for Black audiences. In some ways, the families of Kyle and my closest white friends weren't much different from mine. Their parents, like mine, valued education, went to church every week, and held true to ultraconservative beliefs. Most were well-traveled and less inclined to slip and let any racism show in front of me. My bond with Kyle deepened in eighth grade. We went to clubs and concerts, battled rival school rappers, and became inseparable, hitting pool parties and sports events.

Maplewood, or Honkeyville, as the Rondo kids joked, was all about its hockey, hunting, and hot rods. It was like Maplewood kids popped out of the womb with ice skates on, with the state hockey tournament being their Super Bowl. That love for hockey was probably why our basketball team didn't shine. Some of the hockey aces joined us for summer basketball fun, but come winter, they were all-in on the ice. For me, given my five-foot-ten-inch height, "real nigga" peer pressure, and wanting to keep all my teeth, I stuck with basketball. Plus, there was that time a white kid tried persuading me hockey was a "white man's game," even saying something about Black folks having "weak ankles" for skating.

On Fridays, white students would gather around muscle cars, hoods lifted, taking pride in their engines while blasting their favorite metal and glam rock tracks: Mötley Crüe, Metallica, Dokken, and more. Being a drummer and singer, I secretly liked some of it too.

But back then, I kept my admiration for Jimi Hendrix under wraps. One Black kid dubbed it "white boy music." Despite Dad explaining Hendrix's going from soul groups like the Isley Brothers to rock, a lot of kids of all races believed Hendrix stole his style from white rock idols, unable to accept that this Black man transformed rock guitar. Lots also questioned Prince's authenticity as a Black artist, calling him and Michael Jackson "fags." This was even after *Thriller* but before rap and Black culture conquered the world.

In the year leading up to eighth grade, older white kids in Maplewood hung out at the local Hardee's. They'd drive to parking lots in their souped-up four-by-four pickups and drive donuts. Whenever I hear loud mufflers I think about Maplewood and their tales of "three-wheelin'" and snowmobilin'" and the five-point buck they shot "up north."

I never shared that my great-grandparents owned a Wisconsin lakeside cabin, or that my mom's stepfather, Papa Elmer, was an avid hunter with cases full of trophies and imported hounds. The Blakey family had even traded vast land parcels and operated a hunting guide business in South Dakota for years. Across races, the notion of Black families hunting or farming seemed alien. So, I'd just listen, as if no Black person ever held a rifle or fished at their own cabin.

Frankly, ice fishing or waiting in the cold for deer weren't for me, but since it was in my blood, I loved their stories. That same urge to belong led me to try "dippin'," our slang for chewing tobacco, though never at school. Getting caught with tobacco could open me up to a "trap" arrest by the school officer, Officer Zappa.

When we chewed, we'd tuck Kodiak or Copenhagen tobacco in our cheeks and spit into cups, soaking in the buzz. Some friends added Jack Daniels to their chew. I'd use tobacco only if offered. I imagined that a store clerk, recognizing me as "that arrogant Black kid with the dimes in his shoes," might call the police instead of just denying the sale.

My white buddies never fretted like that. Dad said Maplewood was built for them; we were merely interlopers in their Minnesota paradise.

Yet, Minnesota was where my heart was. Our family's deep ties to Rondo spanned various sectors from politics to law enforcement. I embraced the cold, wearing down jackets during my snow-shoveling gigs and cheering for the Minnesota Vikings' Purple People Eaters. The "Minnesota Nice" ethos, evident in friendly exchanges at stores, warmed me.

My momentum surged. After running for the eighth-grade student council and delivering a standout speech, I was elected, confirming my sense that most of my white classmates weren't racist. I realized that being a Black "public figure" as Dad had warned could also be an advantage. Those increasing calls from Twin Cities kids—especially girls—didn't escape my parents' scrutinizing glances. Racial insults vanished from the basketball court, and I felt secure, genuinely believing my white friends would have my back against racists.

Still, our differences were clear. They were baffled by my parents' strictness, which led to my nerdy sobriety and early exits from parties, my guarded phone calls with girls, or my wearing long-sleeved shirts in scorching summers.

I stayed sober at the few backwoods "kegger" parties I was allowed to attend. Even now, the scent of burning wood transports me to those nights, the cloying aroma of Rumple Minze liqueur, and the hazy-eyed Nordic faces, often laughing or slurring their words. Somebody was always trying to give me a snowmobile or ATV ride. And some slurring white boy would eventually yell, "We need to build a bonfire so we can see Hawkins out here."

When the slurring and the jokes kicked in, that was my cue to exit stage left. Something in my body, my gut, my dad's voice in my ear, told me that being the only Black dude surrounded by drunken white teenagers in a remote, wooded part of Minnesota could end badly.

Police truly unnerved me. When at parties in some friends' sprawling backwoods mansions, I feared resentful police would crash in, spot the "uppity Black guy," and arrest only me. The mere thought of an accident in a beer-soaked Ford Bronco with older white kids scared me almost as much as Bacardi 151 or the flirty older female "friends" who'd sometimes sneak notes into my locker vent. Each time I saw beer gush from a keg, Dad's voice echoed: "You're not a white kid . . . they'll get drunk and throw you in that fire. And if you get arrested for drinking, you're done. And you can believe those white kids'll abandon you in a crisis."

If I wanted to escape to freedom, I couldn't afford to drink. No amount of playful razzing from friends could surpass the dread of an arrest or fear of jeopardizing college dreams because of a guidance counselor's call to college admissions officers. No more traps for me.

Navigating my chameleon identity in different social and racial environments was exhausting. I was constantly shadow boxing—ducking, weaving, and dodging in a ring regulated by old societal rules. There were aspects of thriving in a 99 percent white Minnesota that my parents and many Black elders just couldn't fully understand or pass on to me. As part of the first "integration generation," I had to forge my own path.

Watching *The Cosby Show*, I saw hints of the Hawkins family and our peers, but not the full story. I wondered about the racism Dr. Cliff Huxtable, a Black OB/GYN, faced, or his wife, Clair, a lawyer at a top New York City firm. How did their Black children fare in mostly white prep schools? It's hard to believe they weren't judged, by both whites and Blacks, for anything about them that didn't conform to stereotypes. In the time of the falsely accused Central Park Five, was Theo ever confronted by NYC police? Were the Huxtables as concerned about Theo's free speech and spirit as my parents were about mine? Did they have family in the South—with generational ties to both cotton fields and Martha's Vineyard? Considering that more than 80 percent of Black families believed in physical discipline, were the Cosby children whipped? And in a post–civil rights America, were they still expected to follow the rigid rules imposed by elders who traced their roots to the South?

Most of the Black families I knew had much more complicated stories than that of the Cosbys. Yes, I was determined to thrive in one of the whitest states in the United States, but I still had to know not to put too much faith in the benevolence of my white friends or white-controlled institutions. This sad truth landed with a thud during our end-of-year eighth-grade trip to Valley Fair Amusement Park as I headed back to three buses lined up for our return to Maplewood.

Kyle and some friends were already seated when I boarded.

"Get off the bus, nigger-r-r-r-r-r-r-r-r-r-r-r!"

It was a classmate who I'll refer to as Raquel, a white female class-mate who had run against me for the student council, shouting the slur from behind Kyle. My first instinct was to yell something embarrassing back. But I felt an overwhelming exhaustion, a bone-weariness from the past, wash over me. Why would I lower myself to call her a name or beg to sit near a racist?

Besides, ultimately, my response—not her ugly epithet—would be the punishable crime, both at school and at home. What would happen, I wondered, if I called this white girl a bitch and gave her a chance to crush me with the power we both inherently knew she held over me? It would prompt a call home from a teacher or her dad. I dreaded the thought of Dad being triggered and how far he'd go because of his own fears.

Even in my fearlessness within Maplewood, racists could identify my deepest vulnerabilities: being a Black kid in white Minnesota with Black parents and generations before them living with racism and the fears and traumas it engendered. Thanks to my parents' sacrifices, I was privileged to never fully understand or face these struggles myself. But embarrassing Raquel could set me up for an injustice I despised: being blamed or even labeled racist for speaking out against racism. In the words of Macalester College's Mahmoud El-Kati, "If someone puts a noose around my neck and I struggle, how am I the racist?

So, instead of emulating Rosa Parks and taking my seat in that bus, I turned around and climbed off it to look for a seat on one of the oth-ers. As I descended the stairs, looking down at my dime-stuffed black penny loafers, I noted the resounding silence of that moment. Not a single word from my "colorblind" friends or more than a dozen class-mates. Nobody got off the bus in solidarity with me. Not one person. Sometimes, saying nothing says everything.

18

Oreo

Over the summer, I revisited Dr. King's "Letter from Birmingham Jail." It reaffirmed his argument that the white moderate is a significant barrier to freedom, perhaps more so than even the Ku Klux Klan member. He criticized the white moderate for preferring "order" over justice, opting for a false sense of calm instead of true racial equality.

The letter educated me on white complicity, revealing how my white friends' "colorblindness" conveniently allowed them to remain silent on racism. "Neutrality helps the oppressor, never the victim," as Elie Wiesel so aptly put it. This neutrality found a foothold among leaders and educators throughout St. Paul School District 622 and Minnesota, where countless tales of racial harassment against students of color went unacknowledged and unaddressed by both district and state leaders. To this day, Minnesota has not enacted specific laws or mandates to punish teachers and students who engage in racist hate speech and harassment. Remarkably, no white student or teacher in my district ever faced discipline for racism. In contrast, Black students who defended themselves or sought help were often punished, branded as the true instigators of racism. My fellow 2 + 2 Crew rapper, Michael Thomas, had a haunting memory from District 622. His white male sixth-grade science teacher called him "a nigger who'll never amount to anything." But instead of breaking under that insult, Thomas rose to become a school superintendent in Minnesota.

Even as a fourteen-year-old, I understood that "white moderate" pain. As I prepared to enter ninth grade in the autumn of 1985, word had spread across the Twin Cities about my rendition of King's

"Mountaintop" speech, and I started to collect modest speaking fees, earning between $100 and $150 per speech—big money for a ninth-grader whose only other source of income was from shoveling snow and cutting lawns.

This all inspired an interest in student politics and activism. In ninth- through twelfth-grade student council elections at North High, the student who received the most votes was named class president. My classmates elected me overwhelmingly, and some of those I defeated were sitting on that bus next to Raquel. Winning felt thousands of times better than if I had argued or begged to sit with them. Again, in certain cases, saying nothing says everything.

Among my colorblind friends in the preppy circle, one particularly stood out in contrast to my true friend Kyle. He was on that bus and also ran against me for the class presidency. After losing, he started saying, "You're not really Black—you're very articulate, and you don't dress like a Black person." When I told him his statements were racist, he shrugged it off, swearing he was complimenting me. He couldn't fathom Blackness aligned with excellence, assuming excellence was "acting white" while considering those he deemed beneath him as the only "authentic" Black people. In his eyes, only "real niggas" were truly Black. His question to another friend further confirmed his racism. He asked, "Where does Lee get the money for his clothes?" as if an authentically Black person had to be poor and slovenly. He refused to accept me as anything other than exceptional or an "Oreo"—Black on the outside but white on the inside—bound by a mindset that "real" Black people must be subservient, struggling economically, dangerously violent, and of lower intelligence. This belief system, one I'd encountered repeatedly, even from some Black people, was puzzling to me. I couldn't fathom its origin.

But for every racist or hater white classmate, ten others supported me. Similarly, for every prejudiced teacher, many more educators encouraged me, believing in my potential. Milo Gray, my teacher for eighth- and ninth-grade government and civics, was a prime example.

Mr. Gray introduced my friend Brian and me to the YMCA Youth in Government (YIG), a program where high school students replicated the State Capitol's processes. Over four days, we drafted and passed bills, immersing ourselves in the mechanics of state governance.

This initiative took us to Mankato, Minnesota, for a pre-legislative convention, where YIG participants from across the state elected upperclass students to various roles, from governor to speaker of the House, setting the stage for a dynamic mock legislative gathering.

As freshmen, we eagerly participated, penning bills and passionately debating them, with the goal of moving them through the Senate and House for the Youth Governor's signature. This session uncovered abilities I hadn't realized. My keynote speaking experience made me a stronger debater, empowering me to speak extemporaneously, with the same power Sister Jackson had helped me find. What I found was the "white sons and daughters of doctors and lawyers" whom Mom feared I'd struggle against mostly didn't match the oratorical prowess of the speakers I'd met in Black churches. And like with sports, this program was full of Minnesota's best—nationally ranked debaters, class presidents, stars of Model United Nations—many students who would one day become real-life politicians if they chose to.

Inspired by accomplished older YIG students, I set my sights on the governor's position by 1989, aiming to inhabit Governor Rudy Perpich's office during that four-day session. This ambitious goal meant ascending through every election until my senior year, creating a ticket out of Maplewood and its tumultuous memories. I envisioned our recreation room laden with speech and leadership awards, paving my way to a distant college. That year, my bill advanced through the Freshman Legislature, the senior House and Senate, and received the Youth Governor's seal. By the session's close, my colleagues elected me Outstanding Freshman Representative.

My time in YIG deepened my appreciation for Mr. Gray's class. He was among the few educators who truly connected with me and saw me for who I was—avoiding what President George W. Bush (or perhaps a sharp speechwriter) would term the "soft bigotry of low expectations." Regrettably, teachers like Mr. Gray were rare.

PART 2

"I'll Break Your Neck"

19

SchwarzeNIGGER

My Youth in Government accolades hit the newspapers and began to spread around my school. I assumed my newfound commitment to rising above low expectations would be met with positive reinforcement. I quickly learned otherwise.

One of my high school teachers, who I will refer to as Mr. Simpson, was also a coach. One day, he drew upon this supposed expertise in a biology lesson that somehow led him to ruminate about the human physique. "I played football with a lot of Black guys," he said with authority, "and I can tell you that they are just built differently. Black men are incredible physical specimens. They're athletically superior to everybody. They can run faster, they're stronger, they're just built that way."

He stopped short of saying that Black men were "bred" like horses during enslavement, but I'd seen *Roots* and *Mandingo*. I knew where this was going, and I sat in my chair silently exploding. I felt my forehead start to heat up as he pushed into everything Dad warned me about racist white men and their insecurities about Black male virility. All I wanted was to attend my biology class and manage the demands of being a student leader at North High and beyond. However, the conversation took a turn I couldn't ignore. Some of my white classmates, particularly the guys, expressed more outrage than I felt initially. It was then that one of them made a shocking statement. "That means whites are more intelligent," the guy next to me declared, looking directly at me and then with concern at the white girl sitting across. "More whites work in banks and stuff, while Black guys are on the field, but we white people own the teams."

I lashed back. "Yeah, but that's not because you're more intelligent. It's because of ra—" The word "racism" wasn't even out of my mouth when the teacher and five or six kids in the class interjected, "Enough with your racism crap!"

I argued as best I could, but ultimately, like so many times before, they fixated on my protest of Mr. Simpson's racist statement rather than on the statement itself. "You're not discriminated against, Hawkins. Look how you dress. And you're the *class president* and all that other state government stuff, dude. Nobody's oppressing you. Everything with you is about race!"

They were right about that last part. Unlike them, I didn't have the luxury of thinking about race only when I felt like it. I was always fighting some standard of racial expectations. And I'd run the gamut—filling the role of "model minority," "budding criminal," "welfare kid," "spoiled, privileged kid," "talkin' white Uncle Tom and sellout," and "Black liberation racist."

I don't know why I bothered, but that night I told my parents about Mr. Simpson's comment and the ensuing discussion and asked them what I should do. "Be careful down there, son," Dad said, with Mom nodding behind him. "Some of these white teachers are retaliating against you for all this activism and political stuff you're doing." But in the end, they suggested that I speak to the principal or a counselor.

When I told my counselor what had happened, he listened and then chuckled, "Oh, Ralph shouldn't have said that. He's a character—I'll talk to Ralph." Since the teacher never apologized to me or the class and never made any attempt to correct or clarify that statement he had passed off as biology, I assume the school did nothing.

Around that time, I was targeted by a classmate whom I barely knew. He had no standing in the social hierarchy and was widely considered to be a potential mass shooter before school shootings became as common as water. He taped to my locker a paper dartboard with the silhouette of a Black man with a large Afro and protruding lips. The drawing had point values assigned to each part of the body and a bullseye in the place of the head. At the top, printed in black marker, was "A Running Nigger."

I took the threatening drawing to an administrator, who did nothing. That was when I finally realized that expecting administrators to hold racist teachers and classmates accountable for their racism was a lost cause. Mostly, they told me I was overreacting. Faced with apathy from adult educators and disabling fear from my parents, I decided I had to figure out my own method for coping with racial hatred. My solution: to continue my "success is the best revenge" strategy, but also to perfect my cappin' to the point of making racists, even teachers, cry. I wanted it to stop. And since the school's administration wouldn't help me, I decided to stop it like a "real nigga" would, except without violence. I would embarrass them so much they'd think not twice, but thrice, about ever messing with me again. I vowed to unleash my insults on anyone who tested me, including Black kids who called me "white" and racist white kids. I despised the concept of the Black man as helpless victim. I might have to deal with racism, but I refused to be destroyed by it.

Later that year, my classmates and I were stretching on the soccer field before gym class, and Mr. Gustafson, the gym teacher and football coach, was walking among the rows of students. I generally liked the guy—a military vet who was rumored to have briefly played with the Green Bay Packers before getting injured. His modus operandi was to keep us laughing, but he was also a racist and a bully. He'd once called one of my overweight white friends "Slim" just to publicly shame him.

On that day, Mr. Gustafson walked by my row, saw me stretching, and blurted out to the whole class, "That Hawkins, always smilin'. Who do you think I am, the welfare man?"

My classmates erupted in laughter, and mortified, I lashed back immediately: "Don't you make like thirty grand? My *mom* makes more than you." I knew that the mere mention of his earning less than a woman—especially a Black one—was a metaphorical kick in the groin. Since he was a racist, I assumed he was also a sexist. I transformed before his eyes into the "smart-ass little darky" I'm sure he probably called me in the faculty break room later that day. My snappy retort drew a laugh from some of my classmates, but one glance at Mr. Gustafson's beet-red face forced them into a collective "Ooooh."

Mr. Gustafson didn't attack me, then or ever. But I do believe that day was embedded in his racist mind. He probably took the memory to the nursing home because he made no secret of despising me for the rest of my days at North High. Every time I saw him, I felt his seething glare. If my parents had found out what I'd said to Mr. Gustafson, they probably would have killed me out of fear that he'd kill us.

Toward the end of the year, my class reelected me as class president, and I also geared up for my sophomore run for secretary of the Senate in Youth in Government in the fall.

In an elective English class on satire, my teacher, who I'll refer to as Ms. Wood, assigned us to create a video of a one-act satirical routine. To fulfill the assignment, two upperclassmen, Lance and Mark, chose to do a parody of *Siskel and Ebert & the Movies*. Their script went something like this: "Welcome to another night at the movies. My name is Gene Siskel," Lance said.

"And I'm Roger Ebert," Mark chimed in. "The first movie we will review tonight gives audiences a good hard look at one of Hollywood's biggest tough guys, and really puts him to the test as an actor. As always, Arnold SchwarzeNIGGER fails the acting test. But in terms of the action, SchwarzeNIGGER does a superb job."

"I agree," Lance said. "SchwarzeNIGGER might not be the best actor, but boy, does he know how to keep you on the edge of your seat."

The only Black student in a class of about thirty, I sat back through the roar of laughter across the classroom, searching for the humor. "Guys, that's not funny, that's incredibly racist," I said.

"Here we go again Hawkins, we didn't even say anything!" Mark said. "That's just how we pronounce SchwarzeNIGGER! It's a *satire*."

"Well, I didn't think it was funny, either, and it's not appropriate for the class," Ms. Wood said. "I want you to redo the assignment."

Mark and Lance objected, but Ms. Wood held her ground. The pair came up with something else to get credit for the assignment, and that was that. Not another word was said.

Another incident unfolded in the lunchroom, as I sat with about twenty all-white teammates and friends. I got up to throw something away, momentarily forgetting the stupidity of leaving a full, unattended plate of food around a bunch of high-school dudes. When I returned to the table, everyone was smirking. My first inclination was to inspect my food to see if they'd pulled a common prank, like mixing my broccoli into my chocolate milk. I then studied the wise-ass grins on just about everybody at the table. A few people were stifling full-throated laughs.

"What did you do to my food?" I said, chuckling.

By now everybody was laughing outright. Finally, one of them pointed to a kid in a wheelchair, who was hovering over a notebook, turned face down, and wearing a sinister smile. Then somebody flipped the notebook over and pushed it toward me. The kid had drawn a picture of a smiling, pencil-blackened face and written "GO HOME SAMBO" in block letters underneath it. I dimly remembered my father showing me a book with caricatures of a character named Little Black Sambo, along with old episodes of *Amos 'n' Andy*. He wanted me to be aware of the grotesque stereotypes of Black people that were out there.

My anger spiked and I decided to make this kid regret it. "This motherfucka's talking shit from a wheelchair! Bruh, are you talking shit from a *wheelchair*? Now *that's* funny!" I shrieked into his face as I bent over him. "Well, if I'm a Sambo, get up and walk, motherfucka! Let's see what you can do!"

Now the table exploded in laughter as the kid's face turned red and then whiter than white. I stood up and started punching down in the air and dancing around like Ali and Tyson, in a flurry of mock jabs and blows, demonstrating what I could do to his face and body in his disabled state. "I'll fuck you up, motherfucka," I screamed as I pranced and threw volleys of punches to the approval of my rapt audience. "I'll fuck you up!"

Amidst the uproarious laughter, I kept going around the table, high-fiving everyone, causing the kid even more humiliation than his disability and wheelchair ever did. For the next few days, every time I crossed paths with him in the hallway, I would act out my imitation. My right arm would go limp, I'd raise my hand to my chest, mimicking disability, scrunch my face, and shift my whole mouth to the left. Then, I'd walk with a limp, dragging one leg behind me.

It was the most despicable I've ever been, and it was a natural escalation of the incessant smart-ass cappin' riffs that made bullies shy away and won me friends who found them humorous. To escape racial bullying, I'd turned myself into a stronger, wittier, meaner, and at times crasser and more profane bully, who knew precisely what to say to pierce the heart of my racist tormentors. I was out for blood, and I honed my comebacks to cut straight to the bone.

I would mock a racist's speech impediment or s-s-stutter, his dirty or unfashionable clothes, his Coke-bottle glasses, his acne or struggles with weight, the unfinished siding on his family's house ("your parents started the job and ran out of money"), or even, as with the kid who drew the Sambo picture, his disability. I'm not proud of this behavior and I concede that my comebacks were often hurtful. But this was the 1980s, when cappin' was all the rage and "trauma sensitivity" was nonexistent. It would be unfair to profess that I was an angel in our world and time, where every kid had to stand his ground or be swallowed alive.

Still, though my Blackness often sparked the expectation that I should carry myself like a grown man, I remind myself today that I was still a kid. It also always surprised me how much more tolerance there was for drawing someone as a Sambo than there was for my sharp replies. After all, the pain I felt from the slur was on par with the pain I caused with my comeback—and I wasn't the one who had struck the first blow.

20

Dad's Diet and Biblical Waterboarding

A dding to the mix of anxiety at school was the crazed, mysterious antics I experienced at home.

One evening, Mom sat all three of us kids down for a misty-eyed, whispering session. "Dad might lose his job," she said in a hush-hush tone. "And if he loses his job, all of our lives are going to change a lot. The people at work are messing with him, and Dad has to go on a diet. If he can't lose the weight, he could get fired."

I was shocked to learn that Dad's weight had climbed to a whopping 270 pounds. Given his tall frame, he resembled many former professional athletes who had gotten out of shape, complete with a potbelly, yet he didn't fit the typical definition of "fat."

"How can they justify that?" I protested, referring to societal or specific policies that seemed to marginalize overweight people. "Isn't that a form of discrimination against those who are overweight?"

As if on cue, Dad walked in, pulled up a dining-room chair, and faced us all. "They're saying that the regulations are changing. I'm too heavy to be up there on that telephone pole. It's considered a hazard, so I have to lose forty pounds within months. But I can do it. This diet should knock the fat right off me."

"Is this part of that stuff you were saying about all the high-paying union jobs like yours going away?" I asked.

"Yeah, son. It's another way to get the guys with seniority off that payroll if they can. But this is good for my health, so it's a blessing in disguise."

He passed us a sheet with the words "LOSE 10 POUNDS IN 3 DAYS" across the top. On the paper were meal instructions for breakfast, lunch, and dinner. As I skimmed it, my eyes fixed on the dinner menu for Day Two: "2 frankfurters, 1 cup broccoli, 1/2 cup carrots, 1/2 banana, 1/2 cup ice cream."

That diet wasn't all bad. As soon as Dad jumped into it, he'd go to Cub Foods every week and buy a half-gallon of that milky vanilla Breyers ice cream he loved so much. And once Dad got into the diet, the pounds melted. We made sure to hit the YMCA on Wednesday nights, skipping the postgame runs for eight-packs of pop.

Then, on the evening before I was set to deliver my reelection campaign speech for tenth-grade class president, I found out the hard way that my parents' addiction to ice cream was even greater than mine. I was in my room with the door shut. Following the lessons of Sister Jackson, I kept reading my speech aloud, over and over, hoping to drill it into my subconscious.

On what was probably my tenth go-round, I started in, "It is a distinct honor . . ." when Mom barged into my room. "Lee, why did you eat Dad's Breyers when you knew he needed it for his diet?"

"Huh? I didn't eat any of the Breyers. I only eat the Kemps, and I haven't had any of that for a few days."

"You're lying!"

"No, I'm not, Mom. I didn't have any. I've been in here getting ready for tomorrow."

She silently closed the door.

I sat there, turning the situation over in my head: Breyers ice cream was the only sweet food allowed on my father's diet, so it was off-limits to us kids. Besides, as I told Mom, Breyers wasn't my brand of choice.

Mom called us into the kitchen where Dad, seated at the table, was sure there should have been more than just a few bites of ice cream left. I repeated my denial and my ignorance of the true culprit. My sisters each said the same.

Whenever my mom thought that one of us had done something wrong, but no one confessed, she'd pull out the Bible from the drawer of the living-room hutch. Mom knew we revered the Bible and feared the wrath that God heaped upon liars, so she used it to squeeze the truth out of whichever kid allegedly committed a crime. Mom taught us from toddlerhood that telling a lie with our hand on a Bible is a sin, like premarital sex, punishable by burning in hell for eternity.

The Bible was Mom's favorite torture method. She'd page through it to find verses that justified whipping us—as if the order to beat welts all over our bodies was coming down directly from Jesus. On that night, Mom had all three of us place our hands on the Bible and swear we were not the ice cream thief. "We know Tammi didn't eat it," Mom said. She sent Tammi to bed.

Then, Mom took two of our dining-room chairs into the front living room, placed them back-to-back, and ordered Tiffany and me to each sit in one. She told us both that neither of us could go to bed until one of us confessed to eating the ice cream and launched into a high-pressure interrogation.

She widened her eyes and recited her mantra, over and over. "God hates liars, and whoever ate that Breyers and lied about it is gonna burn in hell." The rhyme of "liars" and "Breyers" sounded almost like a chant. Anyone seeing her through our window (shuttered, of course) would have thought she was flat-out insane. She yelled and taunted us for hours, standing nose-to-nose with us, breathing and unintentionally spitting in our faces, slapping, pinching, and pushing us every time we started to nod off. Fixated on the Breyers, she paid little attention to my concerns about the next day's speech for the class presidency.

The entire time, as I tried in vain to respond to her trap questions and contradictory demands, I thought about the speech I had to deliver and had hoped to memorize. Instead, I'd been caught up in yet another misbegotten drama. I often thought that she secretly relished these nightmarish productions—throwing herself into the staging, setting the scene, and overacting in the starring role of the long-suffering, thwarted artist. And her punishments were administered with a divalike flourish. What, we all wondered, had happened to our authoritative mother to make her behave like this? Where did these sick, sadistic-seeming rituals (we had gone through this kind of questioning before) come from? Surely not from the Bible.

I fought to keep my eyes open. In addition to my speech, I had a final the next day, and I had planned to look over those notes and then wake up early to rehearse the speech at least five more times.

The clock ticked off 1:00 and then 2:00 a.m. My dad had gone to bed hours before; he had to get up for work in the morning. I boiled with rage. This absurd ice cream imbroglio would ensure that I'd be at my worst for one of the most important days of my high school career.

And then it dawned on me: it would be better to take a beating now than lose the few hours of potential sleep—and the class presidency with it—over some missing ice cream. So I declared, "I ate the ice cream!," delivering my line with all the conviction I could muster. At that point, I was totally worn down by Mom's biblical waterboarding.

Her stare turned to a sinister smile. "Why didn't you admit it in the first place?" she said. "Why did you lie?"

So, I lied about lying. "I lied because I was embarrassed," I said, "and I didn't want to get spanked." I tensed my body, preparing for the inevitable.

My mom went to my parents' bedroom and retrieved Dad's belt, indulging in her apparent fondness for middle-of-the-night whippings—a preference of hers I could never understand the inspiration for.

I don't remember if I got any sleep that night, and I still don't know who ate the damn ice cream. To this day, neither sister has admitted to it, and Tammi said she doesn't even remember this incident.

At the end of that dark night, I no longer cared who had eaten it. I just rededicated myself to my goals: deliver the best speech I possibly could, get elected class president, and compile a résumé that would be my ticket out of the epicenter of organized chaos that was my home.

21

The Last Poets, Jack and Jill, Boogie Down Productions, and Me

Though groggy and covered with welts, I rallied, delivered my speech, and was elected class president again. The hard-won victory ushered in a whirlwind of a tenth-grade year. I won the secretary of the Senate election in Youth in Government, which made me the chief operating officer of the Senate, just below the president of the Senate. Before any bill or resolution could be introduced in a session, it first had to be delivered to the secretary's office to be prepared for introduction.

We ran our sessions using the same protocols as the legendary Speaker of the House of Representatives Tip O'Neill used in the official sessions of Congress that I watched on TV. Our state Senate operated somewhat differently from the House in terms of processes, but our deep knowledge of Robert's Rules of Order made our sessions run smoothly.

Being secretary meant that I could get a firsthand view of the duties of president of the Senate, making me a natural fit for the next job in line. All I had to do was serve well and meet, impress, and help as many YIG participants as I could, and execute the election plan. All of this was achievable. I never felt out of place in that atmosphere; in YIG, unlike school, I never once experienced a blatant episode of racism.

My tenure as secretary of the Senate brought local news coverage, drawing attention from influential politicians and executives in the state. One such person was Bill Wilson, the president of the St. Paul City Council, who approached me to help lead the annual Martin Luther King Holiday March to the Capitol, and also lead the marchers in

"We Shall Overcome" during the program on the Capitol steps. It was the same march I had skipped school to take part in every year since elementary school. As we walked, linking arms with then–Minnesota State Attorney General Hubert "Skip" Humphrey III and other dignitaries, memories flooded back to when I had handed that school absence note to Mrs. Blumer in the third grade.

We still had a lot to fight for. President Reagan had signed the bill making the day a federal holiday in 1983, but the first observance wasn't until 1986. And even then, several states refused to acknowledge the holiday, including Arizona and Mississippi. Some states even introduced bills combining MLK Day with celebrations of Confederate General Robert E. Lee.

Because of all the resistance, we kept marching and speaking out, vowing that we would never let up until every state in the nation recognized this American hero. We couldn't have imagined that South Carolina would resist all the way until 2000 before making MLK Day an official state holiday. Before then, state employees were allowed to choose between celebrating Dr. King's birthday or one of three Confederate holidays.

It felt surreal to be standing in front of thousands of activists, leading the march I had walked in as a troubled third-grader. Somehow, I had risen to Dad's "Do it on the field!" challenge, turning myself into a briefcase-carrying fifteen-year-old in a dark blue suit, a red power tie, and a flattop. Other than remembering the note in third grade, I never stopped to dwell on the childhood that had never happened, much less mourn the loss. I simply watched myself marching and singing on the ten o'clock news and understood that my exit plan was moving forward smoothly.

A few weeks later, after a local newspaper ran a piece about me called "Student Brings New Meaning to Black History Month," I was called to the principal's office and handed a thick envelope that had been mailed to me in care of the school. Inside were about ten pages of clippings that someone had assembled from photographs and stories in several newspapers. Pasted on the clippings were various verses from the Bible that were intended to illustrate that "race mixing" is a sin, and also denigrating Jews.

As I flipped through the pages, I saw that the Bible verses had been manipulated to suggest that Jesus warned the races to stay apart. A big part of my astonishment at that moment had to do with the sudden flash that Mom's tendency to distort the Bible for her own purposes was not limited to her. Clearly, the Bible could be weaponized by people everywhere to justify racism and the mistreatment of innocent people (and not merely of the crime of eating the last few bites from a carton of ice cream).

Who would send such a hateful message? Could it be the same people who deliberately drove over the lawns of the Black families in Maplewood? The gym teacher who asked whether my smile meant he was the welfare man? The girl who yelled, "Get off the bus, nigger!"? My white friends who did nothing after she said it? The science teacher who implied that Blacks were bred to be athletically superior? The classmates who responded by asserting the intellectual superiority of white people? The freak who taped the "Running Nigger" dartboard on my locker? The district officials or school administrators who did nothing about racism Black students faced? The more I thought about it, the more potential culprits came to mind.

Over the next few days, the envelopes kept coming, with my photo cut out and pasted next to racist diatribes and distorted Bible verses condemning the mixing of races. Reading those letters, I remembered the *Mandingo* movie and the fact that my parents had always warned me that interracial mixing in Maplewood could have dire consequences.

The principal told my parents that several Black student athletes who'd received media attention had received similar letters in the past, but the authorities hadn't been able to figure out who'd sent them. Although the sender never threatened me, I angrily prepared to defend myself, if necessary, keeping watch over my shoulder from minute to minute.

The school then provided a first-of-its-kind police escort for me. My mother told me that the administrators demanded that I accept the escort. For those few days, I always asked the officer to let me off at a side door so as not to draw attention to the situation. I tried my best to hide any fear or apprehension, because I knew the letters could be from someone with ties to the school.

It seemed like my life had formed a half circle. I'd started my pre-teen years fearing cops, but now I had a white Maplewood police officer protecting me. Feeling as if I was turning into my father, I kept worrying that one of his fellow police officers had sent the letters, or that the school administration was retaliating against me for my activism and complaints about racism. The cop escorting me turned out to be extraordinarily kind and compassionate, a reminder that one needs to move beyond the dark history of US policing and allow for human complexity.

Of course, my parents were terrified, so I felt guilty about my activism at school. I'm sure they wondered how we had ended up there: 825 miles and thirty years away from the Little Rock Nine, and a Black kid in Minnesota still needed police protection at school.

22

Self-Destruction

The hate mail wasn't enough to slow down my Maplewood and Hawkins household exit plan. In the summer after my sophomore year, I headed to the Jack and Jill Teen Regional Conference, attended by kids from Chicago, Detroit, and other major cities and suburbs. They elected me president.

Winning the presidency paved the way for me to be mentored by another village of accomplished, loving, and patient Black females. The Jack and Jill mothers were corporate lawyers, CEOs, politicians, school superintendents, doctors, scientists, and more, and they all took the same "you can do it, and because we love you, we expect nothing less" approach that I'd first encountered in the miraculous ladies of Mount Olivet. Even better, my presidential victory earned me a two-year term on the Jack and Jill Foundation's National Board of Directors. Since that board included men, I also gained more Rondo-like father figures in men who had distinguished themselves in a variety of industries. In my board position, a position that would last until my first year of college, I traveled all over the country, to both mothers' conventions and board meetings.

On one bus ride home from a Jack and Jill convention in East Lansing, Michigan, all the teenagers on board celebrated amid what was almost certainly the most memorable and enjoyable trip in our high school experience so far. My older friends had already been accepted into HBCUs and Ivy League universities, while others had Division I athletic scholarships from major universities like Notre Dame and Arizona State University. With the wind at our backs from Jack and Jill, Rondo, and our families, we were strong, confident, and rooted in a solid foundation.

But not long after that high-spirited bus ride, I found myself on another bus ride that was its polar opposite in terms of the emotions it roiled up. As the long coach rolled members of Mount Olivet's youth and adult choirs down Interstate 94, the pink glow of the setting sun hit my face as I listened to my Walkman. We were returning from a church service in the sanctuary of our sister church in Beloit, Wisconsin. Despite the noise of video games and youth chatter, most of the adults managed to fall into naps, hoping to get some decent sleep before their Monday morning return to work.

The bus stopped at a gas station in Hudson, Wisconsin, less than an hour from the Minnesota border. When I got back to the bus, armed with snacks, our First Lady, Elnora Battle, announced, "We have some unfortunate news. We just learned that Kimberly Coleman was murdered." My mind immediately brought up the image of Tammi's longtime friend from church, as the two of them clapped and laughed at their joint birthday party as children. "We don't have any details other than the fact that she was murdered. She's gone, y'all. We are going to pray right now for the Coleman family. We know the Lord will make a way . . . somehow."

Amid the gasps and low-level shrieks, we immediately joined our suddenly sweaty hands. I tried to concentrate on the prayer, but the inevitable harsh thoughts intruded. I looked over at my cousin James and whispered, "You think it was Jamal?" He nodded yes.

On at least two previous occasions, mutual friends had told me that Kim's ex-boyfriend, Jamal—a kid I'd met at summer sports camp—had slapped her and slammed her against the lockers in their school hallway. While they dated, we'd heard he had grown uncontrollably jealous and possessive.

The two were a mismatch from the get-go. Kim had it all: a sweet, talented beauty with a gorgeous smile, she was beloved by her tight-knit family and scores of friends from every part of her life. She was easily one of the most popular girls in St. Paul, with admirers all over the city. Her grace and beauty almost certainly intimidated Jamal and aroused all his insecurities. Now, we all knew in our bones that he had taken out his anger on her in the most brutal, and final, way.

As we prayed, I remembered six-year-old Kim sitting alongside Tammi at their joint birthday party at the Maplewood Mall, wearing glittery birthday hats and blowing out the candles on their cake. Thoughts of that happier time made the death of our childhood church friend almost impossible to bear.

Ultimately, Jamal admitted to stabbing Kim to death in his mother's kitchen. Her offense: she had told him she wasn't sure she would attend prom with him. He was sent to prison, joining the growing number of 1980s-era Black boys entering the prison industrial complex.

Kim's grisly death was far from the only one in our circle. During each of my four years of high school, a kid I knew was murdered in St. Paul. I grew up with three of them, and one—Ricky Churcher—was the nephew of one of my father's co-workers and best friends. All but Ricky's murder involved a personal slight or a moment of passion gone wrong.

Ricky died at age ten in 1986, when an intruder stabbed him thirty-one times, mostly in the neck, while he was babysitting his mom's boyfriend's eight-year-old daughter, whom the murderer also left to die after sexually assaulting her. Through the grace of God, that girl survived. Kim was murdered a year later. Another Black Maplewood friend from Jack and Jill, Marcy "Marlizza" McIntyre, was nineteen when she was killed in 1990 in an apparent ambush. After entering a duplex with a woman she considered one of her best friends, Marcy was robbed and then shot in the back of the head. The "friend" and a group of mostly male accomplices placed Marcy's body in the trunk of her car, which they abandoned. Around that same time, Andre, the fifteen-year-old nephew of my uncle L.C., Aunt Corene's husband, was fatally shot in the back by his best friend. Why? Andre's friend felt "disrespected" when Andre teased him about backing down from a fight weeks earlier. Andre and I, who considered ourselves to be cousins, played hide-and-seek for hours and hours as kids. I remember the kid who shot him as a kind soul; he just felt too embarrassed in front of others and made a terrible choice that left two families grieving—one standing over their Black teenage son in the morgue, the other with their son facing years in prison.

In each of these crimes, the murderers were Black—not white KKK members, not white police officers—as well as the victims. Growing up, I attended way too many funerals, mostly for Black loved ones who died way too soon. I found it hard to grasp why Black brothers would kill their own just as quickly as racist police officers or members of the KKK would. It seemed as though Black murderers and violent racists were united in their hatred of Black people. The Black attackers had internalized the same racist belief system of white supremacists, becoming enforcers, turning against their own. Like the slaves who betrayed Kunta Kinte, Black-on-Black murderers were just another unconscious version of a white man's overseer. But where, I wondered, did all this Black-on-Black violence—and the self-hating belief system it was rooted in—come from?

Our funerals were elaborate, full of pomp and circumstance and often exceeding three hours in length. Whenever I attended one, I was devastated by the reality that our community had become so grand and adept at burying our loved ones, especially children. I'd take the lonely walk up to the gold-leaf, flower-adorned casket and wince at the deformities of the cheeks or skull of the departed. I'd stand there and ponder what this person could have done differently, if anything, to avoid such an untimely demise.

All of those 1980s-era young Black homicides spawned hip-hop's "Stop the Violence" movement, and the prescient words of the song "Self-Destruction," which brought America's top rappers together to condemn what was then acknowledged as Black-on-Black murder and crime. In the midst of this, Kool Moe Dee provocatively highlighted the irony of having to be more wary of the possibility of being murdered by another Black man than by the KKK.

The Reverend Jesse Jackson once went even further. "There is nothing more painful to me at this stage in my life," he said, talking about rampant crime in Washington, DC, "than to walk down the street and hear footsteps . . . then turn around and see somebody white and feel relieved."

Despite my positive experience with my high school police escort, I was still stressed out by the possibility of any interactions with police officers. When I got my driver's permit, and Dad took me out driving, he gave me another dimension of "the talk." Almost none of what he had to say involved switching lanes, using turn signals, or watching my speed.

"Okay, son, let's go through the steps," Dad said. "If they pull you over, you have to do everything I'm showing you right now, so pay attention."

"Okay."

"I'm serious, son. Do not take this lightly, because if you miss a step, these police will blow your brains out, and what's left of them will be splattered all over this passenger-seat window. You'll be on the ten o'clock news and the preachers will preach how wrong it was, and we'll march, and we'll protest—but you will be dead. Dead and gone. And I don't want to have to be out there marching for justice for my son with the preachers and all your politician friends. I want my son. Do you hear me, boy?"

"I hear you."

"Okay. As soon as you slowly pull to the side of the road, you gotta make sure that the cop can see your hands, and that you move very calmly, and very slowly. It's on you to make him feel safe because they fear us. At least that's what they'll say after they blow your brains out. They are intimidated by and afraid of Black men, so you have to assume that they think you have a gun or that you're gonna open that door and kick their asses."

"Mm-hmm."

"Put your hands on the dash, spread 'em out."

"Mm-hmm."

"When the cop says 'Open the window,' don't move your hands, but tell him, 'I'm opening up the window.' Pronounce it loud and slow so he can read your lips, because the window is going to still be rolled up. Then take your hand, put it down there, slowly open the window, okay?"

"Mm-hmm."

"Then put your hands back up. When he says, 'Show me your

registration,' you need to tell him, 'I'm reaching for the registration in the glove compartment.' And then move your body slowly and reach over here for it. Grab it, and then slowly move back."

"Mm-hmm."

"Then hand the registration to the cop. Keep your hands in the air where he can see 'em. Do not assume that he will not pull the gun out and shoot you twenty-four times, because he will. Eighty percent of the time, if you move too fast, he will. And even if you don't move too fast, he might, and he could just lie on the police report and say he thought he saw a gun. And if they need to plant one on you after they kill you, they won't hesitate. So do not play with these white cops. Fuck that, the Black cops, too, because they will shoot you just as much as the white ones will. In fact, they'll do it to impress the white ones, to show their loyalty. Do you hear me?"

"Yes."

"When the cop tells you what to do, do it. Follow everything they tell you. Don't do anything. Don't say anything. Don't get smart. Be polite, no matter how fucked up they may treat you. Just go along with everything. Go along with it, son. Go along with it."

Dad lowered his head, and then reached out to squeeze my shoulder. He breathed in, and he sat there for a minute, while I looked over everything on the dash.

"You okay, son?"

"Yeah." I exhaled for the first time in what felt like hours.

"Okay, good job, man. Let's pull out."

23

Lee Roy Chauvin

That's not a chip on my shoulder. That's your foot on my neck.

—MALCOLM X

For me, Dad's touches on my shoulder signified that, in his private moments, he did think about the pressure I carried every day. Perhaps that's why I didn't see it coming—the physical attack that made all the previous beatings in my life seem like minor swats on the rear.

Despite the hundreds of times my parents whipped or slapped me, I always felt certain that my father's propensity for violence had limits. But one day, he set out to prove me wrong. It wasn't until that moment that I grasped the depths to which violence could take him. And for once, my mom wasn't the one who egged him on, though she didn't lift a finger to help me.

He had just returned from work and was wearing black steel-toed work boots and blue khaki work pants. We were sitting at the dining-room table, talking about some political issue, and had a difference of opinion. Like an athlete training for a sport, I was so polished in speech and debate that I was unaware that my preparedness and grasp of the issue might trigger my father's insecurities. "That's your mentality," I told him. "You have to change your mentality on that, Dad."

Somehow, the word "mentality" set off a ticking bomb in Dad's brain. I was urging him to shift his way of thinking on the issue, but he took it as an insult, as if I were questioning his intelligence. He lunged at me, choking me with an intensity that had no precedent. I fought at his hands as his thumbs pressed firmly on my Adam's apple, applying viselike pressure. I desperately tried to tell him I couldn't breathe. He let go, but before I could get my bearings, he did the unthinkable.

He shoved me down to the living room floor, my head barely missing the sharp corner of the dining-room table. I broke the fall with my hands and knees and for an instant was propped up on all fours. My father put his work boot between my shoulder blades and stomped down on it with every ounce of strength he had. Facedown, with his entire 250 pounds pressed hard on my spine, I struggled to turn over and dislodge his foot.

He had threatened to kill me and break my neck many times, but still, I was in disbelief.

"He really is gonna kill me," I thought, with pure, distilled terror. "He's not gonna let up." Somehow, I squirmed my way out from under his foot, but then he grabbed me and slammed me down again, this time with my back to the floor. I braced myself for a punch to the face, but it didn't come.

Instead, he kept moving his boot around my body, seemingly intent on finding the perfect position from which to press down even harder. "Boy! I'll kill you!" he screamed. "I'll kill you!"

Then, as I turned my face downward and tried again to propel myself off the floor, his foot caught the crevice between my side and the back of my neck and shoulders. My head was on the floor with my neck slightly turned to the side. He put his foot on my neck, pressed all his weight down on it, and kept pushing. My sister Tiffany and my mom witnessed everything.

Years later, Tiffany recalled, "Mentality, mentality. That's what you said. I don't know how he flipped you on the ground, but the next thing I knew, his foot was on your neck, and he was putting all his weight on it. I remember screaming, 'Dad! Stop! Stop!' He was out of control. It was like he was the Incredible Hulk or something.

"He easily could've snapped your neck," she continued. "It was like it wasn't even about what you said. I don't know if he was thinking about something else or what, but he completely lost control. He was out of his mind."

Under my dad's foot during his out-of-body experience, I used all my strength to grab his boot by the ankle. From that vantage point, under my father's worn steel-toed boot, I thought he looked ten feet tall. That moment was without question the lowest point I have ever been in my life—on the floor, looking up at my father standing over me, crazed beyond comprehension, pressing his steel-sheathed foot as hard as he could on his namesake's neck. He was panting from the effort, and his protruding belly bounced up and down with each raggedy breath.

Poison tore through my veins and body as I teared up, fighting with everything I had to get a him off me. But he kept pushing harder and harder, despite Tiffany's screams.

And then suddenly, he let up.

But it wasn't because he feared he would kill me—it was because he was so out of shape that he couldn't catch his breath. This man, once a lean, fit soldier and athlete, stood there, obviously broken, and finally eased his foot off his proper-speaking son's neck—but only because he was panting for air.

As he backed away, I rubbed the back and sides of my pulsating, stinging neck. My father didn't say a word, just disappeared down the hallway and into his bedroom, his exit punctuated by the sound of a slamming door.

Something shifted in me after that near-death experience at the hands of my own father, with my mother looking on and doing nothing. I truly and finally accepted the cold reality that nobody—*nobody*—was coming to save me. There was no tenderness to be had anywhere at 2180 Hazelwood, and my sole aim was to get the hell out of there.

24

Echoes of Dr. King

A few weeks after Dad's attack, I clinched the junior class presidency, bringing me within striking distance of a four-year streak of class presidencies.

In the fall, in what quickly became my most action-packed year yet, I won my Youth in Government election for president of the Senate, incorporating that winter session into my already bustling schedule. I also triumphed in Minnesota's Martin Luther King Celebration speech contest. At Minnesota's King holiday celebration that January, with my smiling parents in the front row, I spoke at the St. Paul Cathedral before Vice President (and former Minnesota senator) Walter Mondale and fellow award winners, one of whom, Judy Oliver, was accepting the state's Martin Luther King Jr. Humanitarian Award on behalf of her husband, the playwright August Wilson.

As I readied myself to speak, gazing out at a sea of faces, my mind wandered back to being that lost little boy, guided spiritually by the indefatigable Sister Jackson. A silent nod of gratitude to her superb speech training preceded my spoken acknowledgments to the attendees: Councilman Wilson, Vice President Mondale, the mayor, the attorney general, my family, my church, my community, and all the distinguished guests. With that, I dove into the most impassioned address of my school years.

While drafting my speech, inspired by Dr. King's nonviolence principles, I thought about challenging the audience to extend his vision of peace into our communities and homes. I wanted to declare war on Black-on-Black homicide and violence against Black children. I pondered, What if Black Americans vowed to practice nonviolence with each other, echoing our commitment to white America during the civil rights movement? What if Black men made this promise to other Black men, to their wives and partners, and parents to their children? Or did we love white people more than ourselves?

However, I was aware that mentioning Black-on-Black violence would touch an extremely sensitive, denial-provoking subject. Addressing domestic violence could also embarrass my parents as they sat alongside dignitaries. Furthermore, I recognized that many Black attendees likely practiced "spanking" their children regularly. I suspected that this intraracial violence might stem from the history of enslavement, yet I lacked concrete evidence. I feared that calling for the Black community's collective attention to these issues and the whispered hypocrisy around them might lead to accusations of pushing respectability politics and "pathologizing Black folk," potentially alienating most of the Black audience. Many in our community are keen to talk about Dr. King and nonviolence, as long as it doesn't require them to take substantive action against violence in Black homes and communities. Haunted by family and societal beliefs that Black children need and deserve to be whipped—and to remain silent about it often while practicing it—I was still unsure whether it was fair to label such violence as "abuse."

So I safely focused on interracial unity and the universal celebration of the King holiday. Channeling Dr. King for my finale, my voice boomed "Let freedom ring! Ring!" and the intensity of that final "Ring!" prompted a spontaneous standing ovation. The applause, echoing everywhere, finally softened the sting of my flubbed speech on Kareem Abdul-Jabbar.

Each congratulatory handshake from some of my favorite politicians, as well as watching the highlights on TV that evening, reinforced my conviction that I would be heading to college, not prison. My strategy to break free was succeeding. The trophies filling up our rec room symbolized one crucial thing to me: unapologetic freedom and liberation. It wouldn't be long before I'd exchange Maplewood's chaos for tranquility elsewhere—anywhere, truly.

Later that year, a flurry of newspaper articles reported that the Federal Bureau of Investigation had identified the man who had sent me the hate-filled envelopes. The racist letter-writer was Elroy Stock, "a frugal bachelor with resources, a mission, and a copying machine," as the *Chicago Tribune* put it. A retired West Publishing Company employee who lived in a St. Paul suburb, Stock had just made a $500,000 gift to his alma mater, Augsburg College, a small liberal arts institution in the heart of Minneapolis, which was preparing to name an auditorium after him.

According to the *Chicago Tribune*, during his fourteen-year sub-rosa campaign for racial purity, Stock had sent more than one hundred thousand letters, mostly photocopies of articles and pictures with comments in the margins. All the letters repeated his theme: "Racial genocide, today's holocaust. God did not create mixed race people. Sinful man did. To destroy God's races is to hate God."

Stock made a special point of vilifying children and teenagers of mixed race, and of color like me, most of whom excelled in all-white settings. For instance, he sent a series of letters to a girl whose family had adopted her from Korea in 1979. Stock mailed his first letter to the family in 1980, after the child's baptism, then another following her confirmation. Finally, he haunted her with a graduation letter.

In 1987, the *Minneapolis Star Tribune* reported that after postal authorities caught wind of Stock's extensive letter-writing crusade, he was forced into retirement. He'd been at West Publishing for thirty-seven years. Beyond his letters—some even sent in company envelopes—Stock often shared his racist beliefs with co-workers. Reminding me of my dad's warning about racists in corporations fearing that Black men would "fuck all the white women," one colleague recounted how Stock asked her whether she had ever dated "colored men." When she admitted she had, he ordered her to sit at a desk "away" from him.

Maybe, when Dad went ballistic on me as a second-grader for yelling "I hate Hitler!," he had been onto something. Thousands of racist, Nazi supporters might have been living quiet lives, just like Elroy Stock, all over Minnesota. At that point, the Holocaust was only about forty years behind us, and the United States had allowed thousands of Nazi Party members and supporters to emigrate here. Plus, Hitler and his white supremacist comrades were inspired heavily by the social caste system that the United States had already tragically built. With US realities such as those, which were never taught in our schools, it wouldn't be a stretch to believe that Nazis and bigots were living all around us.

Elroy Stock's fate was gentle compared with the shocking death of another of my white tormenters later that same year. In May 1988, all of Maplewood reeled at the news that my third-grade teacher, Mrs. Blumer, had been beaten to death by her husband in a gruesome murder/suicide. According to the *Minneapolis Star Tribune*, "the body of Darlene Blumer, 51, was found on the floor of the recreation room with apparent injuries to her face and upper chest. Glenn Blumer's body was hanging from a clothesline tied to a ceiling pipe in his work-shop." The couple, described as "reclusive," had been dead for several days before authorities found their decomposing bodies.

Just days earlier, Mr. Blumer had consulted a physician about his depression (he had recently lost his job). He'd been referred to a thera-pist, but instead of keeping the appointment, he opted to end it all and take his wife with him.

Mrs. Blumer was known around Weaver Elementary for her frequent absences, but when she didn't show up for days, colleagues notified the authorities. An administrator at Weaver remembered Mrs. Blumer as "a tenderhearted, soft-spoken woman who loved butterflies and frequently called parents at home to discuss their children's progress." I could cer-tainly vouch for the second part of that description.

Even as a third-grader, and a survivor of abuse myself (from Mrs. Blumer as well as my parents), I had a gut instinct that something was amiss with her. Now, from my vantage point in eleventh grade, I recalled some telling details—the way she burst into tears when my classmate and I knocked over her fan; her tense, tight-lipped expression as she con-signed me to hours behind that infamous wooden partition. I suspected that she, too, had often been afraid to go home at the end of the day.

But outsiders are rarely privy to the demons people are battling. As was true of my own family, when the craziness unfolds, the windows are almost always shuttered. "I don't think any of us were ever in the house," a neighbor told the *Star Tribune*. "They were always inside, and the shades were always drawn."

A High Tolerance for Pain

asked the pediatrician for ways to ease the tension that had built up in my neck, making me so desperate for relief that I'd started twisting my head to each side until my neck made a loud popping sound.

A doctor told me to run hot water over my neck and to take ibuprofen instead of popping it, and eventually the tension would subside.

But it got worse.

He sent me for x-rays.

After reviewing them, the doctor said the test was abnormal but didn't provide a clear enough view of some of my vertebrae. I would need further tests and an evaluation by a neurologist.

As a kid, I never had neck problems, and as far as I knew, no one else in my family had, either. In fact, I had never broken a bone or even sprained an ankle. This neck condition seemed to arise out of nowhere for no reason. At least, that's what I wanted to believe.

After rounds of tests and consultations, we were told I had problems with my upper spinal vertebrae, which included a subluxation of key upper vertebrae. The doctor advised my parents that I needed surgery and cautioned that without it, a car accident or a nasty fall could have tragic consequences. I had no idea what "subluxation" meant, but if it required an operation, it had to be serious.

The surgery was considered high risk because of the complexity and critical nature of the area involved. To stabilize my neck, I would need to have a bone graft of tissue scraped off my right hip bone and placed between a few upper vertebrae. Then, I would be put in a plaster cast from the waist up, with metal bars installed into the shoulders of the cast that would stick up just past the top of my skull. Between the bars, doctors would install a circular metal halo around my head and drill four holes into the front and back of my skull, into which four screws would be inserted. I would need to wear this contraption for three and a half months while the bones fused together.

The doctor warned, "This is not the most comfortable process. There will be many days when you'll be in pain."

As I tried to absorb all this, Mom's mind must have drifted back to seeing me as her little Bamm-Bamm. "Oh, he can do it," she assured the doctor. "He has a high tolerance for pain."

The doctor warned us that there was always the chance that a surgeon could slip and make an error that—this being the spinal cord—could leave me seriously injured or even paralyzed. That did it. I told the doctor and my parents that I'd forgo surgery and take my chances. Beyond the risks, I didn't want to miss the YMCA Youth Conference on National Affairs in Washington, DC.

Eager for me to have the surgery, my parents and the doctor proposed a compromise: I could go to DC and then have the surgery when I got back. I reluctantly agreed, knowing that as a minor (not to mention a human whipping post), I had no real voice or choice in this or any other matter.

A few months later, I opened my eyes in a dark, dimly lit hospital room. I tried to glance around me but couldn't move my head. It seemed as if I'd been awake only minutes earlier, but if the surgery had gone according to schedule, that had been around six hours ago.

My mouth started watering profusely. The nurse, evidently reading my mind, rushed over with an aqua green hospital bowl for me to puke in. "The anesthetic is still wearing off," she explained. "Some people's systems just reject that anesthesia."

Turned on my side, with my head near the bowl, I had never been so happy to be puking in my life. If I was vomiting, that meant I had made it through the surgery. I was still sedated and feeling reasonably good, thanks to all the painkillers they must have pumped into my system.

Thankfully, I could also feel my legs, so I'd soon be taking my first steps on the road to recovery. It wouldn't be easy. Once I made it out of that bed, I would need to learn how to walk in the cumbersome fifteen-pound halo cast. But that was still a ways off. In the meantime, I simply lay there, inert in that dark room, IV in my arm.

Once the nurse left, I took the opportunity to check out the damage. Just as the doctors had explained, my head was locked sturdily into place with a halo-shaped apparatus secured to my skull. My entire torso and back, from the waist up, were covered with the cast. I knocked slowly on the hard plaster, as if it were a door. It fit almost like a vest. The only opening was a hole around my stomach area. I wear it for at least three months, during which I prayed the desperately needed fusion in my spinal cord would occur.

I moved my hand up to my head, which was enclosed within the metal rods the cast was supporting. It was a shock to realize that the strong screws were attached to my skull. A group of people walked through the door, and, forgetting about the cast or the metal rods in my head, I turned my head to look. Or tried to: my neck strained slightly, but the screws wouldn't permit me to move even a centimeter. I rolled my eyes to the left to see Mom and Dad slowly approaching my bed.

Dad spoke first, looking somber but attempting his usual laid-back attitude. "How you feelin', man?"

Mom just stared at me, speechless. She then broke into a shrieking cry, putting her head on Dad's chest, as he consoled her. (I made a mental note: Never cry in front of someone you're visiting in the hospital. It has a spirit-crushing effect.)

Mom's reaction alerted me to how scary I looked. I closed my eyes and felt Dad's hand on my leg and Mom's tear-dampened hand touch my face. But because of all the attacks I'd endured at my parents' hands, Mom's tears outraged more than consoled me.

"I'm okay, Mom, I feel good," I said, my throat still scratchy. Then came the shocker.

"We love you, Lee," said my mother.

For years, all I had received from her was skeptical scorn. Yet now, as I lay foggy from anesthesia, she spoke of love. Even though it felt strange, considering I hadn't heard those words since I was a young child, I genuinely believed my mom was sincere and awkwardly replied, "Love you too."

Gone was the aura with which I had surrounded myself of invincibility, immunity to pain, and toughness my parents had always taken for granted. Every time they were violent with me, I always seemed to bounce back in time for them to attend another awards ceremony and sit as honored guests with all the other VIPs and act like the Hawkinses were the Huxtables.

I closed my eyes, feeling drained from the morphine and anesthesia. When I opened them again, Mom and Dad were gone, and I was alone. A sliver of light crept into the room through the crack of the door. That little bit of light helped me think about the darkness of my double life: on one hand was my public life as a student leader who supposedly represented "the best of America's future"; and on the other hand was my secret life of getting pounded and threatened and humiliated behind those shutters that Mom was always careful to close.

Today, I am proud, and a bit astonished, that I managed it all. I think back to how exhausting—physically, mentally, psychologically—it was to maintain that public persona while privately living in constant deference to my mysteriously broken, unbalanced parents. Yet somehow, with nearly every touch of the ball, I lit up the field. Even as I lay in the hospital bed fuming, I still felt undefeated.

I was pushing through on borrowed strength. Not from within and certainly not from my parents, but from God, and from those elders who hugged me so hard I could barely breathe. Almost from the moment I came out of surgery, Mom started inviting people to visit me in the hospital. I angrily told her that the only visitors I wanted were my personal rock stars—Grandpa Buddy and Great-Grandpa Sam, Aunt Loyce, my Sunday School teacher, Deaconess Williams, and all the other deacons and deaconesses from church.

They started filing in immediately. In fact, one of my stars, ninety-something-year-old Deacon Maceo Simmons, limped in, looked at me with his Malcolm X glasses, and started yelling at my parents, thinking something seemed amiss. "What happened to him? Why did you let them do this to him? What is going on here? You should have never let them put him in this contraption!"

Mom half-laughed, albeit awkwardly, and said, "The doctors said he needed it. It happened when he was born and went undetected all this time. It was congenital." At least, that's what she wanted to believe.

I sat back in the bed, with Deacon Simmons squeezing my hand, calling me "Little Lee Roy."

"I'm okay, buddy," I told him. "I'm gonna be fine. God's got me."

These were my warriors, and I knew that he and that whole all-star squad were praying sincerely for me even when I wasn't praying for myself.

As Deacon Simmons and I chatted, Mom interjected. "Yes, keep us all in your prayers. We've been sleeping here and it's been hard on the whole family. We didn't know he was going to be in intensive care. The doctor didn't tell us it was this serious. It's been really, really hard. But God is able. In fact, when Lee was in the operating room, God spoke to me. He told me 'If Lee lives, he will help many people.'"

In that gut-punch-of-a-moment, I almost vomited again.

The ad nauseam worsened as the day went on. Predictably, the visitor list quickly grew far beyond my Mount Olivet all-stars. I would estimate that for the duration of my hospital stay, more than a hundred people saw me laid up in that cast, under the influence of pain medication. I snapped at Mom for inviting people to visit me in what to this day remains the most vulnerable, weakened state I have ever been in.

I felt naked and exposed. I couldn't see myself, but I saw the horror and disbelief on the face of every visitor. One kid walked in, looked me over, and merely said, "Oh my God, Lee. You look terrible."

Despite my rage, I had to smile from that bed. I couldn't be ungracious to people who took the time to visit me. But I couldn't scold my parents, either. I needed them, and I still couldn't trust them not to hurt me, even in this incapacitated state.

During my week in the hospital, I discovered a paradox: strong Black men are often most cherished when seen as vulnerable, yet are viewed by some with suspicion and fear when they succeed and excel.

During the three and a half months I wore that ugly, immovable cast, my mom became my primary caretaker, and she was a pro. A trained nurse, she followed all the protocols for keeping the screws clean and free of bacteria. And she was nicer to me during those months than she ever had been.

I didn't know how to process this change in her. I still worried that my parents might lose their cool and hit me even though I was wearing the cast. Because of their mood swings and white-hot tempers, and their history of hundreds of "spankings"—I'd never gone that long without a beating—I feared they could too easily forget that my vertebrae were still fusing. One temper-inspired pull, one push, one jostle of the two plaster-implanted steel bars that held the screws tight in the four holes in my head, and that would be the end of me. By that time I had decided that my parents' over-the-top assaults conferred an authority and omnipotence that was denied them in their daily lives, so I was terrified that they might become desperate for the "fix" that only Tiffany or I could provide.

Thank God, they were incredibly loving and kind and never touched me during those three long months. Yet the fear that they might—and the familiar poisons that fear triggered—was hell to bear.

It was also hell to confront my utter lack of trust in my parents, the very people who were supposed to be my primary protectors. It underscored the vulnerability and aloneness that the extremely high-risk surgery and my immobility evoked. My one saving grace was the knowledge that after the halo cast was removed, I would soon be off to college and on my way toward a new life. I couldn't wait to shake off the remnants of trauma that clung to me like lint.

Yet oddly, perhaps stubbornly, I never considered what I had gone through as trauma. Not then, anyway. I had neither the inclination nor the language to describe my constant whippings or the squashing of my neck by my dad's foot as "abuse" or in those terms.

My doctors were mystified as to the cause of my spinal problems and hypothesized that they were likely caused by a congenital deformity or some sort of sports injury. The Cleveland Clinic offers this definition: "A Subluxation is the medical term for a partial dislocation. You have a subluxation if something pulls your joint apart and the bones still touch, just not as completely as usual."

I, a strong, athletic kid who had never broken a bone or suffered an illness more severe than asthma and childhood pneumonia, didn't push my doctors for more detail or give them additional information that might have led them to a more definitive causation.

And neither did my parents. My team of health professionals never knew that my father had pressed all 250 pounds of his weight into my neck with his steel-booted foot.

I held that memory inside for decades without ever speaking of it to anyone. Whenever people asked me about the halo cast, or later asked about my stiff neck or the long scar it boasted, I always changed the subject or obfuscated, out of embarrassment. Because of wishful thinking and my profound love for my dad, I have always kept it simple: I was just born this way.

It has taken me all these years to admit, even to myself, that if Dad's boot didn't cause my joints to "pull apart," it certainly didn't help.

26

Urkel

B eing in the halo cast meant that I couldn't work the job I had at St. Paul Book and Stationery, but otherwise I kept a normal schedule. In a strange way, even with fifteen pounds of plaster and steel weighing me down, all those days without any physical attacks or cruelty from my parents were some of my best.

In the fall of 1989, I began the academic year riding a bus for students with disabilities, attending school half-days. I regretted mocking the wheelchair-bound classmate, chastising myself for not feeling empathy for someone even though he had been so cruel to me. A few times weekly, a kind, middle-aged white female tutor assisted me with coursework at home. The class president election was that fall. Many classmates, intrigued with and puzzled by my cast, wondered whether I'd run for a fourth term, and if elected, whether I'd be able to fulfill my role.

The sight of my hobbling down the hall in my triple-sized shirt, baggy pants, flattop, and large, Steve Urkel–looking tortoise-shell glasses couldn't have given them much confidence that I'd be able to pull it off.

On the day of the speech, I made my fitful way down the aisle of the auditorium and was taken aback to find that almost twice as many classmates as usual were running against me. Apparently, people thought I'd take a pass that year. But upon seeing me, dozens of classmates started clapping and yelling and coming up to me with high-fives.

"All right, Lee! You're here? You're running?"

"Damn straight, I'm running," I said, slapping hands as I tried to find a suitable chair. That moment, and the endorphin surge that came with it, was further evidence that not everyone at North High was a blistering racist. I had supporters I didn't even recognize, and maybe even took for granted. Though I sometimes felt like the world was against me, that clearly was not the case.

Once I started speaking, it was clear that I was the same Lee Hawkins they'd elected class president three times before. They gave me another round of rousing applause and proceeded to vote me in for my fourth and final term.

And just days before the crucial YMCA gubernatorial election, I received a last-minute invitation to speak at a delegation more than an hour away. Declining could have jeopardized my election chances, so I nervously asked my mom for a ride. Without a hint of criticism, she immediately agreed, even helping me to the car with a simple, "Okay, let's go." Fighting back tears, I realized that her actions at that moment spoke volumes of her love for and belief in me—a working mother indifferent to my dreams never would have rearranged her midweek schedule to chauffeur me there, wait patiently outside for an hour, and then drive me home. And that was not the only time Mom showed her love for me through action, not necessarily words.

Three and a half months after the surgery, my scans showed that the fusion was successful. On the day the halo cast was removed, I felt like an infant who had just discovered his neck moves back and forth. Striding down the hall of the hospital, I wiped my eyes dry, went into the bathroom, and offered up an emotional prayer of thanks. My plans to move forward with my life were still on track.

That October, I was elected Youth Governor of Minnesota, an honor that meant that I moved into then-Governor Rudy Perpich's office and for four days presided over a mock state government that had me signing and vetoing bills, appointing a cabinet, and executing a wide variety of other gubernatorial duties.

Most important, being Youth Governor gave me a chance to publicly acknowledge my "all-star team," including all the deacons and deaconesses and family members who flooded the State Capitol to hear my "State of the State Address" in the Minnesota State House of Representatives chamber.

For my address later that day, I was told to wait outside of the chamber before making my entry. As I waited, a group of escorts and cabinet members took their places in front, in back, and beside me, and we all walked in together.

"Ladies and gentlemen, please rise for Lee Hawkins Jr., Youth Governor of the State of Minnesota." Flanked by sergeants at arms on both sides of me, I entered waving—determined, Black, strong—and almost free!

In my address, I pulled off a secret surprise I'd been planning for weeks. I called out to Mr. Gray, my former civics teacher, who was sitting in the top gallery with his wife, and asked him to stand. I then declared Milo Gray Day, explaining that he was the teacher who had introduced me to the Youth in Government program. The next day, a section front of the *St. Paul Pioneer Press* carried a photo of me pointing up to Mr. Gray and his wife in the second level of the chamber.

That spring, not long after I had received the Martin Luther King Jr. Humanitarian Award and helped lead that year's march with Martin Luther King III, I had decided upon the University of Wisconsin-Madison. I was thrilled to learn that our class valedictorian and three other classmates, dozens of friends from Minnesota youth politics and speech competitions, and lots of friends I knew from nightclubs and parties from across the Twin Cities would be joining me there.

27

Hammer in My Hand

After graduation, I began an internship at 3M and took a week off for the 1989 YMCA Youth Governors Conference in Washington, DC. There, I reunited with familiar faces, including the Southern youth leaders known for their distinctive white shirts and bow ties. In the lobby I recognized Jack, a master debater from Tennessee, by his unmistakable drawl. "Well whadd'ya know, Ol' Lee Hawkins done made governor, too."

He'd heard I was going to the University of Wisconsin–Madison, and we talked about our college plans and other things. But I spared him from hearing what I'd been through in the previous twelve months: the surgery and recovery that had me campaigning in a halo cast, attending half-days of school, and applying to college all at the same time.

The next day, our bus driver dropped us off at the Lincoln Memorial. "You have two hours to explore," he said, "and then meet back here." I rushed up the eighty-seven steps from the reflecting pool and gazed at the reflection of the Washington Monument. I envisioned Dr. King, standing on those steps on August 28, 1963, delivering his "I Have a Dream" speech. Being born eight years after that pivotal moment carried an unknown weight. The wind's whispers seemed to echo the crowd's cheers from that day.

Reflecting on my hardships from '88 and '89, I felt grateful for this DC trip, courtesy of my beloved YMCA, which influenced my life tremendously. It marked a triumphant end to high school and brought me closer to the cities I dreamed of—New York or Washington, DC. Proudly, I felt I'd escaped my family chaos. But I was yet to realize that moving away isn't the same as getting away.

During my YIG trips to DC, I noticed the "Southern delegation" reacted differently to iconic sites than I did. My interactions with them during the national YMCA conferences highlighted the reality that, although we all flaunted our obnoxious three-page résumés, our elders had been raised on opposite sides of Jim Crow. Their Confederate loyalties were unmistakable, as they waved small Confederate flags in political triumphs against us "Yankees." They'd sing "Dixie" on our bus rides, as I sat frozen in my seat, bracing myself for "colored" or "pickaninny" verbiage. I'd anticipated some tension with these guys, given the caution Lee Roy Hawkins Sr. had instilled in me. However, I was unprepared for the depth of anti-Yankee sentiment, still strong 125 years after the Civil War.

Our Minnesota textbooks hadn't captured this deep-seated bitterness or given an extensive account of the grim history of enslavement. The evident sense of white supremacy some Southern delegates exhibited, and their continued perception of a nineteenth-century North-South division, showed that enslavement was but a moment ago. I never doubted that some of those delegates saw me and the other Black governors as "N-words."

At Mount Vernon, George Washington's estate, I learned Washington had been an enslaver from age eleven. Our group briefly acknowledged but rushed past the burial ground of Washington's enslaved people. I later returned alone. Enslavement, previously an abstract concept from North High's history classes, where a teacher had once said that Washington owning enslaved people was "not confirmed," became real for me that day. Standing at the site of the slave cemetery, I felt connected to "the many faithful colored servants of the Washington family"—words inscribed on a 1929 marker placed by the Mount Vernon Ladies' Association. I knelt, pondering their identities, questioning any blood connection, and wondering about the Hawkinses. Who truly was I? My yearning to uncover my ancestry grew.

Our day culminated with a "personal tour" of the White House led by Gregg Petersmeyer, a YIG alumnus now assisting President George H. W. Bush's chief of staff. Unlike my prior visit, this one promised glimpses of "the White House the public never sees." Most anticipated was the Roosevelt Room, adjacent to the Oval Office. "Hey Hawkins," Jack jested, "this is the closest you'll ever get to the presidency," triggering my smile.

Petersmeyer began his "You are the future leaders of America" speech, stressing the honor of accessing the Roosevelt Room, with its artifacts from both Roosevelt presidencies. We knew there was no chance of meeting the president but were thrilled to hear his surprise: "Well, as you know, the Oval Office is right across the way. We're going to give you a chance to look inside." The excitement was titillating, but he instructed, "You'll have to go in threes."

Each group returned with faces hinting at imagined meetings with past presidents. When it was our turn, Petersmeyer gestured toward the Oval Office's threshold. "Don't cross the line here," he told us. Peering in, the renowned room appeared familiar yet more intimate than on TV. I found myself thinking, *If only Dad and Grandpa Buddy could see this.*

As we settled into the Roosevelt Room, Petersmeyer momentarily excused himself, but then reentered with a special guest. "Youth Governors," Petersmeyer's voice rang out, drawing our attention, "please welcome the president of the United States."

I felt a gush of nervousness in my stomach, as we rose and pounded our hands together. I didn't become a fan of this president until after he was retired from public service. But it didn't matter: the endorphins rushed through me with a force much greater than the poisons I was accustomed to.

President Bush strode in with the classic eighties dark suit and red power tie, his six-foot-two-inch frame making him look like a seven-footer. I was in too much awe to follow President Bush's "future leaders" speech. This moment transcended politics. Whether staunch Republican, fervent Democrat, or an independent like myself, we were all united by the exhilaration of meeting POTUS. Suddenly, the racism I'd endured just weeks earlier in Maplewood and North High seemed so distant—years and years, and millions of galaxies, away. Listening to the Southern governors-to-be sing "Dixie" on the drive back to the hotel, I realized that all the confusion, the craziness, the hurt feelings, amounted to background noise. It could not, and would not, foil my plan: to get out of Maplewood and start my life.

As the white Southerners yammered on the meaning of their Confederate heritage, I silently hummed my own little ditty. *This is for you, Grandpa Buddy*, I thought, mentally lifting a glass to the strongest, hardest-working man I'd ever known:

> *John Henry said to his captain,*
> *"A man ain't nothing but a man, . . ."*

Tiffany

didn't realize it then, but when I left for college to start my new, peaceful life, my parents redirected the brunt of their fear and whipping-enforced belief system to my sister Tiffany. With Tammi at college in North Carolina, Tiffany was alone at home with Mom and Dad.

With me, my parents had feared that I'd end up in prison or be killed by the police or another young Black man. For Tiffany, they feared she would become a teen mom or be murdered like some of the other Black teenaged girls we knew.

Just like me, Tiffany's outgoing spirit and confidence helped her make friends from every corner of the city, across races. Yet, as her popularity and independence grew, the lash of our parents' control intensified in resistance to her expanding quest for freedom.

"It couldn't be a normal childhood," Tiffany lamented. "My friends didn't even want to call the house because Mom and Dad would act crazy. They'd pick up the phone extension, just listen, and say, 'You need to get off the phone,' for no reason. Two seconds later, they'd pick up again and say, 'I said get off the phone.' 'Okay, I'll call you later,' I'd say. And they'd yell, 'No! She ain't calling you later.'"

When she turned seventeen, Tiffany bought a pager that her friends could call instead of our family line. She hid it under her pillow for months, but one day she left it out and Dad saw it. "What's this? You've got a pager?" he yelled. "Get downstairs!"

Our parents then interrogated her for two hours. "They kept saying, 'The only people who have pagers are doctors and drug dealers, and we know you're not a doctor,'" Tiffany told me. "They just went crazy. They truly believed I was dealing drugs."

With every whip, slap, and verbal putdown from our mother, Tiffany's faith in our parents waned. "I realized I couldn't trust them to protect me."

Nestled underneath her pink bedspread and ensconced in a deep sleep, my fifteen-year-old baby sister Tiffany was abruptly awakened by a forceful yank on her nightshirt. Amid the shock, she wondered if she was stuck in a bad dream. It was 1:30 a.m.

Mom stood over Tiffany, wearing the trademark sleepwear we have permanently burned into our adult brains: a white head rag, a long nightgown, and the knee-high compression stockings she wore every night to help with circulation.

"Her eyes were huge. She was in the dark, but the hallway light was on," Tiffany recalled. "'Get up. Get up, *now*.' I didn't know what was going on, so I got up and went into the living room."

"Do you have something to tell me?'" Mom demanded. She then told Tiffany that she had read her diary, in which Tiffany revealed that she had recently had sex for the first time. "Then, she started yelling. She went crazy. I can't remember specifically what she was saying, but she called me a whore. Going to be trash. I'm going to get pregnant."

After a few more minutes of nonstop berating, Mom told Tiffany she was heading to the bedroom to wake up our soundly sleeping Dad, who was due to get up for work in four hours. From the living room, Tiffany strained to hear our parents' conversation in their bedroom down the hall. In their minds, she had committed the very sin they had beaten her throughout childhood to prevent, and she was on her way to the doom of fiery hell. All she could hear were muffled, frantic words, and then, the clank of the buckle on Dad's worn leather belt.

Our father came out yelling, and two hours of face-to-face insults followed. "No wonder you won homecoming," Mom sneered, suggesting that her election to her class's homecoming court was the result of her being "the class whore." Tiffany hung her head in mortification, with our parents hollering for her to look them in the eye.

Then Dad "spanked" her with his worn leather belt. I remembered that belt all too well. It was black but weathered from frequent use and speckled with cracks that exposed brown dots from its tip to its middle, the sweet spot for the walloping beatdowns he unleashed on us.

It was a bitingly cold Minnesota winter, with outside temperatures hovering near zero. When this middle-of-the-night whipping finally ended, Mom shoved Tiffany into the blackness of the garage where temperatures were barely warmer. "The trash can sleep in the garage," she told Tiffany.

"What? I'm only wearing pajamas! I need my shoes!"

"You don't need shit," Mom told her.

"Then Mom put me in the garage and locked the garage door in the dark," she said.

Tiffany's recollection of being in the icy, pitch-black garage on that desolate winter night sparked a flash of clarity that had eluded me as a child: To Mom, the ultimate misery was being a child, locked in cold, dark, scary confined spaces, like garages, basements, and closets. In fact, I remember a time when I was clowning around with some kids from the neighborhood and I pushed them into one of our hallway closets and leaned against the door, laughing all the while. They laughed and screamed, "Lee! Let us out! Let us out, you jerk!"

I thought it was all playful fun, but when Mom found out, she annihilated me with the belt. Remembering the intensity of her white-eyed stare that day, I realized that the thought of anybody being locked up—joke or not—had triggered some deep trauma in her.

Tiffany was in the garage for at least half an hour. When Mom finally let her out, she made Tiff take a shower. "I believe she did that because she knew I had welts and stuff on me, and that it would sting to take a shower. 'Get in there,' she screamed. 'You need to get clean!'

"When I got out, she yelled 'Take your ass to bed!' I went to bed but was scared all night long because I didn't know what would happen in the morning."

On the morning after the garage incident, Tiffany woke up, got dressed, and—with her coat and backpack on—was about to go out the door when Mom grabbed her backpack from behind and dragged her back inside.

"Where the hell do you think you're going?" she asked.

"To school."

"So you can go and tell those white people? You're not going to school today." Mom pushed Tiffany farther into the house and locked the door. It seemed that this time the whipping and welting were so obvious that a teacher might question what was happening at home, even to a Black kid. Mom and Dad had carefully planned out the details of Tiffany's punishment: Mom had a list of chores for her to do during the missed school day, and Dad rigged the phone line so Tiffany couldn't make any calls out.

With the front and back doors of our house locked and windows that were too small to squeeze out of, Tiffany felt like a prisoner in her own home. "I remember being scared, like what if there was a fire or something?" she said.

After Tiffany's absence from school, her Black friend Michelle and a white girl named Carla brought Tiffany her homework. Tiffany opened the door.

"Is everything okay?" Carla asked. Michelle looked scared, Tiffany told me, because she got a beating herself whenever she did anything wrong and guessed that Tiffany was in trouble.

Tiffany was about to take the homework when Dad walked up. "Tell them you can't talk—you're grounded!" he said.

She explained that her friends had just stopped by with the school-work she'd missed. As she turned to them again to get the homework, Dad stepped in front of her and yelled, "I said she was grounded!" and slammed the door in their faces.

Tiffany looked out the window and saw Michelle telling Carla, "Let's go," as she calmly walked away.

On the edge of tears, Carla stood there saying, "Oh my God."

Michelle clearly understood what was going on, but Carla was one of the white kids in our neighborhood who knew nothing about belts or being dragged from room to room, kept home from school, or locked up. All she saw was our six-foot Black dad yelling at them with a menacing look in his eyes.

As kind as our dad could often be, when he was salty about something, he didn't put on the Huxtable act for anybody. He worried a lot less about what people thought than Mom did, and he came across as a formidable threat if he were triggered. Anyone who witnessed his outbursts on the phone or in public situations was always shocked.

He knew he had scared Tiffany's friends, but he didn't care. "Dad, I needed my homework," Tiffany said.

"Fuck your homework!" was his reply.

Lee Roy Hawkins Sr. was far away from the man who once playfully rubbed his prickly whiskers across the baby-skinned face of his precious youngest daughter "Tiptoe." He heard Mom call her "a whore," and that was that. That sweet baby version of Tiffany was dead to him.

Because Tiffany was more courageous than I was, she rebelled against the antisocial protectiveness our parents exhibited in response to the constant ringing of the phone and party invitations from friends who didn't know about our family situation. Sometimes, when she was alone at home, she would invite friends over, and they'd order pizza. Of course they weren't whoring; they were teenagers eating pepperoni pizza and watching *Video Soul* on the Black Entertainment Television network.

For years, she got away with it, and our parents never found out. But one time, when Tiffany was well into high school, my parents came home unexpectedly. Her friends escaped out the back door, leaving snow tracks behind.

Mom screamed, "You're such an embarrassment, and we don't know what to do with you anymore, Tiffany!"

This "embarrassment" was a high-achieving girl who, in addition to being a Homecoming princess, was an all-conference athlete and, similar to me, a student leader who would eventually be elected class president three straight years of high school. But anyone observing the way our parents treated Tiffany and her closest Black friends during those years would have thought they were video vixens for 2 Live Crew.

That night—no surprise—Mom beat more welts all over her body. But Tiffany wasn't defeated for long. Since asking permission was futile, she started sneaking out on her own and dealing with the consequences later. "I was getting in trouble even when I wasn't doing anything," Tiffany said. "So I figured I might as well go out. It was just normal stuff like going to the movies with friends or to a school dance."

So she went, only to be beaten and grounded once she got home.

As Tiffany grew closer to becoming a young woman, the more aggressive the whippings became. With every beatdown, the fatigue and the fear of anticipated beatdowns heightened and expanded within Tiffany's body and mind. She was often afraid to go home for fear of an attack. She and her friend Michelle, whose beatings from her Jim Crow–reared parents were allegedly worse than Dad's, started running away together to avoid whippings, usually to the houses of friends. But eventually, their parents caught up to them.

Once, when the pair of them ran away to a friend's house, the friend's mother called the police and turned them in. The police took the girls to the station, but surprisingly, didn't put them through the humiliation of arresting them, as Mom always warned.

As the girls waited for a parent to pick them up, Michelle grew more despondent and told Tiffany she didn't want to live any longer. "She found a paperclip, and she tried to stick it in the electrical socket to electrocute herself, because she was so afraid to go home," Tiffany recalled. "She was like, 'My dad is going to literally kill me.'"

Tiffany pulled her away from the socket, and they made a survival pact: once a parent showed up, they would ride in the car together. The first time the car stopped, they would jump out at the same time and run.

With the clock approaching 1:00 a.m., the girls' moms showed up in Michelle's family's minivan. "Oh Lord, these kids are going to kill us," Mom told Michelle's mother, likely gearing up for another episode of "chest pains" and a trip to the ER.

As they drove away, Tiffany gripped the side of the door, waiting for her chance to flee. But there were no stops or red lights for the entire trip home. So Michelle slid open the minivan door and jumped out, followed by Tiffany.

Both talented track athletes, Tiffany and Michelle disappeared into the Maplewood night within seconds, leaving my mother screaming promises of a beating for the ages. But Tiffany was long gone, forcing Michelle's mom to jump in her car and drive from block to block. But there was no sign of my sixteen-year-old runaway baby sister. Michelle had dashed for an apartment building across the street, but Tiffany ran up a dark street lined by woods. "I think they eventually found Michelle underneath a car," Tiffany said, "but I just walked around Maplewood all night."

As she walked under the shimmering moon, she weighed the risks of encountering grown men lurking around our white suburban neighborhood against the hell awaiting her at home. Desperation led her to believe that whatever a stranger might do to her would probably be preferable to the torment she'd face from Mom and Dad. She wandered until dawn and then went to a friend's house. Concerned, her friend's mother called Mom.

When she arrived, she was seething with fury. The façade of the Hawkins household was now exposed. The illusion of perfection was shattered.

"You've got these people talking about us," Mom screamed in the car. "When you get home, you're getting your ass beat."

They got to our driveway, and Tiffany got out of the car but started walking down the street. Just as Mom began screaming again, Tiffany saw a bus heading toward St. Paul coming toward her in the distance. She ran and jumped on it.

"I got on and said, 'I don't have any money, but my parents are going to beat me, and I'm scared,'" she recalled. "Someone on the bus yelled out, 'I'll pay for her.'" The bus driver agreed, and off they went.

She took the bus all the way to the Mall of America in Bloomington, and from there, she called a friend who lived in South Minneapolis—a "gay dude" who had told her she could stay with him whenever she ran away from home. Her friend's family were Indigenous people, and his mother welcomed Tiffany when she was essentially homeless. "I told her what would happen if I went home. She said, 'You can stay here as long as you like.'"

Eventually, our parents found out where Tiffany was. They called her friend's mother and threatened to press charges for harboring a minor.

"I'm sorry, you have to leave," she told Tiffany, "but you should tell the police what's going on."

Knowing that she could never do that, Tiffany thanked her and left.

But this time, Mom and Dad didn't beat her. "They didn't do anything to me," Tiffany said, still seeming astonished years later. "Maybe they were afraid I was going to report them because I wasn't staying quiet anymore. I'd figured out that this stuff was fucked up."

During my first semester in college, Tiffany ran away several more times, fleeing in fear from the certainty of a beating. In the midst of Mom yelling at Tiffany about her fear that people at Mount Olivet might know about Tiffany's "delinquency," Mom suddenly declared chest pains and clutched her heart.

"Call 911! I'm having a heart attack!"

Tiffany called the ambulance and as they waited for it to arrive, Dad turned to her with his classic declaration: "If anything happens to my wife I'll kill you!"

In the hospital waiting room, Tiffany paced while Dad disappeared into the medical area with Mom. Fearing that our dad would attack the second the doctors cleared Mom, Tiffany called another friend that she'd run away with before, and they left.

Even today, Tiffany and I will occasionally see visual reminders of the "spanking" of our childhoods and be triggered. For me, these are Breyers ice cream, weathered belts, kids in wheelchairs or halo casts, anyone wearing steel-toed boots, or an especially happy white kid walking through an airport while peppering his delighted parents with questions. For Tiffany, it is city buses, pagers, or high-heeled shoes. She gets triggered more than I do by Breyers, but sometimes also when she sees track athletes racing across her television screen.

Our shared past is marred by more than just violence; it is also overshadowed by our mother's mysteriously uneasy relationship with our successes. I was perceived as the "spoiled, arrogant" Black son for whom "everything seems to be working out for now," but who "might not find success as an adult." During Tiffany's proudest moments, our mom often questioned, "Why do you always have to be the center of attention?" This prompted us to wonder about the origins of these condemnations of recognition and success. Growing up, our mom demanded perfection, but as we entered high school and began to achieve it, she turned colder and began to resent us. It was confusing. Was my mother's strictness merely a strategy to highlight our shortcomings by setting seemingly unattainable standards? That way, if we ever fell short, she could jab us with putdowns. If she truly wanted us to achieve perfection and success, why would she become angry and start downplaying our accomplishments? In contrast, our dad encouraged us to overcome our shortcomings without humiliation. When we excelled, he was overjoyed and celebrated our successes with us.

Tiffany's hard work and talent led her to qualify for the state track tournament with ease. Yet she dreaded our parents attending her meets. Our mother, with her knack for deliberately timed drama and criticisms—"She always had something negative to say just before I had to compete"—disrupted Tiffany's focus precisely when she needed it most. In the ninth grade, even after Tiffany earned her first athletic letter and was recognized as all-conference in track, Mom's support was lukewarm at best, saying things like, "It's just a track meet. It's not like you're going to do anything with that."

Like me, Tiffany learned early on not to share her dreams and aspirations with our mother, anticipating discouragement or even sabotage. "There was nothing I wanted to do that was ever a good idea," she said. "There was always some negative side to it. That's why I learned to never say anything or ask her opinion because I knew there was always going to be that negative comment."

But, Tiffany said, "Dad was always almost over the top excited about it. He wanted me to do well." However, when provoked by our mother, he'd explode into those violent outbursts.

By the time Tiffany turned eighteen, her spirits were buoyed by the knowledge that she'd be leaving for college soon. As she blossomed into a radiant, nearly six-foot-tall young woman who captivated nearly everyone she met, our parents grew even meaner and more violent.

When my parents couldn't grasp the absurdity of continuing to "spank" a fully grown, eighteen-year-old woman, my badass sister served them with a dose of their own behavior. One afternoon, just a few months before Tiffany was set to head off to college, Michelle was en route to pick her up for a Juneteenth celebration. Out of the blue, likely due to anxieties about her soon-to-be empty nest, our mother told Tiffany she couldn't go. When Michelle arrived, Mom explained to her that Tiffany couldn't join because she hadn't finished her graduation thank-you notes.

"Why didn't you tell me before?" Tiffany said. "I have plans. I'm ready to go out the door!"

"I don't have to tell you shit," she recalled Mom saying. "You're not running my life." Then she called Dad, who was there in a flash.

"Do what your momma says," he ordered.

"I'm eighteen, and I'll do them when I get home," Tiffany told him.

Then Mom cocked her arm back, wielding an open hand she'd raised so many times before. "She slapped me," Tiffany said. "And then, without hesitation, I pulled my hand back and slapped the shit out of her. It was almost automatic; it's like all that pent-up hostility just came out and I couldn't stop myself. At that point, I was just so full of rage and exhaustion. I thought, 'I'm eighteen years old and they're still *doing* this?'"

It was the first and only time a child of my parents had ever hit one of them back.

My mom screamed at her as if she swore Tiffany was possessed, and Dad transformed into a bull, determined to protect and save our mother. He hurled himself at Tiffany, restraining her in a full nelson, thrusting both hands under Tiffany's arms from behind and then pressing against the back of her neck.

"Do what your momma says! Do what your momma says!" he screamed, in a mixture of fury and abject terror at the courageous rite of passage he had just witnessed from his youngest child.

Eventually, our physically exhausted Dad let her go, yet both of our parents were confounded by their underestimation of their daughter's courage. After the commotion, she completed the thank-you cards and, an hour later, left the house to celebrate with her friends, having established a newfound understanding with our parents. The violence would cease. Soon, Tiffany would flee from Maplewood and start her new life, too.

"And was that the last time mom hit you?" I asked.

"Yep," Tiffany replied, triumph in her voice. "Mom was pretty shaken up. I think they both realized I wasn't fucking around anymore."

29

"Don't Take My Shoes Off!"

Dad was always hypersensitive about topics related to his mother and Alabama, and Tiffany and I were aware of it, but the congregation at Mount Olivet was unsuspecting. This became all too clear after I'd left for college when Rev. Battle mentioned Alabama during a powerful sermon.

As the Holy Spirit moved through the sanctuary, Rev. Battle called out, "See what the Lord has done? He'll make a way out of no way! I need Lee Roy Hawkins to come up here and sing that song!"

Dad, draped in his long robe, leaped from his seat in the choir stand, ready to grace the church with his melodic first tenor rendition of "See What the Lord Has Done" by Luther Barnes and the Red Budd Gospel Choir. As Mom swayed in the soprano section and the choir jubilantly hummed, the congregation, watching Dad's walk to the microphone, erupted in anticipation.

"Alright Lee Roy, sing now! Sing that song!"

"Sing, Brother Hawkins!"

As the song's intro played, Rev. Battle kept preaching, hyping the congregation for Dad. "The Lord has brought us a mighty long way," he exclaimed, met with resounding "amens" from the congregation. "I recall the South, in Alabama, when we didn't have shoes to wear or enough food to eat! But somehow, the Lord always provided! Lee Roy, being from Alabama, I know you can relate! Tell them what the Lord has done!"

But instead of singing, Dad snatched the microphone and directed a piercing glare at Rev. Battle. His face, overtaken by a resentful scowl, left the congregation in confusion.

"Now, Rev. Battle, don't take my shoes off! I don't know anything about what you're talking about," he lectured. "I'm from a proud family, and we never went hungry. I always had shoes! You don't know me like that, Reverend! Don't lie on my family!"

After church, Aunt Corene, then in her sixties, stormed up to Dad outside the sanctuary. "Lee Roy, now you know you didn't need to do that man like that! He wasn't talking down on our family. What in the world?"

Our pride-filled Dad held his head up. "I don't know what it was. I just didn't like that because he doesn't know anything about our family, and I had to get him straight!"

To this day, it reminds me of when my father cursed my mother out for accepting my cousin's clothes. Something from way back in Alabama had triggered him.

After church, Rev. Battle drove all the way out to Maplewood to apologize, which Dad accepted.

That comment had excited a sleeping giant of inexplicable trauma within our father's heart, and Tiffany made sure to stay clear of him for the rest of the night. In seeking understanding of our past with my sister, our healing began. I cannot imagine having completed this book and all the research it entailed without Tiffany by my side, encouraging me.

We often pondered why we never abandoned our parents. Part of the reason was the trauma bond, intertwined with guilt, and a deep love and sorrow for our parents. Further solidifying this was the long-standing Black cultural belief that elders can do no wrong. We were conditioned to see it as disrespectful to even question them or the origins of their mysterious belief system, one that compelled them to use whipping to restrict and regulate our freedom and audacity. Why did they view our critical thinking, curiosity, independence—and our longing to be free from childhood violence—as a threat not only to us, but to our entire lineage?

Despite our discussing that violence, Tiffany and I still feel unwavering love for our parents. Yet, we've come to understand that love does not require us to bear the shame of what we now recognize as abuse, to perpetuate the unresolved trauma they passed on to us, or to keep quiet about it. My journey toward understanding began by desiring to confront lingering questions. I believe the best way to honor my parents, despite our shared traumas, is through curiosity rather than judgment. I sought to know the source of their anger and violence. What historical events shaped our family's patterns and influenced societal views on Black identity during my upbringing? Is it possible for a family to be ensnared in a cycle of shared trauma and paralyzing fear, all the while blind to its roots? How did our family come to adopt this mysterious, fear-based racial belief system characterized by hypercautiousness and stringent rules?

This system fueled our parents' urge to control our bodies and minds through unrelenting violence, thereby compromising our inalienable rights to life, liberty, and the pursuit of happiness—rights to which every American is supposed to be entitled.

During my early years at the University of Wisconsin, the memories of Mount Vernon's slave cemetery still burned. I felt so free that I didn't reflect much on the hyperregulation of my childhood or heap blame on my parents. I was simply curious, ready to dig into the whole mess, to try to make sense of it. The more I explored, the clearer it became that the pain my parents inflicted on me was intricately linked to the pain our nation, the United States of America, had inflicted upon them.

PART 3

Grandma Charity and Her Children

30

The Journey Home

During my sophomore year, I began writing op-eds for the college paper, a road that eventually helped me become the first Black editorial page editor of the University of Wisconsin's *Badger Herald*. As my interest in journalism grew, my father's curiosity about his past also grew. He rarely spoke of Alabama but often reminisced about Uncle Ike Pugh, his mother's eldest brother still living there. Dad's move to Minnesota in 1961 prevented him from getting to know Uncle Ike. However, in his forties, he began expressing a desire to reconnect. It was clear to me that Uncle Ike held a special place in Dad's heart.

"He has a big farm down there, and the whole family visits," he told me. "He's getting up there in age. Over a hundred, they say. I need to get down there and get some family history from him."

"I'd like to know that history, too," I said. "I've never asked too many questions, because it seems like you don't want to touch on the topic."

"Well, there's a lot there, son. A lot of pain associated with losing my mama," he said. "But I wasn't told a lot. See, I was the baby, and they sheltered me. Back then the old folks kept secrets, and you had to piece together whatever you could. You know what I mean?"

"Do I ever!"

"I know, son, and I hate that things were that way. I wish you kids could have been as close to my side of the family as you were to your mother's. I have cousins down South I used to play with. I don't even know what happened to some of them."

"Why don't you call them?"

"I should, but there's a lot of stuff I left back there, stuff that was hard to take, but that I also miss. The Black community there was special. We didn't have to line up at the barbershop to get a haircut. There were Black people and businesses everywhere. We didn't have to deal with white racist teachers because our teachers were Black. And they were hard on us, but man we knew they loved us.

"You know, when Tammi graduates from college next year, I'm not getting on no plane to North Carolina," he chuckled. "So we're gonna drive, and then go to Alabama and see my brother Mook and Uncle Ike and my cousins. We can bring a tape recorder and interview my uncle."

It was 1991; Dad was forty-three and I was nineteen. I was ecstatic that he wanted to return to his roots.

Then came a caveat: "But man, we'll have to watch our asses. The white folks down there aren't 'Minnesota nice.' If they're racist, they let you know. And you don't want to get a flat tire on the side of the road, because you never know what'll happen down there—especially if you run into state troopers."

I imagined waiting for roadside service along the unlit interstate, just steps from acres of woods packed with poplar trees that once had bodies of Black people swinging from their boughs.

I thought of the myriad images fueling that expectation: the black-and-white media footage of attacking German shepherds, fire hoses, the beautiful faces of the four little girls who were bombed in Birmingham's 16th Street Baptist Church, and the mangled face of Emmett Till, killed in nearby Mississippi. To me, these and other hidden family tragedies were emblematic of the birth of the angered, scared young boy who lashed out at his own children for upsetting our mother or transgressing the boundaries set by white society. There-fore, I expected Alabama to be angrier and even more ferocious than Dad on his worst days.

I was eager to meet Uncle Ike. All I knew was that he and Grandma Opie, my dad's mom, had grown close after their father had died in a tragic hunting accident when they were young. Dad never got the chance to ask her about their father before she passed away when he was twelve years old. Given his own experiences as a motherless child, he un-derstood her grief. And out of respect, Dad would've avoided asking his grandma Ella about the accident that killed her husband and its impact on the family. I often pondered whether that traumatic event was the source of the bad dreams my dad had and his screams I sometimes heard from my parents' room at night. The question always burned inside me: "Dad, what were you dreaming and screaming about last night?" But except for a few times, I never dared ask it. Breaking the rule of never asking questions was a sure way to get popped. But when I did muster the courage to ask, all he said was, "Alabama, son. Alabama," and that was it. I was too afraid to push him to elaborate.

After attending Tammi's spirited commencement, meeting her enchanting Alpha Kappa Alpha sorority sisters, and seeing her march in a soulful final band performance, we loaded up the car for Alabama. Upon arrival, my father's eldest brother, Lum "Mook" Hawkins Jr., guided us. He had arranged for us to visit with and interview Uncle Ike, and that hour-long interview remains the most significant one I've ever conducted about my family's history.

We visited Uncle Mook's home on Oglesby Street, in Greenville, Alabama, meeting his wife, Mary, and their kids—my first cousins. After Aunt Mary fed me some delicious down-home beans, pork, and collard greens, we headed to Uncle Ike's house.

On the way there, I thought about all the times my aunties in Minnesota talked about Uncle Ike: "He's gotta be almost 106 years old," they'd say, and "You can see the Indian in him." We'd often been told at family gatherings that we had "Indian blood"; on this special day, maybe we'd be able to find out if that were true.

Uncle Ike lived on his farm in Bolling, a small town twelve miles south of Greenville, off US Highway 31, near the center of Butler County. As we made our way up the driveway of the sprawling property surrounding the rustic cottage, we marveled at the fact that the roads all around his property were named after him. Ike Pugh Road is still there today.

As we walked up the steps of Uncle Ike's cottage, I asked Uncle Mook in a whisper, "How old is he?"

"He's about ninety-two," he said.

So he wasn't 106, as they'd said back in Minnesota, but still, ninety-two was an impressive age. I did wonder why so many Black families never seemed able to give their age with certainty or document their Indigenous heritage. And why did so many Black families claim to have a relative who was 120 years old?

Later, I read a newspaper article that said Uncle Ike had been born August 17, 1894. That would have made him ninety-six at the time of our visit in 1991. But as with most family members from his era, the birth dates for Uncle Ike vary in public records.

We walked from the porch into the living room, where Uncle Ike's daughter, Aunt Tee, greeted us warmly. Then Uncle Ike ambled in, exuding a polite, relaxed demeanor. The resemblance to my father was astonishing. Smooth, clear, copper-toned skin covered a chiseled face featuring high cheekbones that accentuated his almond eyes.

I was struck by his dashing good looks, a laid-back, high-pitched voice, and a country boy's grace. He was wearing work pants and a white T-shirt a shade darker than his nearly full head of white hair. Uncle Ike, whose rumored Indigenous physical features were apparent, could easily have passed for a seventy-five-year-old.

"How you doin', baby?" he asked my father. Baby, huh? I guess Dad qualified: not only was Dad fifty-four years younger than Uncle Ike, but he was the baby of the family—the youngest child of Grandma Opie, Uncle Ike's younger sister.

As he started to talk, I turned on the recorder.

I struggled to comprehend Uncle Ike's Southern drawl, thick as molasses. Dad told me that the dialect and speech pattern were distinct to this remote corner of Alabama's Butler County. A few missing teeth also sabotaged his speech. But with intense concentration and continued listening, I began to understand his stories about relatives I'd never heard about before.

As he spoke, I looked around the room and my gaze returned to a framed yellowing photograph of a mustachioed white man surrounded by four beagles in a wooded area. Draped around the back of the man's neck was a dead raccoon. The picture had caught my eye the instant we entered the living room. Why was this white man's picture hanging so prominently in Uncle Ike's home?

"Who's that, up in that picture?" Dad asked.

"That's Isaac Pugh," Uncle Ike replied.

"That's your father?"

"Yeah, they call us both Ike, but our real name is Isaac."

This was the father who had supposedly been killed in a hunting accident, so we were shocked when Uncle Ike said, "It was a white man that killed him," he said. "Jack Taylor. We practiced about six months to kill him. I done my best. I didn't mind them killing me. But I wanted to kill the man that killed him."

Dad's eyes met mine, both of us registering utter surprise. Not only was there no "hunting accident," but Grandpa Ike looked white.

"So that's my great-grandpa, my dad's mother's father?" I mumbled. How in the hell, I thought, could this white man be related to us? In the nineteen years I'd been alive, I'd never allowed for the possibility that I was anything other than a 100 percent African-blooded, Black American man. We were from somewhere in West Africa, and that was that, except for the Indigenous ancestors I'd expected Uncle Ike to mention. But now we had learned that his and Grandma Opie's father, Ike Pugh Sr., was a fair-skinned Black man who could have passed for white. But like every biracial person who decided not to try to "pass," he was just another spade to the state of Alabama.

Uncle Ike recounted a story about Grandma Charity, his paternal grandmother. In our family, she was famed for her fiery character. One evening, four white men came to their home, intent on publicly whipping Grandma Charity for some alleged wrongdoing. Confronting them, she brandished a knife. Two men were immobilized with fear, but she bravely bit into one man's ear. All four retreated into the night.

Through Uncle Ike's narratives about defending his father—"I wanted to kill the man that killed him"—and Grandma Charity's courage, I discovered that not all my ancestors and other Black Southerners passively retreated back to the cotton fields after emancipation. Some fought back. Still, I struggled to comprehend why white men believed they had the right to arbitrarily show up to Black people's homes and whip them.

Uncle Ike described Grandma Charity as resembling an "Indian" woman, with striking jet-black hair so long she could sit on it. I imagined a radiant Indigenous woman with a fierce beauty and spirit. She was known as a tenacious fighter who hated white people and wouldn't hesitate to confront anyone who tried to trouble or intimidate her.

Uncle Ike was awed by the fury she unleashed on those four white men. But I detected a whiff of bitterness. He shared how "mean ol' Grandma Charity" would berate and whip him and his siblings if she deemed them to be sluggish on the farm. She'd use twigs, branches, or belts—anything at hand—to sting them into higher productivity.

Up in Minnesota, stories of Grandma Charity were unheard of, as were tales of most Southern relatives. Uncle Ike's conversation that day centered mostly on relating his father's devastating murder in 1914 when Uncle Ike was just twenty years old. He talked with regret about not successfully avenging his father's death by killing the white murderer.

After an hour, Uncle Ike got tired and went down for a nap. We walked out of his house enthralled yet befuddled by all he had shared. On the return drive to Minnesota, we could talk of almost nothing else but the discovery that my dad's mysteriously murdered grandfather looked white. How did that happen?

And how, we wondered, had a man who appeared white have a Black wife and more than twenty children? We theorized that, despite the perilous risks, he chose to marry my great-grandma Ella less than two decades after emancipation. Though he looked like he could have passed for white and enjoyed its privileges, why didn't he? And what did that mean for his life and the life of his family members? Was he ostracized in his small Alabama town?

Uncle Ike passed in 1996, before we were able to follow up and ask. I'm grateful for what we got, though I wish I could redo that interview, knowing what I know now.

My father held fond memories of his grandma Ella. Discovering the truth about how her husband died complicated his understanding, given the misleading "hunting accident" story he had always known. He couldn't remember Grandma Ella ever discussing her deceased husband or his mother-in-law, the fearsome Grandma Charity. How did Grandma Charity cope with her son's horrific death?

What remained clear was that Uncle Ike's father had been murdered by a white man, and the family had been run out of town by a white mob. They abandoned their property and never recouped their losses. I could only imagine that despite being in his nineties when I met him, Uncle Ike was still living inside a seventy-seven-year-old tragedy and maybe grieved his father's murder all the way to his own grave.

At age nineteen, I felt overwhelmed by Uncle Ike's disclosures. But I'm eternally grateful to Dad for brilliantly suggesting we record the words of our treasured uncle. Those recordings remain among my most cherished possessions.

"You're Disrespecting Us"

Over the decade that followed, my interview with Uncle Ike would slip from memory as my budding career in journalism blossomed and I became caught up in the hectic pace of my life and career. After two years of working for the *Badger Herald* at the University of Wisconsin, I rotated through newsrooms in Wisconsin and then to the *Wall Street Journal* newsrooms in Detroit. Since I'd been reading *WSJ* since I'd picked it up from Grandpa Buddy's chair when I was twelve, I was thrilled to be working for that paper in my early thirties.

When I called Dad to tell him, he yelled, "Well, all right, boy, that's the major leagues!" I thanked him for always believing in me, and mentoring me, and he told me how proud and happy he was to have been a part of it.

As our mutual joy reverberated through the phone wires, Dad yelled upstairs to tell Mom to pick up the phone. She got on the line and gave me a cheery hello. Still buzzing with adrenaline, Dad told her the news. She went silent, but Dad stayed on the phone and started talking about how he couldn't wait to see my first byline.

"That's the New York Yankees of newspapers," he said. "You made the pros."

I don't know what inspired Mom to break her silence. "All newspapers are written at a ninth-grade level," she chimed in.

"Huh?" I said, with my equally perplexed dad listening.

"I'm just saying, it's not that big of a deal, because newspapers write down to a lower level, so that even a child can read it."

We just weirdly sat there.

"But it's something I worked toward, so at this stage of my career, it's a dream job, and one of the most important beats at the paper," I said.

Then, she exploded, screaming into the phone: "The *Wall Street Journal* is nothing! Getting married and having kids is everything!"

I was stunned, but she kept going. "Everything's about you, Lee! You're so selfish! You keep moving to these new jobs and different cities! You're forgetting your roots! Don't forget where you came from and the people who raised you, all the people you keep leaving behind! Nanny keeps asking when you're getting married! You've always been such an embarrassment to this family! Are you ever going to settle down and get married and have kids? You're thirty-two. Are you too selfish to think about anyone other than yourself?"

"Marriage isn't even on my radar," I said. "I'm free to focus on what I want to do, and that's my career for now."

"Don't you worry that people are going to think you're gay?" she asked. She knew for a fact that I was not gay and that if I were, I wouldn't be ashamed to scream it from the rooftops. But she clearly wanted her words to offend me. In fact, I think she was more worried that people would *think* I was gay.

My poison levels skyrocketed. All I was doing was taking a job—one that was good for me at that stage of my life. I was pleased with the progress of my career and happy to achieve this first goal.

Mom's ability to physically hit me was now curbed by distance and my age. Hitting Tiffany and me had been her "sugar high," and that easy source of stress relief was gone. So her attacks now took the form of petty coded comments, such as this one, and even viciously cruel criticism. She even found fault with some of the gifts I bought her. Once, she told me out of the blue, "Don't buy us books." The comment was so random, I couldn't resist asking her why. She replied that I needed to realize that a gift I might enjoy wasn't necessarily one she would. In truth, I probably did buy books for her that were total misfires because I didn't know her well enough to recognize that she wasn't a reader. Regardless, she always taught us to be gracious recipients, and to say, "Thank you." Clearly, she was unable to practice what she preached.

Every time I returned home for a family visit, I always left feeling terrible, the way I often had as a kid. And the more independence, success, and happiness Tiffany and I found in our lives, the more spiteful it seemed Mom became.

At age thirty-two, I was a single Black male journalist in Detroit. My life, when I wasn't visiting Minnesota, was free because it was mine. That year, I was named one of *Ebony* magazine's "Most Eligible Bachelors." As part of the deal, *Ebony* paid for a fancy night out with a selected date, including a limousine and five-course meal at one of the top Black-owned fine-dining restaurants in Detroit. I was honored and a bit amused to be chosen.

My date that night was a strikingly gorgeous woman, who, like me, was a singer/songwriter. She was tall and voluptuous, with chocolate-brown skin and natural hair pulled up in a bun. I was thrilled to go out with her. But when the photos of the date were published in *Jet* magazine, the responses befuddled me. One friend, a young Black woman in her twenties told me that my date looked like a "Black Choco-Zulu."

The date went well, but she started out by telling me, "You don't look like your picture," which made me think she didn't find me as attractive as she had hoped. Despite that, I had a fun time and was pleased she'd agreed to be my date.

"Choco-Zulu?" I said. "That sounds great. What's wrong with Black Choco-Zulu? Black is beautiful, right?"

On a trip back to Minnesota, the criticism continued, surprisingly from more Black women. In the car with my mom and Tammi, my mom told me that a few women at her hair salon had said that my date "needed to do something with that hair" and also that she was "lucky" to go out with me. The tone of shade made it clear that these women found my date unattractive and were taking a jab at her.

I lost it. "What's the problem?!—because she's chocolate-skinned and not burning up and traumatizing her hair with lye and cancer-causing chemicals, to try to look like a white woman?"

The car went silent. Tongues were held, but when I was younger, that comment would have gotten my mouth "slapped off." I also realize now that Mom never said a word about colorism—so my response wasn't entirely fair—but something about the salon conversation felt off. The criticism of my all-natural, dreamy date took me back to the "nappy-headed" and "Buckwheat" references of my childhood, and the sad fact that too many Black people had bought in to a self-loathing perception of Blackness.

The writer bell hooks brilliantly nails the problem in *Black Looks: Race and Representation*, writing that "black people/people of color . . . are daily bombarded by a powerful colonizing whiteness that seduces us away from ourselves, that negates that there is beauty to be found in any form of blackness that is not imitation whiteness." It's not a surprise that this poison seeped into my own surroundings, but I yearned to comprehend precisely how it managed to infiltrate our lives.

A few months after I heard the comments about my *Ebony* date, I returned to Minnesota after some extensive international travel. Dad asked me about my trip to Korea, and I told him about the amazing feeling I had after walking up Mount Daedun, just outside Seoul, looking across the beautiful pasture to the faint outline of hills on the other side.

"Who would have ever thought this Black boy from Minnesota would be standing on a mountain in Korea?" I mused.

Mom's silence was so profound that even my father noticed. "What's wrong, Mom?" I asked.

"Lee, how are we supposed to feel about the fact that things are going so well for you, when things are going so bad for us?" she said.

Again, Dad looked at her, shocked. "What's so bad for us?" he asked.

"You don't understand, Lee," she said, ignoring Dad and glaring at me. "You're selfishly not married and don't have kids. You're free as a bird—while we're still here."

"That was your choice," I snapped back. "My going on a trip does nothing to harm you. What's wrong with me being free?" On the plane back to Detroit, the same old poisons kicked in again. It had gotten to the point that if I was unable to fly thousands of miles for a church function or someone's birthday, she'd hit me with, "You've forgotten where you came from," as if I had forfeited my "Blackness" because I'd moved away and realized other goals besides fatherhood and/or marriage in my teens or twenties or bringing more children into our family

186 | Lee Hawkins

for my parents to beat. Over the previous ten years, I'd spent tens of thousands of dollars on my limited budget for flights to Minnesota, showing up for every Thanksgiving and Christmas, birthday party, and basically every family "special occasion." Why was I continuing to fly back to Minnesota for constant humiliation?

Mom even attributed Dad's declining fitness habits to my departure, telling me that he stopped going to the gym when I left for college.

As a kid, I had stopped valuing my mother's approval and often provincial, parochial opinions, especially after disproving her grim "jail or dead" predictions of my future. Had I not figured out as a child that her advice was often neither strategic nor grounded in reality (hence, "the *Wall Street Journal* is nothing!"), I might have been severely wounded. But her criticism did leave me puzzled, especially the "free as a bird" stuff.

I tried to shrug it off and return to Detroit and focus. But what my brain tried to rationalize, my body and spirit rejected. Neither the distance established by passing time nor the steady personal and professional progress I was making could eradicate, or even ease, my darkest childhood memories. In my visits back to Minnesota, which I'd grown to dread, I'd started avoiding well-meaning, supportive people—even my beloved Nanny—because I'd been told they were disappointed in me for joining the *WSJ* instead of moving back to Minnesota and getting quickly married. I grew resentful.

On the outside, I was on top of the world; inside, I was a wreck. I found it increasingly difficult to focus on my job and maintain my positive mindset. Reading became a chore, and I needed to carefully reread, several times, every article I wrote on deadline. That helped me avoid errors, but I was jumpy and short-tempered, constantly locked in fight-or-flight mode. In public, I was hypervigilant, on guard against every conceivable threat from those around me. At night I had trouble falling and staying asleep.

One particularly miserable night, finding myself awake at 2:00 a.m., stewing in resentment at these toxic, recurring childhood memories, I grabbed the phone and dialed my parents. "Put Dad on the phone!" I shouted when my mother answered.

"What's wrong?" she asked, terrified.

"Just put Dad on the phone!"

"Hey, Dad," I began as soon as I heard his voice, "do you remember the time when I was eight or nine years old, and I showed you that video game in the kitchen, and you slammed me to the floor and said, 'Do it on the field'?"

Silence.

"Do you?"

More silence.

"If you wanted to teach me a lesson, why did you have to body slam me like that?"

"I don't know, man," he finally replied. "I did a lot of crazy things."

"Yes, you did, motherfucker! Nigga, you *know* what you did!"

For weeks, my mind and nightmares had been stuck in a constant replay of that Sunday afternoon attack related to that handheld game. For him, his belief that his Black eight-year-old son needed to quit playing childish games and start scoring touchdowns in the game of life was no doubt a perfectly adequate reason to slam him violently to the floor.

But for some reason, I couldn't get past it. Maybe that was because, as I lay sprawled on the kitchen floor with my whole body throbbing, I realized for the first time that my father was a damaged man. My once-absolute trust in him had shattered.

After that phone call, I continued to have daily flashbacks and as many as three nightmares a week. I felt foggy and preoccupied with middle-of-the-day angry thoughts about my childhood. Sometimes I felt so light-headed when I stood up that I thought I might faint. And even though I lived in downtown Detroit, which was relatively safe, I stayed on high alert, afraid I might be jumped or car-jacked. I was always primed for the worst-case scenario. As much as I tried, I couldn't stop thinking about it and I couldn't talk about any of it with my friends or my girlfriend at the time because all that violence—especially Dad's assault on my neck—was a closely guarded family secret of which I was deeply ashamed.

The night I woke up yelling from a nightmare and called my

parents was a turning point. As I argued with my father, I passed through the next barricade.

Mom picked up the phone and yelled, "Why are you calling us? We didn't abuse you! You're disrespecting us!"

"Yes, you *did* abuse me, and you *do* abuse me! I haven't disrespected you! Moving away and supporting myself is not disrespecting you! All I'm doing is living my life! You need to acknowledge that beating me was wrong and tell me why you did it!"

"What do you want us to do, kiss your ass?" she asked.

"You think I'm asking you to kiss my ass because I'm telling you that what you did was wrong and I'm asking you to acknowledge that? You think I'm going to have a relationship with you while you continue to expect me to serve your interests and abuse me if I don't do everything you command? Why should I sit here and maintain a relationship with you when you despise and criticize my independence and everything positive that I do?"

My mother got quieter on the phone and then let out a shriek I had never heard before with an even more shocking message: "YOU'RE JUST LIKE MY FATHER! YOU'RE JUST LIKE MY FATHER!"

"But I'm *not* your father! I'm your son! I'm not Grandpa Buddy! You need help, Mom! You need to talk to a therapist about your childhood!"

Then Mom's paranoia kicked in. "Are you yelling like that in your apartment?" she asked. "Don't you know that your neighbors can hear you?"

Then Dad came back on the phone with a familiar message. "I won't have you disrespecting my wife like that!"

"What? Or you'll kill me, right? Lower your voice, man! Motherfucker don't talk to me like that! I'm not a kid, man!"

Amazingly, instead of exploding more, he calmed down. "I want Mom to go to counseling," I said. "She needs to work out her issues about her father and her stepfather before she meets with me. Because I'm not her father. And then the three of us need to go to counseling. Me, you, and Mom."

There was silence, so I continued, breathlessly. "I can't take this anymore, man. This isn't the way it's supposed to be. And if you don't admit to abusing me, and continuing to abuse me as an adult, and apologize for that, we're not going to have a relationship."

"I don't give a fuck," Dad said.

After hearing Dad's cocky dismissal to me on that desperate 2:00 a.m. phone call, my inner mythical "real nigga" came to the surface. "Oh, you don't give a fuck? Let me show you a motherfucker who can truly not give a fuck! You think I need you, you bitch-ass nigga? I learned at a young age that I could never depend on you, nigga! Because you were too pussy-whipped to stand up to your triflin' ass bitch! She has you in check, like a trick, nigga! You've run behind bitches your whole life, and you're trying to act all hard with me? Soft-ass, weak-ass, rest-haven for a bitch-ass nigga! Don't apologize and don't get your crazy wife into counseling. See what happens you sucker for love-ass nigga! Fuck you and fuck your bitch!"

I hung up determined to finally be done with both of them to protect my own spiraling mental health.

I felt certain my parents would need me before I needed them. Being abused as a child may trigger nightmares in adulthood, but it can also make you extraordinarily tough and detached. It creates a defense mechanism that enables you to quickly disconnect from people, even those to whom you are closest, or never connect at all. It steals your capacity to trust and resigns you to the fact that you can rely only on yourself and, for me, on God. I was not proud of my capacity to be cold and unyielding, but sadly, that was how my childhood, and my surrounding world, shaped me. My streetwise, hardened heart and survivalist outlook on life ensured that I could walk away from my parents.

My father may have talked a good game, but I knew he did not have my wiring, especially when it came to fending for himself, bouncing back from hardships and the women in his life. I saw how broken up he still was over the early loss of his mother, saw how he craved maternal love and validation, saw all the orders he took from my mom, and saw how terrified and abusive he became at the alarm of her "chest pains." And God bless Dad for being that vulnerable, for his capacity to "run behind his bitch" and be "pussy-whipped" (an odious term that, I regret to say, revealed that my hardness back then contained a sizable dose of "real nigga" philosophy). In the heat of the moment, I couldn't find a more appropriate way to describe all the times Dad threatened our lives because he feared losing our mom, and he beat us and screamed like a scared, motherless child in the middle of the night.

I couldn't relate to Dad, and I was grateful. But I was even more grateful that he couldn't relate to me because I wouldn't have wished my hollowed-out, icy-cold heart and cast-iron mindset on anybody.

I didn't know what the future held, but I knew for certain I wouldn't talk to my parents again unless they agreed to get therapy. They needed it. I needed it. We all needed it. But they refused to go, so our relationship was over.

After that night, I didn't speak to my parents for almost two years.

32

Six-Figure Nigger

As my life kept moving along without my parents in it, I recognized that even if they didn't pursue therapy, I needed to. I wanted to stop the nightmares and talk to someone about how my childhood had turned me into a man who, scarily, didn't "give a fuck."

My first therapy session forced me to realize that Detroit was worlds apart from my Black experience in Minnesota. I was hoping simply to open a conversation—to clear my head and stop the poisons from flowing. But I got something different.

Sitting in the waiting room was a middle-aged Black woman with a graying, uncombed Afro shifted to the side. When I walked in wearing my suit from work, she glanced up and turned quickly back to her conversation with herself.

"Fuck this shit. You motherfuckers can't tell me shit . . . shi-i-i-i-it," she said. Looking at the equally disheveled people sitting around her, I wondered whether I was in the right office. I had specifically chosen a Black male counselor, who I hoped could help me deal with what I would later learn was post-traumatic stress disorder (PTSD). I figured he would understand me and relate to me culturally and possibly help me feel something for the people in my life. I wanted him to help me trust more and to be less defensive. I wanted to be able to seek long-needed counseling without giving in to the inner voice that told me, "Stop acting white. Real Black people don't see therapists, especially men. Don't be a kid. Toughen up and be a man, a Real Black Man. You have a high threshold for pain, remember? Stop being so soft."

After completing the paperwork, I took a seat in the therapist's office. But then nothing went as planned. He asked me to explain the situation and fixated on the fact that I was a reporter for the *Wall Street Journal*. He questioned whether I really was, as if I had come in with delusional thoughts.

"C'mon brother, I thought the *Wall Street Journal* was in New York," he said.

"It is, but I cover General Motors, so I live here."

"Really? And you're coming here? To this office? And you're from *Minnesota*?"

I explained that my repeated nightmares were making it difficult for me to function and that I worried that I was closing off emotionally as the result of child abuse I suffered as a kid.

"Child abuse? Like what?"

"Well, I was often beaten by my parents and a lot of other physical abuse." I was too ashamed to tell him about my dad's foot on my neck.

"Okay?" he said, unimpressed.

"And now, it's turned into a different form of abuse . . . a kind of control. Like, my mother said I'm 'free as a bird,' but in a negative sense, like I'm not a good son because I've decided to follow my dreams. But I visit them all the time and get constantly berated and humiliated for everything from not being married to missing birthday parties. And I'm not speaking to them right now and I've demanded my mother go to counseling. I can't concentrate and I'm having nightmares—flashbacks to various beatings that happened. I'm distracted at work. I want the nightmares to stop."

"So, you're coming to see me because you were beaten? A lot of people got beat, man," he said. "And because your mom said you're free? Look at you. You *are* free. You're successful, man. You're making big money. There's a whole bunch of people that got beat, and some of them are sitting out there in the waiting room, but not a lot of them are living the dream like you, brother."

I sat there stunned, trying to sort out my reactions.

I realized I needed to examine my complicated lifetime relationship with the notion of "freedom."

The Black boy in me, molded by years of abuse, was fatigued from years of being told that I'd "forgotten where I'd come from." I'd grown tired of being told I'd "forgotten my roots." My mother, who once championed excellence, now echoed the criticism of white racists and "real niggas" of my upbringing, who felt my "white" aspirations, like being class president in high school, made me a sellout and "not Black." Her disapproval of my joining the *WSJ* wasn't about its politics since I was on the neutral "news" side. And I'd never seen her read the *WSJ* anyway. Believe me, if she'd been aware of the opinion section's reactionary leanings, she would have weaponized that to buttress her claims of betrayal.

Throughout my life, racists and "real niggas" often portrayed strengths shown by Blacks as weaknesses, and vice versa. But my rejection of this racist belief system helped me realize that the real sellouts were those who maligned fellow Blacks who rise above stereotypical tropes, expectations, and limitations.

I couldn't understand. My own Black mother seemed poisoned by this system, trying to reimpose it on me. Why did my parents fear the world and everything in it? Why did my parents associate freedom with danger? Why did they try to whip the life, liberty, and pursuit of happiness out of me? Why did they often dissuade me from engaging in free speech or confronting racism?

God knows, I wasn't as "free" as this brother had suggested. Even though he trivialized the beatings, the mental scars remained. I desperately needed his counsel, but he failed to recognize it.

On top of the gross misstatement that I was earning "big money," I realized that nobody blinks when white people seek therapy; they are practicing "self-care" and maintaining their mental health. (And since when did "making big money" mean a person couldn't benefit from counseling?) But Black people seeking therapy? They're too privileged, ungrateful, or crazy. In America, therapy is often widely viewed as a luxury reserved for white people—even, evidently, by Black therapists.

There I was, sitting in this Black man's office, hoping that he would have the experience to understand cultural nuances and develop a treatment plan for me. But this therapist, in the Blackest city in America, couldn't figure out why a corporate Black man would want to talk about the long-term effects of abuse and being condemned for achieving goals. He was amazed, amused, and probably a little annoyed. In Black America, there is no therapy plan for six-figure niggers.

33

Nobody's Slave

Two years into our silence, Mom was set to retire with her own party. My parents broached the possibility of going into therapy with me, initiating the process of bringing me back into the family fold, especially so I'd attend that party.

Dad called one day and said that a few of his friends had seen me on CNBC and asked whether I'd recorded it. He told me how much he missed me. "Son, this not-talking-for-years stuff isn't working for me. You're my son, and I love you. So whatever I need to do to become a family again, I'm willing to do."

I was surprised, but not astonished. I knew my father loved me. Even more, I knew my parents were tired of coming up with excuses for why I wasn't around.

Dad and I started talking a few times a week. He told me that during our impasse, he'd gone back and looked over the notes from a graduate class he'd taken taught by John M. Taborn, a Black psychologist who was also an associate professor at the University of Minnesota.

Dad remembered Taborn drawing connections between enslavement and belt whipping. He said that our confrontation had brought all of it back, jump-starting Dad's intellectual process of understanding that, by whipping his children, he had introduced a vestige of enslavement into our home.

I was proud that Dad was beginning to grasp intellectually and spiritually the way the past had influenced our present. Unfortunately, Taborn passed away in 2015, leaving us unable to thank him. But his lesson linking whipping to enslavement and Black stereotypes empowered Dad and me.

"I'm sorry son, I really am. I knew you had hit on something, but I didn't want to talk about it, because I feel so bad that I put you through that," he told me. "Your mama is in denial, but I know all that stuff was crazy. She said she'll go to counseling if it will get you back in the family."

When I finally talked to Mom, I told her I needed her to work out her childhood issues pertaining to Grandpa Buddy—whatever they were—before I'd resume contact with her. She'd need to go to counseling for six months, also with Dad, before we could all go together.

After those six months, I flew to Minnesota for two back-to-back therapy sessions that both Mom and Dad attended.

Once I got to the first session, I discovered that my mother's therapist was a white woman. Mom said that she had chosen her partially out of concern that a Black counselor would more than likely know our family from the Black community in Minnesota, or God forbid, from Jack and Jill. She didn't want to be "embarrassed" or have our family's name ground up in the Black community's rumor mill. (Never mind that a therapist is professionally bound by confidentiality codes.)

I sat in a chair across from my parents and the therapist explained that the two-day session would be designed to help my parents and me—mainly my mother and me—establish a new, healthy relationship.

I told the therapist that my decision to cease communication with my parents was rooted in childhood belt attacks that had led to an adult family dynamic where respect was unidirectionally expected to move only from child to parent. They even seemed to expect me to have loved the whippings, echoing the droves of Black people who cited "a difference between spanking and abuse" and celebrated it. I explained that my parents called body-slamming, whipping, and choking "spanking" and that my parents had normalized violence and cruelty in our home. I then shared Mom's saddening question, "How are we supposed to feel happy that things are going so well for you?"

That comment had forced me to an eerie realization that my mother might have truly hated me. I explained my thought, one I hope was unfounded, that when Mom handed the reins of my upbringing to Dad during my fragile third-grade year, it may have ignited her competitive spirit. Each success I achieved with Dad seemed to be a blow to her, as if our father-son bond came at her expense. To demonstrate her dominance over both of us and disrupt our growing relationship, she seemed to engineer conflicts that would provoke Dad to beat me.

Sitting in the therapist's office, I asked my mother a pressing question: "Why haven't you ever liked me?"

"You were a chauvinist," she told me, looking over at the therapist.

"A *chauvinist*?" I asked, incredulous but oddly relieved to finally have her dislike of me confirmed.

She mentioned a third-grade incident when I hadn't shared my candy with Tammi at our great-grandparents' house. She also brought up that when I was eleven, I refused to wear an apron in front of my friends, telling my home economics teacher that "cooking and sewing are for girls," drawing on the "boys versus girls" rivalries that were inspired by our gym teacher.

Ultimately, her examples of my "chauvinism" were more reminders of a rule that my parents whipped into me back then: Black boys can't err and must submit to adultification. Any minor transgression from childhood or youth will forever be remembered and used against them decades later—for life.

What hurt was that our devout Christian mother, in front of that white therapist, denied ever hitting us with a belt. She said, "We spanked you because that's a Black custom. But we never beat you with anything."

I turned to Dad, and said, "How can you sit here and listen to her lie like this?"

"It was rough," he said. "I know, it was rough."

And that wasn't the only lie. Mom also refused to acknowledge merely standing by while Dad pressed all his weight onto my neck. To this day, she has never uttered a word about that terrible day.

Livid, I got up from my chair and, there on the floor, reenacted the neck attack for the therapist and my parents. It was the first time I had ever mentioned the incident, and I still couldn't bring myself to discuss the surgery or the halo cast. That would have touched a too tender place for any of us to bear.

"I was down here," I said from the floor. "It's one of the lowest points you can ever be in life, to be down here with your father's boot on your neck. And, Mom, I can't respect you because you were standing right there and have never even acknowledged it happened. You lie about it and call beating children a Black custom. But I think it's really a slave master custom. You haven't done a lick of research, yet you brazenly insist that this is what Black people do to their children because we invented it. No, a white slave master invented it and did it to our ancestors, and then you did it to us. You tried to beat the confidence out of me, physically, verbally, and emotionally. You think like a slave master and a mentally defeated slave who has accepted they'll never be free. You're like that slave on the plantation who hated anybody who wanted to run and did everything to try to help the master catch them and keep them in those chains. But you couldn't stop me, and you can't stop me. You may despise me for that, but I've made it out. I'm *nobody's slave*, and I will never be a slave to anyone, especially not to y'all. If you hate me for it and still think I'm too good, so be it. This little plantation thing you had going on—it's over."

With tears filling up my eyes, I looked at the stunned therapist, who looked at my mother and father.

"I'm sorry, Lee," my mother said.

It was the first time my parents' actions had been exposed to a third party. My mother was a totally different person—meek—in front of that white woman. I barely recognized her. It was only then, at that moment, that everything crystallized, and I realized that for all those years my parents had consciously chosen to whip me only when they were certain there would be no witnesses. The only exception to that rule was when they were beating me to satisfy a white person.

"For what?" I asked my mother. "What are you sorry for?"

"For the things that have made you upset. And I didn't know that spanking came from slave masters. I always thought it was what Black people did to discipline and protect their children, so I didn't look at it like that."

"What about now? Is it abuse?"

She remained silent.

"Is it?"

"I would never spank a child today," she said carefully. She refused to utter the word "abuse." But she at least gave me the part about the children. Our years-long standoff was partially rooted in my insistence that neither one of them *ever* lay a hand on Tammi's and Tiffany's kids—their grandchildren and my nieces and nephews. I was hell-bent that the cycle of violence in our family be finally and forever broken.

That day marked the first time my mother ever apologized to me for anything. I was unsure whether she felt true remorse or was trying to save face in front of the white therapist. On the second day of therapy, alone with my dad at the base of the stairs leading to the meeting room, we hugged. Seeing his eyes moist for the first time, I recognized his deep regret over the day he held me down with his boot on my neck. He truly supported me. Neither of us could easily express emotion, but years of suppressed pain surfaced during those two cathartic days.

With my parents back on the couch across from me, we sat in awkward silence until finally, the devastated-looking white therapist spoke: "I don't think I slept a minute last night. I have never experienced a case like this, especially with a family that is so loving facing such a challenge," she said. "You are a strong, African American family. I did not know that this happens in the African American community—the fear you feel for children you want to protect. But I can see that you love each other and want to move forward as a better family."

Few Black therapists exist, making it challenging for Blacks to find mental health professionals familiar with their experiences. The American Psychological Association stated in 2015 that whereas 86 percent of US psychologists were white, only 4 percent were Black, contrasting with 38 percent of the US population being racial or ethnic minorities. Yet even my short sessions with a white therapist led to my parents, notably my father, acknowledging their disrespect of and unfairness toward me and offering an apology.

Mom complained about the fact that I hardly ever called her, without recognizing that she rarely initiated calls to me. After I shared with the therapist that my conversations with Mom usually occurred when my dad put her on the phone, the therapist recommended that Mom call me weekly to demonstrate her commitment to establishing a mutually respectful relationship.

Mom made two calls, and then stopped. But Dad and I continued regular chats, sometimes twice in a day.

"Everybody Knows the Character of a Negro"

hen I told Mom she'd need counseling to reconnect with me, I reminded her of my third-grade suicidal diary entries after her whippings, noting she ignored them and further terrorized me. "Everybody considers suicide," she darkly responded. Reflecting, I see how close I came to joining the statistics. While "Oh my God, my parents are going to kill me" was a regular complaint and idiom among my white peers, for me it was literal. A simple beating-triggered accident, like a head crack on a table's edge or Dad's boot cracking my spine, could have been fatal.

Compared with other racial groups in the United States, Black parents have a higher statistical likelihood of committing filicide. Stacey Patton, journalist and author of *Spare the Kids: Why Whupping Children Won't Save Black America*, underscores that Black children face a greater risk of harm or death from a parent than from external threats like police or racists. A study by researchers at Brown University analyzed 15,691 FBI filicide cases from 1976 to 2007, revealing that 38.2 percent of victims and 37.9 percent of offenders were Black—a staggering statistic. Notably, 35.2 percent of Black victims were infants under one year old. These findings underscore the disproportionate impact of filicide on Black families.

In my talk with Tim Mariano, a psychiatrist and adjunct assistant professor at Brown University and coauthor of a 2014 study about understanding filicide, I expressed being puzzled by the racial categorization. The study shows Black parents committing filicide at higher rates while oddly grouping whites and Hispanics together.

"This was done because the number of cases in the subethnic groups were low, so they could not be categorized as single groups," Mariano said. "There was an overrepresentation of African American victims and offenders."

Concerns about filicide are genuine. Whether corporal punishment significantly contributes to this trend remains an understudied topic. Though the American Academy of Pediatrics (AAP) and other groups have presented extensive evidence against corporal punishment, noting its potential harm to long-term mental health and well-being, its stance finds resistance in some quarters of the Black community. Stacey Patton cited prominent Black doctors who have spoken out against the AAP's position, arguing that corporal punishment is a cultural norm in the Black community and that Black parents could feel demonized by doctors who attempt to persuade them to stop hitting their kids.

"There are doctors who feel that the AAP's policy is heavy-handed and judgmental of Black families. They also take issue with calling a simple spanking abuse," said Dr. Scott Krugman, a pediatrician in Baltimore.

Harvard psychiatrist Alvin F. Poussaint, an expert on parenting and mental health in the Black community, opposes corporal punishment because of its proven harm. In the 1990s, he pushed educators to end its use. He told me his strongest opponents were Black educators supporting the practice, even as children's rights groups spotlighted significant racial disparities and long-term health impacts.

As of 2023, seventeen states still allow educators to hit children in public K-12 schools. A disproportionately higher number of Black parents give schools the green light to physically strike their children. Compounding the issue, because of systemic biases, educators hit Black students at much higher rates than white students, even though their behavioral conduct is comparable.

Black boys are nearly twice as likely to be hit compared to white boys, while Black girls are struck at over three times the rate of white girls, despite behaving similarly to white students, as reported by the Southern Poverty Law Center and the UCLA Center for Civil Rights Remedies.

Hitting school children is legal and most prevalent in states where enslavement was legal. Mississippi, Alabama, Arkansas, and Texas represent more than 70 percent of all corporal punishment in US public schools, as reported by the Southern Poverty Law Center, with children at some schools being hit nearly twice a month. Notably, during the 2015–2016 school year, one Mississippi school reported 871 instances affecting fifty-seven students, averaging fifteen times per student. Another school noted sixty instances for four students, also averaging fifteen times per student.

Geoff K. Ward, a professor of African and African-American studies at Washington University in St. Louis, believes the racial disparities are strongly linked to the South's legacy of violence toward Blacks, especially children. In 2019, he and his team conducted an analysis of US lynching incidents on a county-by-county basis over time. He said they found that "each additional lynching in a county's history increases the likelihood that all children will be subjected to corporal punishment. However, it is especially predictive of the odds that Black children will be."

The study also uncovered a wealth of public records that contain governmental "rationalizations of violence" against Blacks even after emancipation. For example, during a 1901 Alabama constitutional debate on the legality of whipping prisoners, a county official argued in favor of the practice, stating, "Everybody knows the character of a Negro and knows that there is no punishment in the world that can take the place of the lash with him." In addition, juvenile court records from North Carolina in the 1930s show that court-ordered whippings were almost exclusively reserved for Black boys and girls. This was due to "widespread feelings among [white] county juvenile court judges that whipping is the most effective way of handling delinquent Negroes," according to one court official. Another widespread practice documented in the records involved "sending delinquent black boys downstairs with a big police officer [to] have them flogged" before releasing them.

In my reporting on this subject, I've come across some Black educators who have concurred with the views of white supremacist juvenile court officers, arguing that Black children can only change errant behavior if they are struck.

Growing up, I also unconsciously internalized the widely ingrained belief that Blacks should not feel physical pain—as my mother said about me, "He has a high tolerance for pain." This notion, rooted in myth, continues to adversely impact Black healthcare today, as articulated by Oluwafunmilayo Akinlade in a 2020 article titled "Taking Black Pain Seriously" in the *New England Journal of Medicine*. In it, he debunks the persistent, yet absurd, idea among some medical trainees that Black people have thicker skin with fewer nerve endings, leading to higher pain tolerance than whites—an idea tracing back to a nineteenth-century doctor who owned enslaved people.

Black pain goes far beyond physical. The statistics surrounding Black youth suicide are deeply troubling, as highlighted by Dr. Arielle H. Sheftall, an associate professor at the University of Rochester Medical Center in the Department of Psychiatry. Black children age five to twelve are twice as likely to die by suicide as their white peers, and suicide rates among Black teens have surged alarmingly. Between 2000 and 2020, suicide rates among Black youth ages ten to nineteen increased by 78 percent, and from 2018 to 2021, the suicide rate among Black individuals ages ten to twenty-four rose by 37 percent.

Researcher Jeffrey Bridge, who published a study in *JAMA Pediatrics* in 2015, reveals that suicide rates among Black children ages five to eleven nearly doubled from 1993 to 2012, surpassing rates among white children. Historically, whites had higher national suicide rates, but this research challenges that trend. A particularly disturbing observation is the escalation in suicide by hanging among Black boys. Bridge suggests that exposure to violence, traumatic stress, and harsh school discipline could be contributing factors.

Those suicidal diary entries of the tormented third-grader I was show how desperately I wanted the whipping to stop. What might I have done with a rope?

I thank God that I didn't go there, but a Black boy who wasn't as fortunate was Jaheim McKinzie. In 2017, when he was being whipped and choked by his mother, the ten-year-old ran into the kitchen, grabbed a knife, and stabbed himself. After he was pronounced dead at the hospital, she was charged with aggravated child abuse.

My journey into therapy deepened my understanding of mental

health in the Black American community, emphasizing that PTSD isn't just an issue for combat veterans. Harvard Medical School research shows Black children in the United States encounter more adversity than their white peers, leading to noticeable changes in the brain linked to conditions like PTSD. A 2023 study in the *American Journal of Psychiatry*, led by Nathaniel Harnett, debunked myths of inherent racial brain differences, revealing instead how structural racism affects brain development. Analyzing surveys and brain scans from more than nine thousand children, the researchers found that Black children had a reduced volume of gray matter in some brain areas, influenced by household income. Harnett highlights the profound implications of this for their mental health and overall well-being.

In a conversation I had with Stacey Patton, she observed that millions of Black Americans "are still walking around with dead children inside of us." She opined that the reluctance to label whipping as "abuse" stems from the concern that doing so might suggest previous generations didn't genuinely love us. I can relate. Recognizing that my parents' attacks on Tiffany and me were abuse masked as discipline led to my experiencing years of intermittent guilt, shame, and anger.

But it also led me to investigate the connection between my childhood whippings and my family's history in the United States. My research stretched back to the 1600s, probing the lessons on racial identity and the belief systems passed through generations. With modern technology and DNA testing, I pieced together many of the traumatic stories in our family tree. This often painful yet enlightening process impelled my father and me to confront our family's past—the good, the bad, the ugly, and everything in between. We started taping interviews about his life and the journey of the Hawkinses and the Pughs during enslavement and Jim Crow America, a sometimes grueling process that always brought us back to that question I had been asking for so long: What happened in Alabama?

35

The Pughs and the Hawkinses

By 2015, the science of ancestral DNA testing had exploded. I reached out to Matthew Deighton at Ancestry.com, who recommended I take the test. So I ordered the kit and returned my saliva sample.

When the results came in, I was amazed at the extensive list of DNA matches, including many white faces. Matt told me he hadn't ever seen anyone with so many pages of cousins who had also taken DNA tests—more than 216 fourth cousins or closer. I was a Black man with 82 percent Black African DNA, but 18 percent of my DNA showed I had strong, undeniable genetic ties to a white family from the 1800s. Ancestry.com genealogist Michelle Erpenbach expressed astonishment at the solid connection, which mainly traced back to Wales.

Among the ancestors in my family tree, an eighteenth-century white man named Jesse Pugh stood out. Further research uncovered another surprise. On my Black side, Charity Pugh emerged as the mother of my white-looking great-grandfather Isaac Pugh Sr.—the man in the photograph above Uncle Ike's fireplace. But I still had no clues as to who his father was.

At least I had found Grandma Charity—excavated from my cluttered memory after almost twenty years, like a long-lost family heirloom recovered in an attic. I imagined her calling out, "Don't forget about me!" In my quest to understand her, I contacted family members and scoured the internet for a photograph. But despite exhaustive efforts, I couldn't find one, nor diaries or letters from Grandma Charity. My understanding relied on the limited oral history passed down through family members who portrayed her unfavorably—as a half-Black, half-Cherokee, mean and crazy child-whipper who hated white people. But my DNA test didn't show a drop of "Indian" blood in me. Not one. I was completely perplexed. Why would they say she was "Indian" if she wasn't?

Dad and I knew our 1991 interview with Uncle Ike two decades earlier might contain clues that we'd overlooked at the time. Curious to learn about Grandma Charity and how her life impacted him, Dad overnighted me the low-quality interview tape. We both listened to it again, clinging to Uncle Ike's every word about her.

But relistening to the tape brought me no further answers; Uncle Ike had shared nothing about Grandma Charity's background or what she had endured during her life. She was just "mean" and "crazy." How had she become "mean ol' Grandma Charity" to Uncle Ike and his siblings? Who was this woman? Had she been enslaved? Or was she free?

The more I continued my research, the more Jesse Pugh emerged in the DNA pool alongside Grandma Charity. Was Jesse her father? Or was he the father of her son, my great-grandpa Ike Pugh Sr.? Or did my DNA connection to Jesse arise from another Pugh man who shared his DNA? I hoped my investigation of the white Pugh men and their connections to my family would help me decipher how the traumatic interactions between my white and Black ancestors contributed to my upbringing.

36

Faint Clues

During an early-morning internet search, I broke through a brick wall when I found a digital copy of Jesse Pugh's 1852 will. It allowed me to peer into his life as an enslaver and his decision to will his captives to his wife and children before dying.

The document, titled "Last Will and Testament of Jesse Pugh, Pike County, Alabama . . . signed this 24 day of March A.D. 1852," provides a matter-of-fact account of his human property. It states that the "Negroes: Rueben, George and Huldah" were to be left with his wife, Lydia Sims Pugh. Additionally, he bequeathed "a Negro Girl, Charity, and a Negro Boy, Nelson," to his son "Mastin B."

"A Negro Girl, Charity." Tears streamed as I read those words. Discovering that Grandma Charity had been enslaved was the first step toward understanding her anger, and how the whip had found its way into my family's bloodline, and ultimately, into the Hawkins family's Maplewood home.

Discovering Grandma Charity's origins had been my goal since 2015, but it brought mixed emotions—relief at finally finding her, but also a stream of poisons at the revelation of her enslavement. She wasn't a distant figure like the nameless people buried in George Washington's slave cemetery; she was my grandmother's grandmother, a matriarch whom my family knew.

This discovery made enslavement more real to me. Had Grandma Charity been shackled and passed around among Pugh family members like a farm animal, alongside mules, cows, plantation tools, bushels of corn, and kitchen furniture? It crushed me to think so but provided fragments of her life and the unfortunate circumstances that bound her to the Pugh plantation, where my multiracial family's secrets were formed.

This will and the photo of her white-looking son in Uncle Ike's home became my only connections to her. I realize now that her decision to retain the "slave name" of Pugh after emancipation proved critical to my unraveling the mystery of her life. It connected me to a lineage bound by blood, not just contractual ties. I finally grasped the horrifying truth of Black American family "slave" names—a tradition I was raised to take pride in—entangled with the trauma-bearing DNA of their enslavers.

Without "Pugh" listed in the census and other documents, I might never have found Grandma Charity. Some of the other enslaved people named in Jesse Pugh's will seemed forever lost, possibly because they hadn't adopted the Pugh surname. But I was able to trace some basic information about my ancestor.

Judging from census data, Grandma Charity's birth year could have been anywhere from 1830 to 1846. The 1880 national census indicated her birth to be around 1840 (which would make her roughly twelve years old at the time of Jesse Pugh's will). The 1910 census pegged it as somewhere around 1846, and the 1920 census had it at around 1830.

According to Alabama records, Grandma Charity married at least once, possibly twice, but I could find no documents related to her second marriage. In the 1890 census, she and "Thomas Mullens" were living together as husband and wife, and their household included four of their nine children.

Mullens worked for the warden of Butler County Jail during the post-Reconstruction era when Black prison laborers replaced enslaved people. To maintain free labor, whites incarcerated Blacks on all kinds of trumped-up charges. Mullens worked as an overseer of the laboring Black prisoners.

Grandma Charity's death records are similarly unclear. Her death certificate documents her passing on March 25, 1930. Her age is listed as 115 years and the cause of death as "probably senility." But later, one of her sons, Tom Mullens Jr., revised her age at death to 110. Additionally, the "Mother" section of the document contains illegible scribbles, hinting at her mother's name being "Laney." I couldn't determine what prompted the age change, which was likely a guess, since her sons had no way to ascertain her birthdate and his mother herself never knew it.

The will of Jesse Pugh, a highly regarded churchgoer known for his deep religious devotion, exposed the disparity between his supposed honor and his dehumanization of Black people, including Grandma Charity, the young girl he held hostage in a nearby shanty. How could I share DNA with this man?

I saw that the essential details of Grandma Charity's life had been intentionally hidden. She knew little about herself, even her age. The dates and places of birth for whites were documented in nineteenth-century America, but those born into enslavement were denied this basic affirmation of existence.

This erasure of personal information aimed to disempower the enslaved, reinforcing their roles as mere objects used for plantation operations. As the essayist Sherronda J. Brown has observed, "One of the primary ways white people maintain their false supremacy and actual racial-colonial terrorism is through the reframing and revisionism of historical narrative and fact"—a process Brown calls "ahistoricizing history." In his 1855 autobiography, *My Bondage and My Freedom*, Frederick Douglass eloquently conveys the impact of having his identity stripped from him:

> The reader will pardon so much about the place of my birth, on the score that it is always a fact of some importance to know where a man is born, if, indeed, it be important to know anything about him. Regarding the time of my birth, I cannot be as certain as I have been regarding the place. Nor, indeed, can I impart much knowledge concerning my parents. Genealogical trees do not flourish among slaves. A person of some consequence here in the north, sometimes designated father, is literally abolished in slave law and slave practice. It is only occasionally that an exception is found to this statement. I never met with a slave who could tell me how old he was. Few slave-mothers know anything of the months of the year, nor of the days of the month. They keep no family records, with marriages, births, and

deaths. They measure the ages of their children by springtime, wintertime, harvest time, planting time, and the like; but these soon become indistinguishable and forgotten. Like other slaves, I cannot tell you how old I am. This destitution was among my earliest troubles. I learned when I grew up that my master, and this is the case with masters generally, allowed no questions to be put to him, by which a slave might learn his age. Such questions are deemed evidence of impatience, and even of impudent curiosity. From certain events, however, the dates of which I have since learned, I suppose myself to have been born about the year 1817.

The legacy of enslavement continues to undermine Black Americans today, perpetuating the ongoing crisis of Black identity. We are all the descendants of the same genealogical bewilderment and resentment that birthed Malcolm's "X."

I came to understand that the past identity struggles of myself and my people were not just personal, but part of a larger system designed to erase Black histories and identities. Even now, many of us cannot trace the origins or meanings of our Black surnames, evidence of our stolen heritage. This isn't merely individual pain—it's a lasting chain that binds us. Our names, devoid of their original meaning yet fraught with the traumatic significance of bearing European names as Blacks, were intended to instill a bondage mindset in our psyche, a mindset that has infiltrated family identities for generations.

37

The Tragic Life of "a Negro Girl"

Sometimes I feel like a motherless child
A long way from home, a long way from home.
Sometimes I feel like I'm almost done
And a long, long way from home, a long way from home.

—TRADITIONAL NEGRO SPIRITUAL

On Grandma Charity's death certificate, Tom Mullens Jr. named "John Blue" as her father, which suggests he learned this information from her. But how did she, "a Negro Girl," learn such details, given the legally and socially imposed secrecy around paternity at the time?

In my search, I came across an 1837 inventory from enslaver John B. Reid in Pike County, Georgia, which lists the names "Rueben," "Laner," "Charity," "Nelson," and "Letty." These names also appear in Jesse Pugh's will in Pike County, Alabama. The Georgia document includes a nauseating detail—the price list of enslaved people, ranging from $100 for Nelson to $650 for Rueben. Were these the same documented enslaved people that appear in Jesse Pugh's will fifteen years later? Genealogists agreed this couldn't be coincidence, and with that, the identities of Grandma Charity and her mother, Laner—the scribbled "Laney" on her death certificate—came into sharper focus for me.

Grandma Charity was most likely born in Pike County, Georgia—not Pike County, Alabama—between 1825 and 1830, not 1840. As of April 1843, Charity was indeed enslaved on John B. Reid's estate in Georgia. Given the geographic proximity among Reid family heirs,

Grandma Charity and her mother, Laner, were likely on neighboring properties, separated by a few miles; but given the realities of enslavement, it might as well have been a few hundred.

A great deal of research has documented the traumatic impact of separation from their children on enslaved mothers, whose monetary value was often determined by their ability to produce more children for labor. Separation perpetuated identity crises and disrupted family structures that otherwise would have provided stability and solace amid the hardships of plantation life. So the effect on Laner of being separated from her children—who may have been the result of rape by white men—is incalculable.

According to Rutgers University historian Deborah Gray White, the significance of the family extended beyond the realm of labor. An intact family, White notes, offered companionship and allowed enslaved men to transcend their dehumanizing roles, enabling them to be fathers and sons rather than mere beasts. Women, too, could find comfort in motherhood and take on roles that extended beyond that of an enslaved person. But such family situations were rare.

Indeed, recalled former enslaved man Lewis Clarke in his 1845 book *Narrative of the Sufferings of Lewis Clarke, During a Captivity of More Than Twenty-Five Years, Among the Algerines of Kentucky, One of the So Called Christian States of North America, dictated by himself,* "I never knew a whole family to live together, till all were grown up, in my life." Clarke escaped to freedom in Canada in 1841.

"Families like ours," he says in his book, "were torn apart due to various reasons, including sales, escapes, early deaths resulting from poor health, suicides, and even murders committed by slaveholders, overseers, slave patrollers, or other dominant individuals." Separation was also enforced within plantations by segregating "field slaves" from "house servants," separating children from their parents to live under the care of a slave caretaker, or taking children fathered by the enslaver to live in the "Big House."

Roughly one-third of enslaved children in the upper South birthed between 1619 and the emancipation era of Grandma Charity experienced separation from parents or siblings. Enslavers deceived children into leaving their families, sometimes luring them with candy, according to Heather Andrea Williams, professor of Africana Studies at the University of Pennsylvania. "They try to placate the kids, who don't realize for a couple of days that they are not going to see their mother again," Williams said. One heart-wrenching detail in Williams's research is her description of a child who for years returned to the field where she had last seen her mother and stared up at the sky in hopes that the heavens would bring her back.

Historian Daina Ramey Berry, author of *The Price for Their Pound of Flesh: The Value of the Enslaved, from Womb to the Grave, in the Building of a Nation*, is a specialist in Black women's history, particularly in regard to gender and enslavement. In an interview, Berry told me that some enslaved mothers, forced to give birth and immediately hand their children away, would distance themselves emotionally from those children, refusing to form connections. "When the women were interviewed at the auction block," Berry said, "slave dealers and buyers would be trying to figure out, 'How many healthy children can she have? Let me ask her a question.' Then they would say, 'How many babies have you given birth to?' And the women on the auction block would say, 'It doesn't matter. I don't count them. I don't know.'"

The effects of all this rape, separation, and other abuse? "Soul murder, the feeling of anger, depression, and low self-esteem," is the succinct summation of historian and Princeton professor emerita Nell Irvin Painter.

I came to realize that the idea of a Black mother being fearful of connecting emotionally with her children has a long legacy; it didn't start in the 1970s and 1980s in Minnesota with my own mother.

38

Overseers

The "Alabama Slave Code of 1852," which revised the 1833 Slave Code, contained the "traps" of Grandma Charity's era. Enforced with bullwhips and guns, these codes severely restricted her freedom to move, express herself, seek education, and more, under the penalty of severe whipping or death. These "codes" laid the groundwork for the enduring stereotypes that I often observed from childhood onward, shaping perceptions of Black people among both racists and members of the Black community who internalized their false definitions of Blackness. These stereotypes propagated the white supremacist belief that Black people should never be free—that they should refrain from pursuing education, speaking out, or enjoying any form of individuality or expression in their lives.

Created in response to a growing enslaved population and the rising abolitionist movement, they also affected the lives of free Blacks. Following the Civil War, similar Black Codes emerged, continuing the oppressive Slave Code practices during Reconstruction into the Jim Crow era, which sentenced Grandma Charity to living under a caste system until she died in 1930.

State law required all able-bodied white men aged eighteen to forty-five to serve "Slave Patrol" duty at least once a week. Armed with firearms and whips, their job was to suppress any sign of "insubordination" or unauthorized gatherings among Blacks. These ordinary white men could burst into Black homes, pull family members out, and whip anybody or even everybody publicly. They were especially vicious with slaves who tried to escape or free Blacks who acted "too free." They'd often whip them and/or hand them over to the justice of the peace for punishment and incarceration. Studying these codes helped me understand why the white men who showed up to whip Grandma Charity, as Uncle Ike had told us, felt so emboldened: Alabama's laws sanctioned their violence and hatred.

Likely from an early age, Grandma Charity would have been hyperaware of these rules, which bound her to Jesse Pugh's property and prohibited her from going anywhere without a proper pass. Any form of weapon possession, other than basic tools, led to more whipping. "Crimes" such as speaking to a crowd of Blacks without a white person present or aiding in an enslaved person's escape often led to punishments of between thirty-nine and one hundred lashes with a whip. The criminalization of Black freedom—even thinking or speaking about it—was beaten into Blacks. The grim reality is clear: for much of US history, random white American citizens, merely because of their race, legally wielded power over Blacks—both enslaved and so-called free—with full authority to whip and even kill them.

After emancipation, the effects of this system continued and spread. Millions of freed enslaved people and those punished in the aftermath bore psychological wounds. Many felt compelled to raise their children under the shadow of these traumas, resorting to whipping as both discipline and a protective measure. Uncle Ike's story of Grandma Charity whipping her grandchildren mirrors the sad continuation of this practice, linking her time in bondage to her "freedom" after emancipation. She internalized a whipping tradition, along with the white supremacist rules, ideas, and fears that had been beaten into her and passed them down through generations—to my grandmother and her siblings, to my father, and eventually to me.

As the last generation of enslaved people moved toward emancipation, subsequent periods such as the Jim Crow era, the Great Migration, and integration saw numerous Black parents, including mine, inadvertently take on roles resembling that of overseer. With the weight of centuries of ingrained Slave Code laws and punishments, each generation aimed to ensure safety, order, and conformity to standards set by an enduring white supremacist system. In their efforts, they unknowingly introduced Slave Code practices into their own homes. Many didn't realize that the age-old act of whipping served a dual purpose: it delivered immediate pain and, more insidiously, reinforced white supremacist principles of the Slave and Black Codes in Black minds. The ultimate intent was not just to punish Black bodies and govern physical actions but to punish the aspirations, self-worth, and self-confidence of Black Americans, infecting their minds with white supremacy before they could even talk.

However, it's essential to differentiate between experiences. While the whippings Tiffany and I suffered from our parents were harsh, they can't be compared to the grueling punishments our ancestors endured.

In *Slave Patrols: Law and Violence in Virginia and the Carolinas*, historian Sally E. Hadden highlights the state's role in perpetuating enslavement, detailing the evolution of slave patrols from the late 1600s to the Civil War's conclusion. In our discussion, she distinguished between the belt beatings I described as "whipping" and the extreme torture enslaved people faced from enslavers and white men on patrol duty in the nineteenth century using bullwhips, which inflicted "horrific wounds," she said. Hadden also described the "cat o' nine tails," a whip with nine strands, each capable of causing separate wounds.

But although I know the undeniable physical distinction between a belt and a bullwhip, I also know the similarities: both tools were and are used to beat and solidify the rules of white supremacy into the minds and family culture and values of Black people. Despite the liberation of 3.2 million enslaved people after emancipation, many of our PTSD-stricken elders left their marks on us. The fact that Uncle Ike knew about and received beatings from Grandma Charity underscores the generational proximity of these experiences.

It's unsurprising that my parents incorporated the heavy influence of white supremacist laws and history into their parenting. For generations, they, along with countless other Black parents, unintentionally acted as enforcers of the very racist facets and foundations of the police state we stand against. The statement "We spank you so that the racist police won't kill you" attests to this. It's particularly telling when Black parents "protect" their children using the same whipping methods once inflicted on our ancestors, with our law enforcement community effectively and symbolically having passed the whip down to successive generations of Blacks, saying, "We've removed public whipping. Now, keep your little pickaninnies in line, or we'll do it for you."

My parents' concerns about my activism, particularly during the Elroy Stock incident, are telling. In examining the Slave and Black Codes, I recognized similarities between the "modern-day overseer" mentality and certain societal norms upheld by my parents and even some of my self-proclaimed "real nigga" friends from my younger days. Recalling the ban on enslaved people seeking education, I considered the ongoing obstacles Black people sometimes encounter when pursuing intellectual endeavors. These efforts often result in their intellectual ability and/or racial authenticity and loyalty being questioned, sometimes even by other Blacks who've internalized the Slave Code mandate against Black education.

Before President Barack Obama rose to global leadership, he lost an Illinois congressional election to former Black Panther Bobby Rush. Rush argued Obama was "an educated fool." After all, in certain US states, Black people faced prohibitions against literacy far longer than they've enjoyed the right to read and write. I find it plausible that some could have internalized this and viewed Obama as an outsider. Or that some Black politicians and others might leverage this ingrained prejudice to undermine rivals within the community, knowing its potency. This is why I refer to Blacks who enforce racist constraints and penalize others for "acting white" as "modern overseers." This is all part of what I call the "modern war on Black excellence," which is an extension of antebellum-era oppression tactics.

Growing up Black, I was unaware of the daily struggle shaping my self-perception—a battle between oppressive mindsets and the proud Black elders advocating for Black excellence. I remember hiding my *A* English assignments, fearing being called an Oreo. For years, I and many others reclaimed "nigga," transforming it into an expression of camaraderie, defiance, and even love. The fact that I have tried to stop using the term for years and still can't illustrates the complicated legacy of language and identity in our community, and how difficult internalized white supremacy can be to shake.

And I now understand why I had so much difficulty being criticized by my mother for being "free as a bird." For a long time, I wondered where she picked up the notion that being free was a violation and deemed it a putdown that would inspire guilt and shame within me. The concept of a free Black American has historically been contentious in the United States. In her book *Slavery and Plantation Growth in Antebellum Florida, 1821–1860,* Julia Floyd Smith writes that many Southerners denounced free Blacks as "an evil of no ordinary magnitude." This sentiment spurred oppressive legislation aimed at free Blacks with the intention to either force them back into enslavement or drive them out of the state. At one point, a law in Oregon stated that free Blacks who chose to stay had to be whipped every six months. Some states even required free Blacks to have a white legal guardian, made them register with local probate judges, or limited their ability to enter the state. Noncompliance could lead to being claimed as an enslaved person by any white person.

Now, with more clarity than in my youth, I discern the depth of the "overseer mentality" entrenched in the American psyche. The whip born on Grandma Charity's Pugh plantation wasn't just punitive; it served as a means of psychological control, passed through generations. I call this a *bondage belief system,* under which generations of Black Americans have internalized ingrained ideas of Blacks needing to follow many of the same rules established under the Slave Codes—becoming subservient, having a lower sense of self-worth, and harboring lower aspirations, traits that echo through successive generations.

Studying the Slave Codes, I saw their shadows in so many present-day experiences. These codes once prohibited gatherings of more than five enslaved people without a white person present, reminiscent of today's Black Americans being questioned for mundane tasks like barbecuing, walking, or bird-watching. If the white people who feel entitled to approach Black Americans in these scenarios today weren't alive before 1965, when it was legal in many places to do this, many are the children and grandchildren of white Americans who were sanctioned by the government to whip Blacks for having barbecues or delivering speeches. Even if these white Americans don't know it or won't admit it, their bones know that they were historically protected in their basic rights and had governmentally backed power and institutional preference over Blacks—up until only sixty years ago.

Past restrictions on public assembly and preaching underscored my parents' fear of my activism. Dad's intense worry about false allegations of stealing or sexual assault being leveled against me, especially from white females, became clearer when I learned of the historically limited protections for Black women, the antimiscegenation rules of the codes, and the rampant lynchings of Black men based on rape accusations.

Whipping went beyond immediate pain; it deeply affected behaviors, thoughts, and aspirations. The prohibition against reading wasn't solely about the act but its broader meanings: enlightenment, empowerment, and liberty. This strategy aimed to degrade Black self-worth, often framing as weaknesses strengths such as pro-Black activism (as dangerous radicalism), a wealth-building mindset (as greed or race betrayal), or a free-spirit attitude (as foolishly inviting danger). Conversely, weaknesses or challenges are sometimes celebrated as strengths, such as passivity (valued as humility for "protection" and "safety"), imposter syndrome (mistaken for self-effacing humility), and economic hardship (seen as more "authentically Black" or virtuous than prosperity).

For those of us with strong ties to apartheid in the United States, we're descendants of those who lived before 1965—a time when whites could freely discriminate against Blacks in employment, voting, housing, or through violence, often without legal repercussions. Remember, this was in 1965, not 1765. The Black Codes not only shaped our history but perpetuated toxic stereotypes and prompted some Black parents to feel a duty to beat a white supremacy–inspired survivalist mindset of unwavering passivity and compliance into their children. The bondage belief system influenced my own upbringing in the 1970s and 1980s. It turns out that white supremacists, and "overseers," now come in all shades.

39

Lost Recipes

n 1840, Grandma Charity was sold to the family of Jesse Pugh for $1,200, a sum that would be equivalent to about $40,000 today. Already reeling from the loss of her parents, she must have felt that the prospect of freedom was a distant dream.

By 1852, the teenage Grandma Charity was one of around a dozen enslaved people on the Pugh plantation. Accounts of how many enslaved people lived at the time tell that she likely lived in a tin or wooden shack, close to the main house on the vast two-hundred-acre land. Most slave shanties had dirt floors, partitioned with old boards and rags filling in gaps.

Before dawn, Grandma Charity would rise from her bed on the floor, dress, and take a sack from the wall. She'd toil in the cotton fields from sunrise to sunset, constantly fearing rape and the looming whip.

Solomon Northup, a nineteenth-century free Black man who wrote about his experience of being kidnapped into enslavement in his 1853 memoir *Twelve Years a Slave* (later an award-winning film), describes the grueling nature of this work, which included the constant threat of whipping:

> When a new hand, one unaccustomed to the business, is sent for the first time into the field, he is whipped up smartly, and made for that day to pick as fast as he can possibly. At night it is weighed so that his capability in cotton picking is known. He must bring in the same weight each night following. If it falls short, it is considered evidence that he has been laggard, and a greater or less number of lashes is the penalty.

On plantations, even the foods the enslaved were forced to eat constituted a form of abuse. In my own family, it is clear that Grandma Charity's likely diet rippled through generations. The pig intestines my parents embraced as "our Black heritage" were once forced upon our ancestors.

In his article "How Did Eating Pork Become a Way to Judge Blackness?" historian Adrian Miller writes that pigs weren't central to the Indigenous diet of sub-Saharan West Africa. Yet, during the grueling transatlantic journey, not consuming the salted pork given to the prisoners could mean starvation. Miller describes how, in the British North American colonies, enslavers provided the enslaved with weekly pork rations alongside cornmeal and molasses because of the ease and low cost of raising pigs.

Forced dietary habits continued after emancipation, with many Black families still consuming the pork scraps of enslavers. The physician Dr. Milton Mills refers to this as "death by fork," advocating a return to a traditional, plant-based West African diet. Before being brought to this country, Mills notes, West Africans traditionally consumed high-fiber, calorie-diluted food and had exceptionally low levels of chronic disease. In America, however, salted pork has contributed to today's higher rates of diabetes, cancer, and cardiovascular disease that I saw so many Black friends and family members succumb to in their forties, fifties, and sixties. Mills cites the disproportionately higher rates of diabetes among Black Americans, who are then more likely than their Caucasian counterparts to end up with amputations and more likely to go blind or experience kidney complications. And when heart disease strikes, it's deadlier and more severe in Black people, which means they are more likely than whites to die from a first heart attack.

Today's pediatric obesity crisis has caused a rise in type-2 diabetes among Black children. Although I've given up chitlins, my battles with sugar and carbs continue. Realizing how Grandma Charity's diet influenced my father, much as Great-Grandpa Sam and Great-Grandmother Roberta's diet influenced me, reinforces my commitment to healthier living.

Though Grandma Charity was among the last in my lineage to survive long enough to be freed under the Emancipation Proclamation, being manumitted did not bring freedom, equality, or peace, since she suffered under Jim Crow apartheid until her death in the 1930s.

She lived through earth-shattering historical events like the constant warring between the Indigenous and white settlers, the Civil War, and World War I, taking her first steps on land forcibly taken by the white supremacists surrounding her and controlling every aspect of her life.

The depth of her hatred of white people became clearer to me as I learned about the systemic sexual abuse inflicted upon enslaved women and the complex trauma they endured. Referring to any part of her life as "posttraumatic" is misleading. It suggests that there was a period when the horrors inflicted on my enslaved and Jim Crow–era ancestors ceased, which was never the case. Escaping enslavement was a crime punishable by death, yet some still cling to the lie that the enslaved were often treated well, experiencing no short- or long-term effects. They entertain the mistaken idea that Black matriarchs genuinely loved their enslavers, and that their roles as "mistresses" to white men were based on mutual love, equality, and even passion. In reality, any seeming "consent" to such relationships arose from a need to survive, similar to what we understand today as Stockholm syndrome.

Referring to Grandma Charity as a "mistress" fails utterly to capture her lived reality. It is very possible that her mother, Laner, was also a rape victim—and Grandma Charity, a biracial woman, the product.

The enslaved and their captors were not equals under the hierarchy of enslavement. Like the rest of the institution, their sexual contact occurred within a system of trafficking, forced labor, and rape culture, where enslaved women most often had no standing or agency. Slave-captor sexual relationships were defined by trafficking and force. The rapes of our matriarchs further intertwined white and Black families through secret blood connections that few families openly confronted or discussed for centuries. In my own family, Grandmas Laner and Charity had biracial children while they were in bondage, including my "white-looking" Great-Grandpa Ike Pugh Sr., whom experts confirmed was biracial, likely with much more European DNA than African. And once eighteen percent of my DNA was revealed to be an undeniable genetic tie to the Pughs of Wales, I began to see the modern effects of enslavement more clearly.

Jaycee Dugard and Elizabeth Smart, white girls who experienced kidnapping and captivity in 1991 and 2002, respectively, were never referred to as "mistresses." I interviewed Smart in 2014 and was inspired by her activism and resilience. While she refused to define herself as a victim, her victimization has never been in question. Nor should it be. During her nine months in captivity, the then-fourteen-year-old was repeatedly raped and tortured by her abductors. In the firestorm of worldwide media publicity that Smart's kidnapping generated, none allowed even remotely for the possibility that Smart "wanted" sexual relations with her tormentors or that she could have been "treated well" by her captors.

Celebrity Drew "Dr. Drew" Pinsky aptly described Elizabeth as "nothing more than [an] inanimate belonging, a slave." Yet society has refused to accept that millions of Black women enslaved in the United States suffered, generation after generation, for their entire lifetimes, from unwanted sexual relationships with their captors.

Researcher Jennifer Hallam and others have noted that nineteenth-century enslaved women were characterized as lustful and promiscuous "Jezebels" who tempted their white owners. Such depictions simultaneously abhor and fetishize Black women, who were seen as hypersexual mares. Enslavers often felt entitled to engage in sexual activity with Black women, who may have capitulated to their advances in the hope that such relationships would increase the chance of freedom for themselves or their children. Most of the time, however, enslavers took enslaved people by force, and euphemisms were invented to describe their rapes.

Feminist scholar Hazel Carby, author of *Reconstructing Womanhood: The Emergence of the Afro-American Woman Novelist*, argues that the institutionalized rape of Black women has been overshadowed by lynching, a crime typically inflicted on Black males. Carby contends that rape has always been entwined with patriarchy, often casting women as partially willing or inviting assault. The enduring association between Black women and illicit sexuality has had lasting consequences.

In contemporary society, women who escape rape and psychological torment are rightfully lauded for their bravery. But women like Thomas Jefferson's "wench" Sally Hemings and my grandma Charity were diminished and devalued in their time. Their silenced voices make it hard to comprehend the full extent of the atrocities they faced.

Even in my youth during the 1980s and 1990s, I and many in my generation—male and female—embraced stereotypes rooted in antebellum beliefs. I cringe now at how often we disparaged the complexity and vitality of Black women, referring to "angry Black women" and rapping about "hoes." This is just one more example of how enslavement's legacy has been internalized by modern overseers within American culture.

Historian Thelma Jennings, in her 1990 article "'Us Colored Women Had to Go Through a Plenty': Sexual Exploitation of African-American Slave Women," details the daily realities of enslaved Black women. Jennings shows that female bondage was often the harshest, as women endured sexual abuse and childbearing on top of labor. Enslaved women were subject to their captors' desires for higher populations of enslaved people, which meant greater profits. Practices like "slave breeding" coerced sexual relations to boost populations of enslaved people. By 1860, more than 10 percent of slaves were biracial, reflecting the relations between white men and enslaved Black women. Masters held the power to force enslaved women into mating, control their reproduction, limit time with their children, and break up families through sales.

Before 1861, some states didn't allow enslaved women to file rape charges against white men. This absence of legal recourse, combined with the portrayal of enslaved women as prostitutes or uncontrollable sexual beings, left them with few options for justice or protection.

In her 1861 autobiography *Incidents in the Life of a Slave Girl*,

Harriet Jacobs describes the oppressive environment enslaved girls faced, surrounded by licentiousness and fear. From a youthful age, they experienced lashings from their masters and their masters' sons, lewd talk, and rapes. By adolescence, white male owners, overseers, and sons would try to bribe them into sexual relations with gifts or resort to whipping and starvation if advances were refused.

In *Once a Slave: The Slaves' View of Slavery*, author Stanley Feldstein recounts the story of Maria, a thirteen-year-old house servant. After the enslaver's wife finds him with Maria, the girl is imprisoned and beaten for two weeks. The case of Celia in 1855 highlights the plight of enslaved women subjected to sexual violence. Celia defends herself by killing her rapist but is found guilty of murder by a jury of twelve white men and executed. Her defense challenges the dehumanization of enslaved women and the legal system of enslavement, highlighting Black women's fight for dignity and justice.

Examining these historical accounts, I realized that the sexual abuse of enslaved Black women is deeply embedded in America's fabric. Learning about the experiences of the women in my family tree helped me expose the rape of Black women as the other side of America's "Mandingo" fear. Abuse and shame underpin a lie in my family that persisted for more than a century—that Grandma Charity was a "Cherokee Indian." This likely originated from ancestors ashamed and afraid to acknowledge their white-Black blood ties, distancing themselves from enslaver families whose darkness and abhorrent character they experienced daily. Even though my DNA tests show no First Nations ancestry, some relatives still insist that "Grandma Charity was a Cherokee." It's easier to believe that lie than the truth of enslavement and rape.

40

Whipping, Rape, Torture, and the Separation of Black Families: Cornerstones and Drivers of American Capitalism

My Black family carries the weight of America's enslavement legacy, while countless whites—not just those in the South or descendants of enslavers—have benefited from the wealth that enslavement generated. This wealth, built on the suffering of Grandma Charity and others, elevated the nation globally.

This became crystal clear when I interviewed Edward E. Baptist, a history professor at Cornell University and author of *The Half Has Never Been Told: Slavery and the Making of American Capitalism*. Baptist explained that violence fueled the growth of American enslavement, which supercharged the economy. According to Baptist, in 1836, cotton produced by more than a million enslaved people accounted for more than $600 million in revenue, nearly half of all economic activity in the United States. By 1860, enslaved labor had multiplied US cotton production 130 times its 1800 level, an increase driven by whipping, waterboarding, and murder.

The introduction of the cotton gin in the early 1800s also brought (somewhat counterintuitively) a more sophisticated form of brutality called "the pushing system," which involved profit-boosting through whipping and other torture techniques. With the advent of the cotton gin, plantation owners were able to efficiently process every bit of cotton harvested by their enslaved workers, leading to significant surges in profit. As a result, enslaved people were driven onto ever-expanding cotton fields. Each day, they faced the daunting task of meeting quotas, underpinned by the constant stress of knowing that falling short would result in a whipping by day's end. These whippings, occurring in the evening or the middle of the night, served as a form of psychological torture that was a crucial part of the system designed to maximize output.

Under the pushing system, cotton production in the South rose consistently from 1800 to 1860. While 1.4 million pounds of cotton were produced by enslaved Africans in 1800, the number skyrocketed to nearly 2 billion pounds by 1860. A vast majority, 80 percent, of this cotton was shipped primarily to Britain, becoming the cornerstone of the Industrial Revolution.

Highlighting the intertwined relationship between violence and profit, Baptist cites a white doctor from Natchez who detailed how daily violence was systematically used to uphold the plantation economy:

> The overseer meets all hands [slaves] at the scales, with the lamp, scales, and whip. Each basket is carefully weighed, and the net weight of cotton set down upon the slate, opposite the name of the picker. . . . [O]ccasionally the countenance of an idler may be seen to fall: "So many pounds short," cries the overseer, and takes up his whip, exclaiming, "Step this way, you damn lazy scoundrel," or "Short pounds, you bitch."

This daily cycle of violence and exploitation became the foundation of a system that transformed the world economy and subjected enslaved people to immense suffering.

Enslaved cotton workers quickly learned the consequences of falling behind or resisting. Allen Sidney, a formerly enslaved man whom Baptist mentions in his book, saw a man fighting back against a Black slave driver, only to be shot dead by a white overseer. Sidney and the other slaves who witnessed the killing remained silent.

Baptist also writes about Okah Tubbee, an enslaved person in Natchez, Mississippi, who stood up for the first few blood-cutting strokes of the first whipping he received before falling and passing out. He woke up vomiting, discovered he was still being beaten, and passed out again. His experience was not atypical, Baptist writes:

> Under the whip, people could not speak in sentences or think coherently. They "danced," trembled, babbled, lost control of their bodies. Talking to the rest of the white world, enslavers downplayed the damage inflicted by the overseer's whip. Sure, it might etch deep gashes in the skin of its victim, make them "tremble" or "dance," as enslavers said, but it did not disable them.

Reading this passage, I was assaulted by vivid memories. I remembered the suffocating sensation when the belt struck me and the sheer panic of gasping for air. In those moments, as I tried to shield my eyes, my parents would shout questions at me. However, fear and hyperventilation choked my responses, rendering me mute as I breathlessly tried to speak. Fast-forward to adulthood: I've heard countless Black comedians joke about Black kids "dancing" and "choking" during beatings. It's as though there's an unspoken rule in comedy: when the laughs dwindle, sprinkle in some jokes about Black children's suffering to reinvigorate the crowd. Seeing Black audiences giggling wildly alongside others, I bitterly thought, "Black children are the laughingstock of America."

This devaluation of the bodily integrity and well-being of Black children dates back to enslavement. According to *The Atlantic Slave Trade: A Census* by Johns Hopkins historian Philip D. Curtin, the transatlantic slave trade in the United States ended in 1808, with fewer than one million enslaved people imported. After 1807, illegal trading mainly targeted children. By 1860, the enslaved population reached 3.9 million, with 56 percent younger than twenty, making childhood trauma a defining part of the Black American experience.

Enslaved children were constantly endangered, intensifying stress, fear, and adultification that was ingrained into the experience of being enslaved. Those born to white fathers often incited jealous anger in the enslavers' wives, who might direct their rage at the child's mother. As depicted in *Mandingo*, this situation often caused explosive strife in enslavers' marriages. White women contributed to the high infant mortality rates among enslaved babies, as author and researcher Joy DeGruy describes in her presentations on "post-traumatic slave syndrome." She explains that white women were often excused from any accountability after beating Black and biracial children to death under the "Casual Killing Act." This Virginia law permitted enslavers to kill enslaved people in the process of "correcting them" without legal repercussions. DeGruy posits that many of the beatings that led to infant deaths were fueled by white plantation mistresses' jealousy of their husbands impregnating Black women. I am thankful that Grandma Charity didn't suffer the same terrible fate as the Black children killed in the name of "correction" by jealous wives.

In 2019, UC Berkeley associate professor of history Stephanie Jones Rogers, author of *They Were Her Property: White Women as Slave Owners in the American South*, revealed that white women made up approximately 40 percent of all enslavers. "The story of our founding and the story of American enslavement are too often masculine ones," says Jones Rogers.

But even as Black women and their children were tormented by their enslavers of both genders, they strived to build structure and nuclear families into their experience, against the sadistic and capitalistic efforts to break their families down, and apart. As I examined the effects of rape and family separation in Grandma Charity's generation, I saw the various ways states strove to fracture Black families, starting on plantations. In response to this injustice, "jumping the broom" became a prevalent makeshift marriage ritual for enslaved couples. And once Blacks eventually gained the right to legally marry after 1865, Grandma Charity and millions of others forged legally recognized families.

Willis Krumholz, in his 2019 article "Family Breakdown and America's Welfare System" illustrates this evolution. Between 1890 and 1950, Black women had higher marriage rates than white women, with a mere 9 percent of Black children in 1950 living fatherless. By 1960, Black marriage rates dipped but stayed close to the white rate. Yet, a dramatic rise in Black fatherlessness marked the mid-1980s. Today, only 44 percent of

Black children live with their fathers. Similarly, Black out-of-wedlock births jumped from 24.5 percent in 1964 to 70.7 percent by 1994.

My family was impacted by the antebellum efforts to stifle the formation of Black families. Before his death in 1854, Jesse Pugh transferred Grandma Charity to his son, Mastin Burrell Pugh, in Greenville. There, she bore George Pugh. At age twenty-three, she gave birth to another child, my great-grandfather Ike Pugh Sr. I've never seen a photo of George Pugh, so I can't say whether he looked white like my great-grandpa Ike. It's possible that George and Ike Sr. shared the same father since both had the Pugh name.

There's no doubt in my mind that part of my 18 percent Welsh and European ancestry traces back to a white Pugh man who likely raped my great-great-grandmother Charity. That "white blood" moved through their white-looking son, my great-grandfather Ike Sr., and down two more generations to me with my unexpected DNA results. To my knowledge, however, Great-Grandpa Ike Sr. never tried to pass as white. He identified as Black and married a Black woman.

Yet, no DNA test can definitively identify the nineteenth-century racist and rapist enslavers from whom I partially descend. DNA testing is imprecise in determining exact paternity but can identify broader family DNA groups, such as grandparents and cousins. These techniques conclusively link me to the white Pugh family.

In the 1600s, the principle of *partus sequitur ventrem* dictated that enslaved children inherit their mothers' names, regardless of their fathers' identities. (Since enslaved people often took their owners' names, this is why Great-Grandma Charity's last name was Pugh.) Experts speculate that my strong DNA connection to the white Pughs might stem from endogamy or inbreeding within the white side of the family, as enslavers often intermarried, leading to DNA concentration.

We can never be sure of Great-Grandpa Ike Sr.'s paternity. When reviewing the will mentioning Charity, I pondered how many of the other enslaved people listed had blood ties to the Pugh family. And because the Pugh men faced no repercussions for their actions, I've termed them America's "original Baby Daddies." This Baby Daddy pathology started with enslavers preying on enslaved women and is misapplied today, mainly to Black men who are unjustly hypersexualized. This phenomenon, often mistakenly attributed solely to Black America, has its roots in centuries of white supremacy. Prominent white figures like Thomas Jefferson, and even more recent figures like Senator Strom Thurmond, fathered children with Black women, often without publicly acknowledging them as theirs, and/or as "mulatto." It's crucial to recognize that America's original Baby Daddy issue was propagated by white enslavers who, aside from sexually exploiting Black women, also manipulated our family structures.

In 1994, a Black friend joked about having "Baby Mama Drama" as the result of having two babies born in 1989. "And they weren't twins," he said with a smirk. I laughed with him about his having only two different "Baby Mamas," compared with "many brothers," ignorant of the fact back then that this behavior harked back to white enslavers serially raping Black women. I neither condemn nor condone Black American men who father children with multiple women, provided they accept their responsibilities. However, it's imperative to note that the stereotype of impregnating multiple women and refusing to acknowledge paternity or take full responsibility applies more to white enslavers than to Black men.

While it's true that Black parents are less likely to marry before having a child, labeling Black fathers as neglectful is misleading. A December 2013 report from the Centers for Disease Control underscores that Black fathers, whether they live with their children or not, are notably engaged in their kids' lives, often more so than fathers from other racial or ethnic groups. I must admit, I once believed the damaging stereotype of the entirely uninvolved Black father, which led me to mistakenly equate the rising number of single Black fathers with neglect.

When I was growing up, many media images and messages taught me that being a "real nigga pimp and a playa" was the only true way to be Black. I've lost count of the number of times strangers from different races have approached me saying things like, "What's up, smooth-ass playa?" or "What up pimp? Where da hoes at?" trying to connect me to this "money, cash, hoes" mindset. It took years for me to finally recognize that this mindset is more characteristic of Thomas Jefferson than of Jay-Z.

During my interview with her, Daina Ramey Berry explained how the media and culture during and after enslavement perpetuated lies and false narratives characterizing our enslaved ancestors as unfaithful animals: "The media, culture . . . every avenue of lie that could be told during enslavement was continued in the postenslavement era. There were enslavers who said enslaved people weren't faithful and were polygamists." This made it easier to justify the practice of "breeding" new enslaved people, Berry explained.

Even if a Black woman or Black man had a life partner on another plantation or on that same plantation, they were nonetheless "forced into relationships that they didn't want to have," Berry said. "And we've seen narratives of enslaved men saying, 'They just took me around from plantation to plantation, to breed.' One guy said, 'I don't know how many children I had. I may have one hundred children. I have no idea.' The narrative about Black people after that was: Oh, they are promiscuous; they have sex all the time. They are not loyal; they are not good parents. That's part of the propaganda around trying to keep the races separate. One race is deviant, the other one 'normal.' This is a case of 'othering' Black people to a point where it becomes internalized and there's self-hate involved."

Understanding these entrenched systems of power and complicity make it easier to understand why Grandma Charity had children with different men and why tracing paternity for her and some of her children is difficult. It's a reflection of how enslavement controlled our family formations in fields, shanties, and Big Houses, while denying us family-empowering and prosperity-building tools like marriage and the basic rights to earn wages, acquire property, and get an education. Nevertheless, Grandma Charity and her ancestors managed to create a solid foundation for our family.

Amid the challenges facing Black families today, it's critical to recognize the deep-seated effects of forced separations of the past and the persisting influence of the "original Baby Daddy" in imposing on Black men and women a set of lies inspired by the bondage belief system.

PART 4

What Happened in Alabama?

41

Sweet Home

n 2015, as I launched into research for this book, I felt an irresistible pull to return to Greenville, Alabama. Dad, two and a half decades older than our previous visit, was recovering from knee surgery and prostate cancer radiation treatments.

He'd been battling obesity for decades. In 1999, as he fought prostate cancer and diabetes, his doctor had crushed him with the blunt truth: "Oh, Mr. Hawkins, don't worry. You could live another ten years!"

"Well, you've survived six years longer than that prediction," I told him. "But not rehabbing that knee will make it harder to exercise, which could put you at more risk for heart attack."

We both pledged to hit the gym harder. Remembering Mom's words that Dad quit going to the gym when I left home, I vowed to motivate him during our regular phone calls.

Though he always seemed much younger than his sixty-seven years—a sentiment I'd often reinforced with the adage "Black don't crack"—I had come to realize one sad reality about many Black Americans: we can look young on the outside but be years older on the inside.

A cousin from Minnesota, who spent his childhood in Greenville, warned, "Be careful down there, and don't travel alone. Ain't nothin' changed." Another relative even suggested I carry a pistol or take along someone who would. Their warnings perplexed me. As a journalist, I'd done investigative stories on shady executives and even murders and had never felt a hint of fear. Why should Greenville be any different? What buried secrets or skeletons in family closets would people be willing to kill over? Eager to find out, and with a renewed sense of curiosity, I booked my flight.

Reaching out to my Southern relatives, I was struck by the contrast between their genuine warmth and the paranoia of some Northern kin. Every Southern cousin I contacted eagerly awaited our meeting; some had even followed my journalistic work. Their openness made me question the apprehensions and misguided warnings that for years had prevented our Northern family learning about our Alabama heritage. The most heartwarming welcome came from Rosa Lee Pugh-Moore, Uncle Ike's last living daughter. My dad and I celebrated our unique familial connection—she is a double cousin, the daughter of my maternal granduncle, Uncle Ike (my dad's mother's brother), and his wife, my paternal grandaunt, Vora Hawkins-Pugh (my dad's father's sister).

On a brisk January afternoon, I arrived at the modern, suburban brick home of my cousin Jean, who helped care for Cousin Rosa. In her late eighties, the five-time-cancer-survivor Rosa sat in the rightmost corner of the couch, exuding regal charm. Her cinnamon complexion mirrored her father's flawless skin. She sported fashionable Armani-like tortoiseshell glasses, silver hair elegantly styled, and a royal blue silk patterned blouse that highlighted her warm half-smile. With open arms, she beckoned me closer.

"Well hello, Lee," she said in a soft, high-pitched voice, echoing the Southern accent of my other Alabama-born, soprano-speaking aunties who had helped raise me in Minnesota. I kissed her soft cheek and embraced her tightly, feeling a connection to my grandma Opie and the previous generations of elegant, pearl-and-dress-wearing Pugh and Hawkins women. As I held her, I saw a glimmer of my grandma Charity in her deep cerulean eyes. Beside her sat three generations of younger, equally striking Pugh women, including a great-great-granddaughter less than a month old.

The baby's early twenties-something mother told me that she had recently moved from Birmingham to Atlanta. "I've been back a few times," she told me. "Grandma made sure I came back to vote."

The room, primarily filled with younger women, fell quiet as I began my interview with Cousin Rosa. Within minutes, around thirty more family members arrived, greeted warmly by the group. I remembered that when I'd arranged the meeting, I learned Rosa's family was planning her eighty-ninth birthday celebration for January 28. Soon, the house was filled with Pugh family members spanning all ages.

Before anything else, they approached Cousin Rosa to kiss her. Rosa introduced me to each one, saying, "This is Lee Hawkins, our cousin from New York. He's asking me questions about the family." They joined the circle around us, and Rosa held her audience rapt with her stories.

Rosa exuded politeness, particularly with her grandchildren and her newest great-great-granddaughter, whom she lovingly held. But like Grandma Charity, Rosa had been fearless throughout her life. She walked grueling miles as part of her participation in the Montgomery bus boycott in the mid-1950s. When she described her daily journey, the grandchildren around her were amazed to learn it covered well over ten miles. Remarkably, she had even served as a physical therapy nurse for the infamous Alabama segregationist Theophilus Eugene "Bull" Connor. "He and I had an understanding," she confided to me—a graceful way of saying he knew better than to mess with her.

Observing Cousin Rosa from across the room, I felt a tangible sense of what seeing Grandma Charity in person might have been like. However, Rosa lacked the notorious meanness that had made our shared ancestor legendary. Watching her quiet but resolute confidence and the respect her children afforded her gave me insights into Grandma Charity's family reputation in the 1800s and early 1900s. In her later years, Grandma Charity was cared for by many young children and grandchildren who had all experienced her wrath. While Uncle Ike and his siblings privately decried her severity, they never dared confront her. Instinctively, they knew the trauma she'd faced, even if it was unspoken.

"Daddy said that Grandma Charity was one of the meanest heifers he ever saw," Cousin Rosa said, laughing. "I never heard my daddy say anything bad about anybody. But Grandma Charity? Daddy did not like her. I don't know what she did to him, but he didn't like her. She had a tough background. I don't know if they . . ." Rosa paused, looking

238 | Lee Hawkins

at the ceiling. "Well, I can't say. I suppose she was still protecting herself, given what she lived through."

During my visit, I found it confounding that while some relatives were familiar with Grandma Charity, not a single one, even Cousin Rosa, was aware of Jesse Pugh or our familial ties to white enslavers. Surprisingly, I provided them with more insights from my research than they gave me, affirming that my genealogical investigation was on track.

For instance, I shared with them that on May 15, 1831, the white Pugh brothers established a church named Beulah, viewing it as their passage to heaven. The *Troy (Alabama) Messenger* newspaper said the church represented the heavenly Zion. Over time, the Pughs were regarded as embodiments of white Protestant values, their church serving as a tangible representation of their spiritual aspirations. Positioned beside a family cemetery, the church became the burial site for many elder members of my white blood ancestors, notably from the white Pugh and Stinson families. When I stumbled upon the *Troy Messenger* piece in 2015, the name Stinson meant nothing to me. Yet, its deep ties to my family's story would soon be revealed.

The *Troy Messenger* declared that the Pughs "came here and reclaimed this fair land from the planted savage." The settlers referred to these people as the "Creek Indians," a name likely derived from the rivers and creeks where they lived in the southeastern United States. These people were part of the larger Muscogee (or Muskogee) confederacy. Today, they are more accurately known as the "Muscogee," reflecting their true identity as Indigenous or First Nations people and honoring their role as the original stewards of the land. The paper overlooked the contradiction between this so-called reclaiming and Christian values, echoing the widespread antebellum belief that Alabama was inherently meant for white Christian men.

The actions of the white Pugh men contradicted Jesus Christ's teachings. Their portrayal of a Eurocentric Jesus wrongly linked American genocide and chattel enslavement to him. My greatest concern was the mention in historical accounts that enslaved people, potentially my ancestors, attended the inaugural services of Beulah Primitive Baptist Church. Some have misinterpreted such stories, mistakenly labeling Christianity as a "white supremacist religion." This perspective overlooks that emigrant enslavers like the Pughs manipulated Christianity, presenting themselves as the pioneers of numerous advancements and molding a country that aligned with their interests, fortified by discriminatory laws and violence in the name of Jesus.

However, I must accept my family's and nation's history, including the reality that Jesse Pugh is my ancestor. While I can't alter history, I'm committed to understanding it.

Seeking information about the Pughs and Stinsons, I studied newspaper articles and public archives. Jesse Pugh, who might be my third great-grandfather, and his sibling Lewis, originated from near Richmond, Virginia. They ventured to Alabama around 1820, journeying through the Carolinas and Tennessee. A veteran of the War of 1812, Jesse was among the wave of white settlers who expanded southward, spurred by the war. As Alabama achieved statehood in 1819, the Pugh brothers became part of the surge of white settlers. They developed lands forcibly taken from the Creek Indians, relying on Grandma Charity and others to cultivate it. From the 1800s to the 1840s, Alabama was characterized by rampant violence, primarily aimed at overtaking Indigenous territories.

Jesse and Lewis weren't particularly wealthy, but Jesse's two-hundred-acre plantation positioned him within the upper middle class. By the mid-1850s, about a third of white families in slave states possessed enslaved people. Jesse Pugh enslaved twenty, including Grandmas Charity and Laner. Nationwide, ownership of enslaved people symbolized prosperity and a desired status. A 2015 *Slate* article by Jamelle Bouie and Rebecca Onion titled "Slavery Myths Debunked" cites the 1860 census, which showed that more than 32 percent of white families in future Confederate states owned enslaved people—a proportion akin to today's percentage of college-educated Americans. Contrary to widespread belief, the majority of enslavers were not opulent plantation owners but smaller-scale farmers like

Jesse, whose 1852 will showed how the stroke of a pen impacted my family for generations. Upon revisiting the will, I recognized names beyond those of my familiar ancestors: "I give and bequeath to my Daughter Malinda Stinson, now a widow, Lucy, a Negro Woman, and her child Silas. These Negroes shall belong to my daughter Malinda during her lifetime and, upon her decease, shall pass on to her children." In the next sentence, Pugh gave his son Burrell (Malinda Stinson's brother) "Laner, a Negro Woman, and her offspring." The Stinson-Pugh connection was becoming clear.

Jesse and Lewis Pugh married sisters from the Graves-Sims family: Jesse wed Lidia Graves-Sims, and Lewis chose Rebecca Graves-Sims. Tracing back the Graves lineage led me to Virginia's "first families" of the 1600s. As for the white Pughs, their earliest known ancestor in America, a Lewis Pugh who shares a name with Jesse's brother, arrived in Richmond, Virginia, from Merionethshire, Wales, in 1695. The Pugh surname DNA project clarifies "Pugh" as originating from the Welsh term "ap-Hugh," denoting "son of Hugh." Today, the surname is found globally: 70 percent of Pughs are white, and 27 percent, Black.

The mistresses of the Pugh plantations, Lidia and Rebecca, likely held significant sway over my Black ancestors' lives. The possibility that Lidia was one of my grandmothers (through one of her descendants who raped Grandma Charity) became an undeniable reality when I saw my DNA results.

As days of my research turned into weeks, a glaring incongruence emerged: the devout claims of the white Pughs starkly contrasted with their unjust actions, a pattern evident in many white Christian slaveholders of that time. They twisted biblical teachings to legitimize abuse—a practice I observed centuries later in the Black Hawkins home. I couldn't help but wonder whether these white Christian ancestors of mine ever faced divine consequences for killing and enslaving people in God's name.

42

Unfolding of the Curse

O n the evening of January 26, 1837, a sniper crept onto a house roof overlooking Lewis Pugh's Barbour County plantation and cemetery and fired on the overseer of Pugh's enslaved people, Jacob Herron, who died instantly. Soon after, sixty Creek Indians descended on the Pugh residence, killing Lewis, his son Joel, and an enslaved infant in his terrified mother's arms. When four enslaved men tried to defend themselves and the plantation, the Creeks killed them, too.

The ambush shattered the illusion that the Creek revolt in Alabama and other Gulf states had subsided. Lewis's murder marked the beginning of an extended Creek attack on whites in Barbour County. Eventually, the Creeks' quest to defend their land failed, and they were forced to move west in what later became known as the Creek Trail of Tears. The deadly attack on the Lewis Pugh estate became national news, instilling fear among whites across the United States.

The *Weekly Standard* of Raleigh, North Carolina, carried a report that was first published in the *Montgomery Advertiser* in Alabama on February 15, 1837. The article quoted the account of the enslaved woman:

> This child was slightly wounded—she says the last she saw of her master [Mr. Pugh] was running down a hill, [with] some 15 or 20 Indians in pursuit. He has not since been heard from and is probably killed. Two of a party of eight, sent to reconnoiter the house on the following evening, were killed. The Indians who committed these murders are supposed to be a portion of those who were left in the friendly camps until the return of the Creek Warriors from Florida.

I wondered what set such violence in motion, so I sought out more information about the way white settlers treated the Indigenous peoples at the time.

Historian John Ellisor, author of *The Second Creek War: Interethnic Conflict and Collusion on a Collapsing Frontier*, believes that Lewis Pugh's murder could have been in retaliation for land fraud. He has cited reports that suggest that Lewis had been fighting with the Seminoles, leading to the Creek attack. The violent culture in Alabama persisted, and the Pughs became one of the many families affected.

After reading newspaper accounts of Lewis Pugh's death, I contacted Ellisor and other experts to get a better sense of how the Pugh brothers positioned themselves to be landowners and enslavers in America. Ellisor's response to me included this remarkable comment: "My family has been in Alabama since 1819 and I have always thought of the place as having a curse of violence extending through it since the old days of enslavement and Creek displacement."

I asked him to elaborate.

"I'm not sure if I'm talking about a sociological thing that is explainable from violent origins, or something else," he told me. "I just know that at certain points, you can feel things. And this is the old question of what do we know empirically, or do we know from some other dimension or realm? I just call it a curse."

The Creek, original inhabitants of the land, suffered violence, deceit, and theft at the hands of the US government and white settlers. My research on the Pughs gave me a deeper understanding of the government's treatment of Indigenous peoples, changing my view of the $20 bill, for instance, which features the countenance of President Andrew Jackson. General Andrew Jackson's role in the first Creek War (1813–1814) opened the way for white settlers like Jesse Pugh to establish farms in Georgia and Alabama using enslaved labor. This violent period of wealth accumulation lasted about twenty-five years. The Second Creek War, sparked in 1836 by land speculators and squatters seeking to dispossess the Muscogee Creek Indigenous people of their remaining lands in nine Alabama counties, was a result of fraudulent dealings by unscrupulous whites that led to starvation and rebellion. This conflict ended in the Creeks' defeat and forced removal west.

At an Independence Day event in Pike County, Alabama, a Creek War veteran raised a toast, saying, "To the Creek War. May this history never be written, and if written, expunged." This underscores that attempts to erase white Americans' heinous acts against people of color aren't new. Long before Florida's push in the 2020s to whitewash history in schools, efforts existed to omit crimes against Indigenous and Black populations. According to Ellisor, Georgians, aware that their actions stemmed from land fraud, felt shame both for their deeds and for their poor performances in the war.

Tensions between established Alabama settlers and incoming Georgians intensified across the state, with the Federal Road, connecting Washington, DC, to New Orleans, contributing to the ignition of the first Creek War. The government surveyed the land, allotting portions to Creek families and opening the rest for settlement. This allowed the Creeks to either keep their Alabama land or sell it and relocate to Oklahoma, where many still reside today. Yet, it also drew in Georgian land speculators, whiskey dealers, and outlaws eager to stake their claims on prime cotton and plantation lands. "They just swindled the Creeks out of all this land," Ellisor said, "and particularly the big land companies like the Columbus Land Company that was operating out of Columbus, Georgia."

The Creeks were systematically defrauded of their land in numerous ways. Christopher D. Haveman, an expert on the Indian removal policy, details the methods used to dispossess the Creeks in his book *Rivers of Sand: Creek Indian Emigration, Relocation, and Ethnic Cleansing in the American South*. He explains that the federal government sent commissioners to obtain treaties from Indigenous nations, and when the Indigenous people resisted, the commissioners would find a Creek willing to betray their own people. In the Creeks' case, it was William McIntosh, a high-ranking headman who had previously ceded Creek land for money. McIntosh and about fifty associates signed a land cession treaty in 1825. None of the signers, besides McIntosh, held any rank in the Creek Nation.

Haveman describes many fraudulent tactics whites used to gain control over Creek lands. Alcohol was used against Creeks, who signed away their land while intoxicated or were forced to use their land as collateral to pay for debts from buying whiskey on credit. In some instances, whites pretended to be lawyers offering to help prevent fraud but instead tricked many Creeks into giving up their land. Also common was "personation," which involved a speculator bribing a Creek to impersonate a landowner. The speculator targeted starving Creeks who were desperate enough to betray their own people. They would meet with a federally appointed certifying agent to confirm the Creek's willingness to sell. Once the agent walked away, the impersonator would hand over almost all the money. Another common fraud was taking back the purchase money after a sale. Haveman recounts an incident where a powerful Creek headman sold his land for $1,000, but one of the buyers pickpocketed the money during a diversionary hug.

It is unclear how the Pugh brothers obtained their land, but given the widespread fraud and theft of Indigenous land at the time, it is likely they used similar tactics. Records show that at least one person with the Pugh surname may have engaged in questionable land dealings. Haveman discovered letters from Francis W. Pugh to the Bureau of Indian Affairs, inquiring about Creek land allotments and discussing land frauds. Pugh's name appears on a list of fraudulent contracts. He bought land from Eufaula Harjo, a Creek Indian, for $200, and the investigator noted that the money was taken back after the certifying agent had left. F. W. Pugh was an attorney and the second white settler to build a house in Eufaula, Alabama. He lived close to Lewis Pugh, but it is uncertain whether the two men were connected or shared land transactions related to Indian lands. I did find a US Department of the Interior record that granted seventy-nine acres to Lewis Pugh, signed by Pugh and President Andrew Jackson in 1829. There was no mention of any cash amount, and none of the land records inspected indicated any malfeasance by the Pugh brothers.

That said, both Haveman and Ellisor said that most of the land in new Alabama was stolen from Indigenous peoples in one way or another, and the Pugh brothers likely were no exception. "Most all of that land in Barbour County was very likely stolen. The land companies had various tricks. Sometimes they would get an Indian drunk, pay him $10, and tell him to go to the land office, and negotiate the sale when the land did not belong to him," Ellisor said. "There were cases of Indians just getting murdered, and people moving onto their land. It happened in all kinds of ways. These people were in debt, and you would tell them, 'Well, you are in so much debt. You can't pay it, give me your land.' . . . There were all kinds of ways to get land away from people. And I just think it's probable that Lewis Pugh did not get his land legally."

Despite not being among the super-planter elite, the Pughs fared well compared with most Alabama farming families, having considerable property, livestock, enslaved people, and cash. Jesse Pugh honored his brother by naming two of his children after him—Lewis Harrison, born in 1814, and Louise, born in 1827. Yet, his brother's namesake, Lewis Harrison Pugh, couldn't escape retaliatory violence, another part of Ellisor's "curse of violence."

Jesse's son, Lewis Harrison Pugh, grew up on the plantation where Grandma Charity had been enslaved into the 1850s. Amid war, violence, and loss, Lewis Harrison's life was marked by violence. In 1862, he and other Pugh men joined the Confederate Army's 50th Infantry Regiment. He fought in the Battle of Chickamauga, a Confederate victory that nonetheless had more than thirty thousand Union and Confederate casualties and losses.

Lewis H. survived the Civil War but experienced the tragic loss of his parents, six siblings, and four children. This string of family deaths began when he was thirty-six and continued until May 14, 1889, when his wife of fifty years passed away. Two weeks later, an air of death and violence still permeated the Pugh estate.

According to the *Montgomery Advertiser*, on the evening of May 28, 1889, shortly after the seventy-five-year-old Lewis and his thirteen-year-old grandson, James A. Pugh, went to bed, they were startled by a

246 | Lee Hawkins

noise near one of the front windows. It didn't sound like the wind or a critter, but an intruder trying to pry open the window.

"Grandfather jumped up and reached for his gun, but before he could use it, in an instant, the window was thrown open. I saw a flash of light and heard a gunshot," James told the newspaper.

Lewis collapsed by the bed, dead. The entire shot from the burglar's gun had burrowed into his neck, killing him instantly. The shaken boy, witnessing his grandfather's head nearly blown clean off, sprang up amidst the blood-soaked scene. One of the intruders commanded him to blow out the lamp or he'd shoot the boy.

So James extinguished the lamp and darted back to his bed. But they shot at him anyway; he rolled off the bed, wounded, and crawled under it.

While James hid under the bed, the robbers took Lewis H.'s trunk and then left through the window. Convinced they were gone, he got up, put on his pants, and sneaked out the back door without shoes or coat, heading in the opposite direction of the robbers' path.

"I ran to an old Negro's house about a quarter of a mile from the house and told him what had happened," the boy said. "I was sick and scared and weak, and the old Negro picked me up and helped me to my father's house, about a mile and a half away."

The wounded boy, James, and his "Negro" savior reached the house of James's father, John Pugh, and after he and a neighbor determined that James's wound was superficial, the boy and the men returned to the crime scene. Outside the house, they found the forced-open window and not far away lay Lewis's broken open trunk, abandoned by the robbers.

Days after the incident, the *Montgomery Advertiser* interviewed James Pugh, who said he didn't know how much money was in the trunk, but people around the neighborhood knew Lewis often had a "considerable sum" on hand. The paper reported, "It was supposed that the robbers got several thousand dollars."

James Pugh told the paper that his father "had several Negroes arrested on the suspicion and a search for the stolen property was instituted." But up to that point, with the crime scene still fresh, "nothing had been found and no clue to the identity of the murderers had been obtained." But amid all the uncertainty, one thing was clear: "The little boy says the crime was committed by Negroes and thinks he recognized the voice of a Negro who lives in the neighborhood." The article continues with "the natural supposition" that "the murder and robbery were committed by Negroes who lived on Mr. Pugh's place or in the immediate vicinity, who knew the facts and surroundings."

The story raised concerns about the fate of the "several Negroes arrested." The boy had only heard a voice, yet his word was more credible than the denials of any "Negro" suspect. Indeed, any Black man in town could be hanged on the word of a white child, with no escape from lynching or a coerced confession.

The missing money in Lewis Harrison Pugh's case was never recovered. Yet, the era's racial dynamics, and the "curse" of violence, ensured that some "Negro," recognizable by young James Pugh or not, would suffer, evidence notwithstanding.

A century later, my parents whipped me in hopes of "protecting" me from similar injustice.

43

Papa Lum, a Child of Dead Fall, Alabama

When my dad and I interviewed Uncle Ike Pugh in 1991, I regret not asking more about my dad's father, Columbus "Lum" Hawkins, especially considering that Uncle Ike's wife, Vora, was Papa Lum's sister, thus, Uncle Ike was my granduncle by marriage. Talking more with Uncle Ike could have shed light on Papa Lum, our elusive patriarch, as he was Uncle Ike's brother-in-law.

Public records offer only a smattering of information about Papa Lum. His birthdate is one of many mysteries, with census records indicating various years ranging from 1898 to 1903. He was the child of Henry Hawkins Sr. and Mary Coleman, growing up as one of seven siblings. By the time my father came into the world, Papa Lum was a whopping fifty years old.

I'm still not sure exactly how my family got the name Hawkins, but my research and oral histories have revealed some of Papa Lum's early struggles, which had lasting effects into my childhood.

Papa Lum was born twenty years after the establishment of Jim Crow in a stormy town named Dead Fall, Alabama, about ten miles from Greenville, a fact that put everything I had heard about his propensity toward violence—mainly fighting and gun assault—into better focus. Dead Fall's name "was bestowed for the reputation it bore for bloody fights, there being several every day," according to *The History of Butler County, Alabama, from 1815 to 1885*.

In 2018 and 2019, I searched for genealogical information on Papa Lum and his family, and in the process, I found an article about a Henry Hawkins who was murdered in 1905 in Evergreen, Alabama. An elderly cousin in Houston later confirmed that this Henry Hawkins was indeed our ancestor—my great-grandfather.

Discovering the truth about the murder of Papa Lum's father, when Papa Lum was only seven years old, was pivotal for understanding Papa Lum's life and the devastating effects on him of that murder. As I studied the article, it dawned on me that both of my father's parents had lost their fathers to murder when they were only children. Few knew of Papa Lum's hidden pain—that his father was ruthlessly killed by a white man who faced no justice. Despite the surrounding silence, each generation inherited an unspoken toll. Carrying such secrets, much like guns, can be lethal.

Census records show that my great-grandfather Henry Hawkins Sr. was born in South Carolina around 1854 to Lewis and Angeline Hawkins. Although the records indicate that his father was from Alabama and his mother from Mississippi, I have yet to discover the reasons that led the family to leave South Carolina and settle in Alabama. The 1900 census reveals that Henry Hawkins and my great-grandmother Mary "Mollie" Coleman-Hawkins were married in 1891 when he was twenty-six and she was nineteen and that they lived in Dead Fall with their five children.

After my cousin's revelation helped me confirm that the man mentioned in the article was indeed our family patriarch, I revisited it—"Saturday Tragedy," in the June 21, 1905, edition of the *Evergreen Courant*. It provided no information about the fate of the shooter:

On Saturday afternoon, Edward Stamps shot and killed Henry Hawkins, a negro, in the powerhouse of the electric light plant. Two bullets from the pistol took effect, one in the head and the other in the breast. The negro lived probably fifteen minutes. Stamps at once surrendered to the Sheriff and was in his custody until Monday afternoon, when he was given a preliminary trial before Justice, which resulted in binding the defendant over to the grand jury, the bond being fixed at $300, which was promptly made.

Aunt Corene later shared the faint but astonishing detail that she remembered hearing as a child: Stamps put my great-grandfather

Henry Hawkins's bloody corpse in a wagon and parked it in front of the Hawkins home for his wife, Mary, and his children to find. That memory of his dead father sprawled across that wagon was no doubt burned into Papa Lum's mind forever. I could find no records or other evidence that Stamps was ever convicted, or even tried, for my great-grandfather's murder—a reality that certainly would have compounded the family's pain. The article did not mention a motive.

But Stamps met a violent demise himself seven years later, when he was shot to death on August 21, 1912, by a white man named J. Mizell, who was evidently the mayor of the town where the killing occurred. The article in the local paper read:

> Edward G. Stamps was shot and killed this morning in Samson by mayor Mizell. This news was conveyed to J. H. Stamps, father of the dead man, in a telegram received here about 7 o'clock from the depot agent in Samson. No particulars concerning the tragedy could be learned. The remains will be brought here for interment probably tomorrow.

In contrast to the Hawkinses, the white Stamps family received justice. Mizell, the perpetrator, was convicted of second-degree murder in February 1913, following seventeen hours of deliberation by the jury. The judge sentenced him to twenty-five years in the Alabama State Penitentiary.

The murder of his father could be the thing that stirred the astonishing no-nonsense posture Papa Lum often took with anybody of any race who crossed him. Like Grandma Charity fighting back against would-be attackers, still grieving for her murdered son, Lum Hawkins was widely known as a notorious Negro who could be mean and violent when pushed—especially when it came to protecting his daughters. In fact, some family members say that the muscular, six-foot-four-inch, 225-pound giant fought for recreation, often going home with a black eye or bloodied nose after pummeling a drinking buddy at a bar. Dad, a young boy, would wince in worry, watching Grandma Opie treat Papa Lum's bruised and bloodied face.

Papa Lum's childhood was marked by his father's untimely murder. This tragedy propelled him and his brothers into becoming the primary family providers, laboring in the fields to sustain their mother and siblings. Consequently, he had to leave school when he was only in first grade, and the 1920 census record of Papa Lum's family indicated "Read: No. Write: No." This stood out to me. Even after the end of Jim Crow in 1965, I'm unsure whether he ever acquired those skills. No family member ever mentioned his illiteracy, leaving me to speculate.

This discovery wasn't entirely surprising. Data from the National Center for Education Statistics highlight that illiteracy was widespread among Americans in the late 1800s and early 1900s. In 1870, 20 percent of all American adults couldn't read or write. For the Black population, this figure was an alarming 80 percent. By 1900, the rate among Blacks had decreased but still remained high at 44 percent. Reflecting on my great-grandfather's tragic end, I recognized how race-based violence and discrimination hindered more than just emotional well-being. It disrupted children's education, leading many to leave school and intensifying the issue of illiteracy.

Upon leaving school, Papa Lum and his brothers found work in Bolling, Alabama, doing odd jobs for local families. They eventually moved to Greenville for employment on the railroad, but they always sent money back to their mother, Mary. Lum often returned to visit her, persuading her to relocate to Greenville. Sadly, she passed away before making the move.

This legacy of adversity resonated across generations, evident in my parents' anxiety and hypervigilance. I realized that, like the Black families I'd written about during my journalism career—those affected by the Tulsa Massacre, lynchings, or violence from within their communities—I too hail from a lineage touched by violence. My writings on "homicide survivors" and their PTSD symptoms suddenly took on a personal dimension. The shock, grief, and anxiety I'd researched were manifested in my parents. The knowledge that both of my father's grandfathers had been murdered shed light on the trauma my father passed down to me. Papa Lum's anger, ignited by his father's killing, was mirrored in my own father's temper. Likewise, because of the murder of Great-Grandpa Ike Pugh, Uncle Ike carried and understood that same anger until his last days.

44

A Snapshot of the White-Looking Man

Although I regret not asking Uncle Ike more about Papa Lum during our 1991 interview, its significance dawned on me only years later. Uncle Ike's tale of his father's tragic murder remained with me, often revisited in conversations with my dad. Our mutual interest in the story persisted. However, it was my deep dive into genealogical research that led me to governmental records and old newspaper articles that echoed Uncle Ike's narrative.

This exposed precious details about the brief, enigmatic life of my great-grandfather Ike Pugh Sr., born in either 1860 or 1862 as per varying records. I felt a connection to him that seemed to transcend time. This was more than just an exploration of family history; it was a spiritual journey that deepened my understanding of the people and experiences that shaped me and my upbringing. I came to realize that a researcher can develop a fervent love for the ancestors whose lives they painstakingly reconstruct, even without the privilege of ever meeting them.

Great-Grandfather Ike Pugh was born into enslavement. It's a realization I can't quite get my head around: *my dad's grandfather, my great-grandfather, was born a slave.* I was educated to view enslavement as an artifact of the distant past, but it extends back a mere two generations—a remarkably brief period of time that amounts to a cosmic millisecond. I especially understand this because of the fact that my maternal great-grandparents shaped so much of my life.

Grandpa Ike was likely born in Butler County on the plantation of Mastin Pugh, Jesse Pugh's son, under the care of his mother, Grandma

Charity. By the 1880 census, he and Grandma Charity lived in Hawkins-
ville, Alabama, in Barbour County. The census recorded him as a twenty-
year-old "farmer/laborer" and "stepson" in the household of a Black couple,
Brad and Martha Dale. I presume that Grandpa Ike worked on the Dale
farm and possibly another. This second residence helped explain why
many family members believed John Ransom Sirmon, a white man, was
Grandpa Ike's biological father. This belief came from Grandpa Ike living
apart from Grandma Charity for a time during his childhood, working
also for the Sirmon family. This raised questions about why a Black boy,
who looked white, born just a few years before emancipation, would live
with families other than his own, particularly a white family. Even though
Grandma Charity was free, her son lived with others, even though she and
her husband, Tom Mullens, had their own children.

The improbability of Grandpa Ike being biologically related to the
Sirmon family added to the mystery of his ancestry. For years, I'd accepted family claims and assertions on genealogy websites that Sirmon
was Ike's father. Doubts arose after my DNA analysis revealed no match
with any Sirmon bloodline. Nor did I know of any matches among
my cousins. I couldn't completely dismiss the claim, but I categorized
it like the unverified legend that Grandma Charity was Cherokee. I
also thought of the white Sirmon descendants who must have been
perplexed and disturbed by claims that their married patriarch had im-
pregnated an enslaved Black woman—bold claims without DNA evidence connecting the families. My discovery of Sirmon's relationship
with my family shed light on a significant aspect of Southern history—
the complex interweaving of Black, white, and Indigenous lives during
the worst periods of enslavement and Jim Crow segregation.

Despite the prevailing white supremacy of their time, my family's
connections with Sirmon, seen by some as friendly or even intimate,
revealed surprising interactions between whites and Blacks. These
relationships sometimes led to varying degrees of coexistence, occasionally within the same household, revealing the existence of whites
who, by the standards of the time, might be considered "good," despite the racist context that complicated such judgments. My insights
into the relationship with Sirmon were not the last examples of such

intricate complexities I would uncover. I'm reminded of Cousin Rosa's telling remark about providing physical therapy services to Bull Connor: "We had an understanding."

By pure coincidence, the tape of my interview with Uncle Ike yielded a breakthrough. Replaying the recording for the umpteenth time, I heard my father ask Uncle Ike who Grandpa Ike's father was. "Master Stinson," Uncle Ike clearly and confidently answered, without pause.

Stinson. I knew the name but wasn't sure why. I searched online for "Pugh" and "Stinson." Eventually, I found Jesse Pugh's will, which mentioned his daughter Malinda Stinson and the inheritance of enslaved people. Malinda was married to Micaiah Stinson, who passed away in 1848, making it impossible for him to be Grandpa Ike's father, given his birth year of 1860. Nevertheless, Malinda and Micaiah had two adult sons, Joshua L. and Jasper Newton Stinson, who were born in Pike County, near Jesse Pugh's plantation where Grandma Charity was enslaved. When Jesse Pugh wrote his will in 1852, both sons lived in Butler County. Their mother died the same year, and they inherited her enslaved people.

One of the Stinson brothers likely could have been the father of my great-grandfather Ike Pugh Sr. A DNA expert had told me that Grandpa Ike's paternal DNA very possibly could be traced to a son of one of Jesse and Lidia's daughters, but there was no way to be scientifically certain. However, I wondered why Grandpa Ike adopted the Pugh surname instead of Stinson. After emancipation, former enslaved people often took the surnames of their former enslavers, a choice that affected their descendants for generations. Their children typically adopted these names too, for consistency and continuity. Moreover, as noted by the *Troy Messenger*, the Stinson and Pugh names were interchangeable in Pike County.

Joshua Stinson died in the Civil War at Barlow's Mill on December 15, 1861. Jasper was killed during the Battle of Second Manassas (also known as the Second Battle of Bull Run) on August 28, 1862, a bloody Confederate victory led by Robert E. Lee involving Alabama's Conecuh County unit. Coincidentally, my maternal great-great-grandfather Private Isaac Blakey fought against Jasper Stinson in that battle on the Union side.

In short, I may well be descended from two great-great-grandfathers who fought on opposing sides in a legendary battle of the Civil War, with the enslaver dying and the formerly enslaved surviving and thriving into the twentieth century. That date—August 28—was again proving its significance in this intricate web of connections, far beyond anything having to do with my birthday. But another astonishing revelation awaited me—that Jasper Stinson wasn't the only relative of mine (and his) who perished on that very day.

In addition to Grandpa Ike never knowing his white biological father, his light skin drew resentment from his darker stepfather, Tom Mullens, and perhaps even his half-siblings. Since Grandpa Ike was a light-skinned Black man who didn't pass as white, white Alabama mostly viewed him like any other Black man. His mixed heritage allegedly exposed him to both favoritism and scorn, particularly from Mullens, who resented him as the son of "Master Stinson."

Mullens worked for a white jail warden and enforced the cruel system that allowed private businesses to "lease" imprisoned Black men for unpaid, grueling labor. Records show that other men fathered children with Grandma Charity during her marriage to Mullens, which probably compounded his anger. In 1866, Charity gave birth to Hulda Pugh, followed by Thomas Mullens Jr. in 1868 and Adam Pugh in 1869. Thomas Mullens Sr. identified himself as the stepfather of the Pugh children, who were listed as the offspring of Reuben Pugh, a former enslaved man of Jesse Pugh.

The spiteful Mullens schemed attacks on Grandpa Ike to appear accidental. Once, while working in the fields, Mullens told Ike to climb a tree and started chopping it with an ax, hoping this would harm or kill him. Although Grandma Charity knew of the abuse, it continued until a white man, likely Sirmon, witnessed it and offered to take in Grandpa Ike, compensating Charity and Mullens for his labor. Charity's decision was profitable but turned Grandpa Ike into property, akin to the convict leasing programs.

As outlined in a report by the Constitutional Rights Foundation on Slave and Black Codes, the Black Codes implemented during Reconstruction and beyond granted white families control over Black orphans, children of vagrants or impoverished parents, and even Black families who willingly rented them out. Courts could forcibly apprentice these children to employers, giving them control until males turned twenty-one and females eighteen. While employers could administer punishments and recapture runaways, they were also required to provide food and clothing, teach a trade, and ensure education.

Since Grandpa Ike was raised by a "crazy" mother and a shell-shocked stepfather who had endured enslavement, I wondered how badly he was whipped as a boy and whether he felt abandoned by his mother for being put in a situation reminiscent of enslavement—a reality he had narrowly escaped, being born just before emancipation. Grandpa Ike Sr. grew up in an era when Black males not employed by a white institution or landowner often struggled to avoid imprisonment and enslavement-like labor. The threat of incarceration hung over his life, and generations later, my Black parents and millions of others would continue whipping their own children based on that same fear. The traps of the 1860s foreshadowed the traps of the 1980s. More than a century later, I and many of Grandpa Ike Sr.'s other descendants wrestled with a perpetual state of identity crisis, feeling caught between worlds. Grandpa Ike was "too Black" to be white and "too white" to be Black, caught in a nineteenth-century "real nigga" versus "acting white" dilemma, motivated by a stepfather who saw a reminder of Master Stinson in their every interaction. Determined to achieve independence, he honed the hunting, fishing, farming, and trapping skills he likely learned from Sirmon or Dale.

Grandpa Ike had a natural green thumb, so despite his lack of formal education, he was a sought-after farmer from an early age. "As a farmer, he could do anything," my cousin Raymond Pugh told me from stories he'd heard. "Any kind of crop there was, he could grow it. Any kind of animal, he could hunt it and prepare the game for a meal." He continued, "When Mullens mistreated him, it fueled his desire to prove his worth and survive."

In his late teens, Grandpa Ike used his experiences in Greenville's farming community to prepare for his escape plans: marrying, having children, and purchasing land and a farm for his children to work.

In 1883, when he was around twenty-three years old and working on farms, Grandpa Ike married his first wife, Nancy, the daughter of neighbors to Grandma Charity and Mullens. This union finally gave him a stable family. He and Grandma Nancy had their first child, Missouri Pugh, in 1874, followed by six more over the next eight years. In a grievous turn of events, Nancy died during childbirth, leaving Ike a widower with seven young children and a newborn, Hillery, a surviving twin. In these trying times, the terrifyingly ubiquitous Grandma Charity likely provided significant support.

With his mother babysitting, Grandpa Ike intensified his farming, hunting, and trapping businesses. Uncle Ike recollected that his father eventually acquired a total of ninety-five acres in two locations in Butler County. Grandpa Ike remarried in 1893 to my great-grandmother, Ella Long-Pugh, who was twenty-three. According to their marriage certificate, the two had known each other since childhood. They wasted no time expanding the family, with Uncle Ike their firstborn of eleven children and Grandma Opie their tenth.

Great-Grandpa Ike was more than just an outdoorsman; he was a master of the wild. This free-spirited woodsman once roamed the expansive Alabama forests, a hunter's rifle confidently resting on his shoulder. With every step, he was flanked by his meticulously trained pointer dogs, a team so attuned to their environment that they could track anything from a fleeting pheasant to a stealthy raccoon. With a sharp eye and steady hand, Ike could shoot a tin can out of any distant tree, displaying a prowess few could rival. It wasn't long before his talent extended beyond hunting, and he began selling fur to New York–based furriers. With this venture, his business soared, further cementing his legacy not only as an unrivaled hunter but also as an astute entrepreneur.

Grandpa Ike harbored a deep mistrust of banks, a skepticism rooted in the collapse of the Freedman's Savings Bank. Established in 1865 to serve African American veterans and the newly emancipated Black community, this bank crumbled during his teenage years because of mismanagement, financial speculation, and exploitation by white politicians and businessmen. Consequently, Ike chose a more personal approach to safeguard his earnings from farming and hunting. Like planting secret seeds, he buried gold and silver bars, along with bundles of cash, in hidden spots across his farm.

My dad's sister, known affectionately as Weenie, once shared about my great-grandparent: "He was white, Lee-Lee. Grandma Ella told us he was white." On the basis of his parents' backgrounds, Grandpa Ike was more than 60 percent white European. The photo of the white-looking man above Uncle Ike's fireplace was clear proof.

Grandpa Ike Sr. and Grandma Ella, both identifying as Black, nonetheless looked like an interracial couple at the 1870 dawn of the Jim Crow era, when miscegenation laws prohibited such relationships. Contemplating the challenges they must have faced in the late 1800s, particularly in light of the enduring controversy around interracial relationships today, I can't help but admire their courage and the strength of their love. Their union defied the white supremacist state that used lynching, whipping, fines, and imprisonment to keep Black couples apart. The fact that the risk of real or perceived interracial relationships could have been as dire as death highlights both their radicalism and their steadfast commitment to one another.

In a Greenville where his marriage was perceived by some as interracial, despite his own identification as Black, Grandpa Ike knew he had to be vigilant to protect himself and his family from potential harm—a feeling rooted in a gut-wrenching incident Aunt Weenie would often recount. One day, while riding his mule, Grandpa Ike spotted some white men up ahead, fueling what appeared to be a fire. Drawing nearer, he confronted a ghastly sight: they were burning people. The men, recognizing Grandpa Ike as the ostensibly white man who had defiantly embraced a Black identity, singled him out. "They tried to get him then," Aunt Weenie recalled, echoing the remorse Grandma Ella felt upon learning that the men had shouted "Nigger lover!" at him. Grandpa Ike narrowly escaped, but the ordeal etched an unforgettable mark on his psyche. From that point forward, he remained perpetually alert, ever watchful for emerging dangers beneath the foreboding Alabama night sky. Their family rebuked the oppressive Slave Codes I oppose today, compelling me to carry on their tradition of rebelliousness, iconoclasm, and resistance against the overseer mentality that still promotes limiting the freedom and choices of Black people in the twenty-first century.

Dad's sister Aunt Toopie lived with the blind and disabled Grandma Ella in her later years. The widow occasionally chatted giddily about her union with Grandpa Ike. She'd lean back in her rocking chair, wearing a random smile. "What's funny, Grandma?" Aunt Toopie would ask.

"I'm just thinking about my man," she'd reply.

The inquisitive Toopie asked, "Grandma, I want to know how come you married a man that was white, and they don't do that down here?"

"Well, let me tell you something, since you had the nerve to ask me that," Grandma responded. "That man was the best toward me I've ever known. He loved me, and I loved him. We got along very well until what happened to him." When Aunt Toopie asked what happened, Grandma Ella said only, "Well, he died."

"But still I had to ask," Aunt Toopie told me. Then she asked, "How did you marry?"

Grandma replied, "We jumped over a broom. I was a very happily married woman. And I had all my children with that man."

Grandma never mentioned that for years there had been rumors of Grandpa Ike's infidelity and out-of-wedlock children, which wasn't uncommon in the "original Baby Daddy" culture. But despite the tests of loyalty, Grandma Ella held firm.

Year-round, the couple busily tended livestock, harvested strawberries, and sold vegetables, cotton, and peanuts. And Ike continued to profit in Alabama's burgeoning fur trade.

From the beginning, Grandma Ella was a welcome relief for him and his overburdened mother, Grandma Charity. In farming families, couples often married young. In her mid-twenties, Grandma Ella was older than normal, so she assumed the demanding tasks of fieldwork and managing the bustling farm and household. She step-mothered six children and bore her own. As one pregnancy advanced, Grandpa Ike invited her sister Ruth to help, fearing a repeat of the tragedy that had taken his first wife. But Ruth's visit took an ignominious turn; she, too, became pregnant. It didn't take long for Grandma Ella to realize that Grandpa Ike was the father, but she forgave them both. A second pregnancy, though, was too much, and she sent Ruth away. "I still loved my sister," Grandma Ella told her granddaughters, "but she had to go."

45

A Patriarch's Possessions

Grandpa Ike had been in the midst of purchasing his next parcel of land, which had been eyed by a white farmer named Jack Taylor. Envy over the land had played a significant role in the conflict between the men. "They were jealous of him," Uncle Ike told me and my dad in 1991. Adding to the tension was a history of the Taylor family's goats feeding on the Pugh's crops, leading to confrontations. Yet the conflict wasn't only about land and trespassing goats; it was more complicated. Grandpa Ike, living freely and confidently as a Black man and not striving to "pass" as a white man, had been an irritation for the Taylors and many other white locals.

One day, after a tense discussion at Taylor's house about the land, Grandpa Ike, perhaps hoping that the talk had cleared the air, was riding his mule home when the quiet of the woods was ruptured by the crack of gunfire. An excruciating pain ripped through Grandpa Ike's back; he'd been ambushed, shot from behind. Grandpa Ike barely grasped what had happened when another shot found its mark between his shoulder blades. Emerging from a concealed position behind a tree or in a ditch (accounts differ), Taylor revealed himself, gun still smoking, as the one who'd betrayed a conversation with violence.

The mule raced back to the farm with Grandpa Ike still on her back and his feet still firmly planted in the stirrups. Ike's children, ranging in age from three to eighteen, along with Grandma Ella, rushed from the house. This scene was hauntingly similar to one just nine years earlier, when Papa Lum's family witnessed Great-Grandpa Henry Hawkins—my other great-grandfather—arriving home bloodied in a wagon. As they realized Grandpa Ike had lost consciousness and was slipping into delirium, they quickly removed his blood-soaked clothes and prayed with fervent desperation. But their prayers went unanswered, and Grandpa Ike died.

August 28 bore witness to a tragic tableau: their patriarch, motionless and prone, sending floods of poison through Grandma Opie, Uncle Ike, and their relatives. In a historical parallel, this date also marked the end for Jasper Newton Stinson in the Civil War in 1862. These two Pugh men, possibly father and son, led vastly different lives and held different societal positions but shared the same death date, fifty-two years apart. One died fighting to uphold white supremacy; the other was killed for defying it.

Grandpa Ike's bloodied body was laid on a cooling board in the family's house while burial plans were made. Realizing that Grandma Opie was only nine when she witnessed her father's lifeless form on that board, I reprimanded myself for previously feeling ashamed of her lamenting of Dr. King's activism, fearing he too would be killed. In fact, she accurately predicted his death, drawing from her own childhood nightmare that haunted her even more ferociously than my father's or mine ever did.

But the family couldn't grieve in peace. Less than a day after Grandpa Ike was killed, Uncle Ike recalled, his grieving survivors began to receive random late-night visits and a flurry of threats to their lives. Uncle Ike, who by then was married and living in Bolling, stayed with the family through the night, sitting wide-eyed with his shotgun ready. On the following morning, the frantic search began for Grandpa Ike's buried money. Everyone began to dig.

The events of the next few days likely stoked even greater anger in old man Taylor toward the family. The Greenville police arrested and jailed him as Pugh relatives from near and far arrived in Greenville for Grandpa Ike's funeral, comforted by the knowledge that Taylor would stand trial.

Throughout my childhood and teenage years, my aunts randomly bemoaned the "white folks killing our family members." It wasn't until 2018 that I finally found written proof of this claim. Under the blaring headline "WHITE FARMER SHOOTS NEGRO IN THE

BACK," the *Montgomery Advertiser* published a story on August 29, 1914, chronicling Taylor's confession and explanation for killing "the Negro." The story blamed the murder on livestock and one of Grandpa Ike's children:

> Greenville, Alabama—Aug. 28 Ike Pew, a negro farmer living on the plantation of Mr. D. Sirmon, was shot and killed last night by a white farmer named Jack Taylor. An Angora goat belonging to Mr. Taylor got into the field of Pew and was killed by a child of Pew. This is said to be the reason Taylor shot the Negro. The Negro was riding a mule when he received a load of buckshot in his back.

When I found the article, I immediately reached out to Dad. Finally, we had tangible evidence of Grandpa Ike's tragic end in 1914. The "hunting accident" his mother had spoken of in Dad's childhood was indeed the cold-blooded murder Uncle Ike had described. The newspaper pinpointed the murder to August 28—the day on which I would be born fifty-seven years later—a small but momentous detail.

That sad truth was laid out on September 16, when the *Montgomery Advertiser* published a follow-up to the story of Grandpa Ike's murder:

> The case of the state against Jack Taylor the white planter, who shot a Negro Ike Pew, was postponed for the third time today. They set a date for the hearing on September 26. Taylor is still confined in the jail. He is an old man, and being crippled he has to use crutches. There has been much sympathy aroused in Taylor's behalf.

On November 17, a short article in the paper confirmed that Jack Taylor had been acquitted in his trial for "unlawfully killing" my great-grandfather. The jury deliberated for "less than few minutes." The agony of Grandpa Ike's family upon hearing that their patriarch's murder would go unpunished is almost unimaginable to me.

But I also understand why, despite Taylor's admission that he had shot Grandpa Ike in the back, the white jurors acquitted and perhaps even applauded him. In the US South, Black landownership, especially by the formerly enslaved, was a revolutionary act. Slave Codes had prohibited such ownership during Grandpa Ike's early years. Yet, once allowed, Grandpa Ike and my maternal ancestors swiftly pursued the "uppity" act of daring to own. And Grandpa Ike wasn't the only one killed over land.

Though I am determined to continue searching for documents, I recognize that the legacy of Ike Pugh Sr. and his descendants is still both celebrated and fraught among people who know about him in Greenville. Even a century after the murder, cousins researching Grandpa Ike haven't always had an easy time doing so. One was told by a white worker at the Greenville courthouse, "You're researching Ike Pugh? That was more than a hundred years ago. Let that go."

In the courthouse's cold, dusty basement, records from the 1800s and 1900s are scattered and jumbled, like the contents of an overturned treasure chest, filled with yet-to-be discovered evidence of crimes against humanity. This chaos is a quiet guardian of Greenville's truths. The courthouse worker's effort to dissuade family members from examining the records reminds us that the white people in Greenville whose families have been there since any time before 1964 are descendants of those who profited from Jim Crow apartheid. What incentive do they have for those documents pertaining to the legacies of Black families to be organized, preserved, and made available to the lawyers, journalists, genealogists, and others who have descended from those ancestors?

46

Shadows and Seizures

ithin days of Jack Taylor's not-guilty verdict, with Grandpa Ike freshly buried, the family was hit with a barrage of midnight threats. Taylor and his mob of supporters had effectively executed a notorious strategy from the Jim Crow era: kill the Black patriarchs and assemble a group to intimidate their families until they are compelled to leave their homestead—essentially, their assets.

"Uncle Ike was the oldest boy, and he took Grandma Ella and the rest of the kids, and they all moved from that place at night to another little country town, somewhere out there," Aunt Toopie told me, recalling her grandmother's stories. "They had to move, because people started threatening them after they killed Grandpa."

Amidst the chilling threats and the raw mourning, Uncle Ike's fury swelled—resenting both the killing and being forced from the family's land. It's understandable that as a teenager, Uncle Ike plotted a plan for retaliation. Even in our 1991 interview, nearly eighty years after the tragedy, he seemed almost apologetic for not exacting vengeance.

Yet Grandma Ella, fearing the prospect of her dear sons facing a lynch mob, leaned heavily into her Christian faith, telling Uncle Ike to focus on the family's survival and let God handle Jack Taylor. Her counsel also bore the weight of the prevailing times, notably the ominous shadow of the KKK, which had gained ground nationwide up until the mid-1920s, reaching even the urban sprawls of the Midwest and West. Uncle Ike confided his conviction that the Klan and other vigilante groups were behind the Taylor-supporting white mob that drove the family from their home. Such reactions weren't isolated; thousands of Black families during the Jim Crow era—and even in more contemporary times—moved in search of safety and to distance themselves from irreversible memories. As Aunt Toopie put it, they sought "a place there where they be out there, far away, but close to family."

The family's middle-of-the-night flight meant abandoning 150 acres of land, along with the wealth of cash, gold, and silver that was buried somewhere on the property. They lost everything, as Uncle Ike recalled. "Some of the Black folks had ten thousand to fifteen thousand acres in their extended families," he told us. When these families left, white people "paid the taxes on the acreage, and that's the reason so many white families and companies got so rich. They just took the land after everybody left."

The family's financial circumstances changed overnight. Grandma Ella openly discussed with Aunt Toopie the monetary impact of the ordeal. "She said there was a white guy who was after Uncle Ike because there was a lot of gold buried on the property they lived on, and they wanted that gold," Aunt Toopie recalls. "Grandpa would never tell where it was, but it was under a tree. That's all he told her. I asked her, 'Did they ever get it?' And she said, 'No.'"

In 2018 when I found the 1914 newspaper article with the headline announcing Grandpa Ike's murder by a "white farmer," I thought it odd that it mentioned that "Ike Pew" was "living on the plantation of Mr. D. Sirmon." Recollections from Uncle Ike and other family members who had close ties with Grandma Ella before her passing in the late 1960s never alluded to the Sirmons owning Grandpa Ike's land.

Uncle Ike recalled a vast childhood homestead, with tall trees and serene ponds, being owned by his father. Just as his father had emphasized the significance of landownership, Uncle Ike instilled the same value in his children by purchasing his own 162-acre farm, complete with ponds and more forest, and leaving it to them when he died.

Yet, despite extensive efforts, and with the assistance of genealogists who braved the cluttered vaults in the Greenville courthouse's basement, I've yet to unearth any landowner records associated with Grandpa Ike. But I still hold on to hope that somewhere there exists some evidence of our great-grandfather's hard-earned acres.

I've started to suspect that such records might never have existed, especially after finding an article in the April 24, 1895, issue of the *Greenville Advocate*. It discussed Dewey "Dunk" Sirmon. Although Grandpa Ike regarded Dunk Sirmon as a trusted friend, the article painted a different picture. It detailed Dunk's role in a horrific event where "five negroes" accused of murdering a white overseer were lynched while under Dunk's "protective custody" alongside other white men. Their lifeless bodies were later discovered hanging.

In a 2017 article in *The Nation*, "African Americans Have Lost Untold Acres of Land Over the Last Century," Leah Douglas reports that after the Civil War, freed enslaved people and their descendants amassed fifteen million acres of land, mainly in the South—representing 14 percent of US farms by 1920. However, by 1975, the number of Black-owned farms plummeted to 45,000 from a high of 925,000.

The well-chronicled landownership of the maternal side of my family in Minnesota and South Dakota stands as an exception. For many Black and Indigenous families, especially in the South, the tangible proof of early twentieth-century landownership is often missing, obscuring the relentless work Grandpa Ike put into his farmland and the strategic dispossession that deprived Grandma Ella and their children of their land rights.

Uncle Ike's voice carried an inconsolable sadness when he spoke of the vast lands Black families had once held in Butler County, stung by the widespread lack of awareness of and indifference toward Black land loss. Historian Pete Daniel in *Dispossession: Discrimination Against African American Farmers in the Age of Civil Rights*, captures this sentiment, stating, "It was almost as if the earth was opening up and swallowing Black farmers."

47

The "Impertinent" Negro Is At-Large and Has Left No Trail

t's important to point out that some of my elders resisted Alabama's white power structure, determined to protect themselves and their families and refusing to suppress their anger toward the region's homicidal and racist culture. This is especially true of my father's father, Papa Lum.

I vividly remember the way ears would perk up whenever my older aunts would reminisce, amid a cloud of cigarette smoke and the lingering aromas of beer, Bacardi, and Coke, about their dad, Papa Lum. Unfortunately, whenever they lunged into the peculiar stories about him, particularly the ones that mentioned "when Daddy shot that white man," my sisters, cousins, and I were promptly ushered outside to play or sent to our rooms. This remark usually provoked laughter, accompanied by assents such as Mmm hmmm, but sometimes it led to loud arguments and uncontrollable tears. Ear-hustling from my room, I might hear them mention that Papa Lum had been jailed, but the details remained a well-guarded secret. From what I know about Papa Lum, he didn't concern himself with others' opinions. He was a true embodiment of brawn, Greenville's own Jack Johnson, a self-made unapologetically Black heavyweight boxing champion and maverick. The constant threat of lynching that loomed over Black men seemingly mattered little to Papa Lum.

"Everybody knew my dad was a 'mean nigga,' man," Dad recalled. "I don't know what the grown folks' attitude was, but he had to have been damn near crazy to do some of the things they say he did. It didn't bother him if you were Black or white, if you got on the wrong side of him, you were in trouble."

At that point, the only jail record I had found for Papa Lum was from December 1, 1938, when he served six months for assault and battery. I assumed the charge stemmed from one of the many barroom brawls he'd get into in the wee hours of the morning. But surely, a Black man in 1930s and 1940s Alabama would have to be deranged to shoot a white man and expect to live. How in God's holy name could he possibly escape lynching or, at the very least, a life sentence in prison? But when I interviewed Aunt Weenie, then eighty-two, she clarified some of the workings of small-town justice in the South.

Aunt Weenie possessed a trademark angelic voice with a melodic Southern drawl that exuded warmth. The Bible was her favorite book, and Jesus was her best friend. When I interviewed her about her father, she answered even my most uncomfortable questions without hesitation.

I brought up the rumor that Papa Lum had shot a white man. Was it true? It turns out it was.

She was five when it happened. She told me that she, two of her sisters, and some girls from the neighborhood were playing outside when a neighborhood Black man named Paul Rudolph arrived at their house accompanied by a white man claiming to be a justice of the peace. The white man bellowed for Papa Lum to come outside. Just as Rudolph began to shout, the white man fired his gun into the air to startle Papa Lum into coming out. Aunt Weenie's sisters even claimed that he shot *into* the house, narrowly missing family members.

The dispute involved livestock. Papa Lum and Rudolph were at odds over a hog, which Rudolph accused Papa Lum of stealing. Rudolph must have thought that bringing the white "justice of the peace" to our house would frighten Papa Lum into surrendering the hog. Instead, upon hearing the gunshot and realizing his children were in danger, Papa Lum followed his instinct to protect them.

As the terrified kids heard the resounding shot, Papa Lum peered out the window and yelled, "You gonna mess with my family?" One of the girls shouted, "Uh-oh, here comes the forty-five! Daddy's about to get the forty-five!"

Aunt Weenie's account was nearly spot-on: Papa Lum stormed out the front door armed with a shotgun, but the person he fired at was a white marshal, not a justice of the peace, according to an article in the *Montgomery Advertiser*, dated October 14, 1938:

LUM HAWKINS, A NEGRO WPA WORKER OF BOLLING, TONIGHT FIRED TWO VOLLEYS TO BOLLING CITY MARSHAL AUSTIN, ACCORDING TO A STATEMENT MADE BY SHERIFF B.C. BARGAINER JR.

Two or three of the shots are said to have struck Mr. Austin in the face near the eye.

The Bolling Marshal had gone to the negro to demand the return of a stolen hog.

The negro is said to have spoken impertinently to Mr. Austin and after a short argument, he went into his house, walked to the door with the shotgun, and fired both barrels at the Bolling Marshal.

The first blast missed Mr. Austin and two or three stray shots of the second blast shot the marshal in the face.

The negro made an escape and a search for him was started. He is still at large and has left no trail.

After the shooting, Grandma Opie wept and prayed for a miracle. Her Black man had just shot a white lawman in Alabama in 1938. Although it had been twenty-four years since her father had been killed on August 28, 1914, the date was still fresh in her mind. She was convinced her husband would be dead before midnight.

Papa Lum went into hiding that night, seeking refuge in the homes of his fellow Black Freemasons. He considered leaving town when he got word that the police were using bloodhounds to find him. His friends helped sneak him into a covered coal boxcar, hoping he could escape. They figured if Papa Lum was blessed enough not to be shot dead or lynched, he was nonetheless looking at life in prison.

With bloodhounds searching for him, Papa Lum eventually turned himself in. At his trial, Greenville citizens, including four white Masons who knew him from the work Papa Lum had done for their families over the years, attested to his good moral character and strong work ethic.

"They said, 'Hold on, you gonna send him away for life, when he's got ten kids and everything?'" Aunt Weenie recalled. "They all talked to the judge. Papa knew them, because we did work for them and they all knew Grandfather [Ike Pugh] was white, so they took up for Papa."

The white men's appeal worked. The judge sentenced Papa Lum to only six months in jail, on the basis of his large family, his reputation and relationships in the community, and the testimony of the white men who vouched for him. He was never charged with the theft of the hog.

Such was the nature of small-town justice that the judge agreed that jailing Papa Lum for such a lengthy period would leave his children fatherless. The story goes that the court ruled the attack was self-defense and that the marshal had no business trying to enforce any laws in a locality where he wasn't assigned.

I sent the *Montgomery Advertiser* article to my dad because it was proof that the story we'd always heard about Papa Lum was true. Dad and I both marveled at how close to fully accurate Aunt Weenie's account was. My dad was in shock after reading the story; the events had happened before he was born, and he'd only ever heard bits of it since childhood. But there in print were the words, "The negro is said to have spoken impertinently." That would be classic Papa Lum, a man who had seen his father's murdered corpse when he was just five years old.

Later, Aunt Weenie expanded her take on the judge's logic: "When Papa went to court, they said that the only reason he got off with nothing but a small period of jail time is because that man came in and was shooting in front of all his children. The judge told the [marshal] he could care less about it because he went in there and started shooting. Papa shot him because they wanted to come shooting all in the house, and that upset the children and Mama. And that judge knew Mama and Papa."

I asked Cousin Rosa what she knew about one of the white men who had supported Papa Lum, Ewell Messer. I said that he sounded like "a good man" and a champion for Blacks. Rosa, who with other relatives had picked strawberries for Messer as a child, brought me up short when she said flatly, "He wasn't a good man. But he did a good deed."

A Greenville-born cousin explained how small-town politics sometimes worked: powerful whites would sometimes vouch for Blacks who worked for them. Acquitting Blacks, especially in cases involving alleged Black-on-Black crimes and murder, could be as simple as a visit to a white sheriff, lawyer, or judge's home.

All of this reinforced my father's long-held belief that "a white woman's word can put a Black man in prison, but a white man's word can keep him out."

Whether Papa Lum knew he had the connections to get white people to defend him is anyone's guess. It's more likely that when a gunshot shattered the air in front of his young daughters, the haunting echoes of 1905 resounded. Back then, a young Lum had seen his father's bullet-riddled body abandoned in a wagon at their doorstep. Now, history threatened to repeat itself, with his children in the yard and a white man's gun dictating the narrative—turning him into that little five-year-old boy all over again.

The Fading Footsteps of a "Negro Boy"

During a Wisconsin Badgers game in fall 2017, my sixty-nine-year-old father's pronounced limp and labored breathing couldn't be ignored. Living apart had magnified my awareness of his aging. As I watched him, memories of Friday Open Gym and our eight-packs of soda came flooding back.

Vivid recollections of my father swishing three-pointers contrasted with the frailty of the man I now saw. My mother's critical "he stopped going to the gym when you left" flashed through my mind, along with his ominous warnings to Tiffany and me: "I may not be here much longer." But we chose denial. He'd recover.

The next morning, I had to confront him. "Dad," I began, my voice trembling, "you're dying. I can't stay silent. You're my father, my best friend. I love you, and I need you. When you get home, let Monday be the first day of your life, and hit the gym." His eyes, filled with a mix of sadness and understanding, met mine. He didn't promise anything, but his nod hinted at a willingness to try.

Nonetheless, he hid how his insides felt, sparing me from worry, in the same way he'd shielded so much about his past. But in 2019, he finally opened up, giving me a clearer look into the trials, tribulations, and triumphs of a "Negro boy" from Greenville.

Baby Boy

Sometimes our parents are full of love and sometimes they are full of anger. This love and anger come not only from them, but from all previous generations. When we can see this, we no longer blame our parents for our suffering.

—THICH NHAT HANH, *Reconciliation: Healing the Inner Child*

In Aunt Corene's living room, a large oil portrait of my dad's mother, Opal "Opie" Pugh-Hawkins—Grandma Opie—takes pride of place. Painted in the late 1950s, it captures her gravity, fragility, and enduring hope. Visiting my aunt as a child, I'd be transfixed by the portrait's stern, well-coiffed woman in her conservative blue dress and pearls. Her eyes, filled with concern, hinted at someone always on edge, expecting disaster.

What troubled her? What had she seen?, I used to wonder from my family's living room as I massaged the stinging welts up and down the legs of my still-developing body.

These roots became clearer during my last interview with Dad near Valentine's Day, 2019. Dad's earliest memory was being roused by his parents in their Bolling home, just south of Greenville. At age three, his routine was to collect eggs from the chicken coop under Alabama's orange sunrise.

"My dad built that house. It was just a little Southern shack, really rural," Dad said. "Our vehicle was a mule and a wagon. We had a basketball tree with the basket nailed to it, and my brother and his friends played on it all the time."

Too small for basketball, young Dad rode Red, the family's coon-hound, like a horse. Born to his mother in her forties, he was the cherished baby. His thirteen siblings adored him, but no one more than Grandma Opie. "My mom wanted my life to be nothing but pleasure. I was babied a lot. And I spent the rest of my life paying for that."

Grandma Opie was only sixteen when she wed Papa Lum in 1922. Uncle Horace, or "Tonk," came in 1923 and Dad in 1948, with eleven siblings between. To ensure Dad wasn't lonely in kindergarten, his parents delayed the education of his elder sister Dorothy by a year, highlighting his treasured status.

The family relocated to Greenville around 1952, officially, because of Bolling's lack of suitable bachelors. But Aunt Toopie whispered of Grandma Opie's fears from mysterious nighttime door knocks that probably reminded her too much of August 28, 1914.

They lived the country life in Greenville, in a close-knit Black community. The area was often enveloped in a foul odor, my dad said, recalling a vivid memory of the pungent stench of a dead mule's carcass. Their old mule had died and been left out for the truck that drove around town collecting deceased horses and mules.

Most of Greenville's Black residents were Christians, attending Pentecostal and Baptist churches. My family most often attended St. Paul's Church, but they sometimes went to a Pentecostal church where a man jammed on the guitar while a female drummer and a piano filled out the sounds. Even as a kid, Dad was wowed by what he called "the beauty of the guitar."

The fact that one of his aunts sat on the porch playing guitar under the clouds only drew him closer to family. "My cousins would come over, and we'd have a great time," he reminisced. They had the freedom to wander, often venturing into the nearby forest during the day to gather wildflowers, roses, and even pick blueberries, blackberries, and plums. In this welcoming community, "you could walk into anyone's house without knocking." On scorching days, they'd guzzle down Pepsi and Coke "like water" and later return the bottles to earn three cents each. Dad often spoke with pride about collecting enough bottles to fill a wheelbarrow, saying, "We would gather enough to earn two or three dollars," which would buy a lot of candy bars, a nickel each, and soft drinks, for six cents.

Beyond his nature escapades, my father played Little League baseball in a park reserved for Black teams, where even the illustrious Negro League games took place after sunset.

"Hank Aaron and some of the Major people would come through Greenville," he said. "My cousin Genie played, too. The city sponsored all these different Black kids. We had five or six teams at least. I couldn't go play with the white boys, even though the league I was in was a lot better than theirs."

But whenever Dad ventured downtown, the atmosphere changed. He had learned the rules well: step off the sidewalk for a passing white person, avoid eye contact, tread carefully, and be aware of every move, every breath. Suddenly, Dad's negative reaction to Ronald Reagan's "Let's Make America Great Again" slogan made so much sense to me.

50

"Stay in Your Place" Country

When trying to recall his childhood, Dad would sometimes loop in his siblings on three-way calls, immersing us in the warmth of shared laughter and familiar songs from days gone by. Their nicknames—Weenie, Toopie, Mook, Teddy, Tonk, and Bud—hinted at times both simple and fraught. Their laughter sometimes concealed deeper tales—ones of an Alabama not always spoken of but deeply felt. But in one call in 2015, Dad and Aunt Toopie unmasked the Alabama they experienced as children, a place that was bright on the surface but bloody beneath.

"We didn't ever know what might happen," Aunt Toopie said. "We couldn't step outside our door and feel free."

"It was 'stay in your place' country," Dad added.

Grandma Opie did her best to train my father to observe the rules of Jim Crow. It took years and a few harsh lessons, but he grasped the fundamentals of traps right away and became almost as compliant as he wanted me to be in Maplewood.

Through it all, Grandma Opie stood as his unwavering shield. I lost count of the times I was whipped, but Dad could recount each instance he was punished. And yet, as Dad often points out, Grandma was "gentle." In his entire life, he was whipped just three times—all by Grandma Opie. Papa Lum never laid a hand on him.

Grandma issued her harshest whipping after Dad accompanied Papa Lum to a painting job at the home of a white family. Dad was waiting on the porch when the lady of the house emerged and asked if he was hungry.

"Some of them white women could cook soul food well, because they learned from the Black women they had working for them," he told me. Grandma Opie pounced, yelling that eating at a white person's house was off-limits and bad manners—a reminiscent vision of the birthday party I had crashed.

Another time, he was with Grandma Opie while she was working at a white family's house. She looked out the window and saw Dad swinging alongside the white man's daughter. She sprinted outside, snatched him off the swing, and screamed louder than ever while shaking him furiously. "Lee Roy, you stay off that swing! You can't be over here with this girl! I told you to stay where you were, and you disobeyed me!" she yelled, making sure the white father could hear. Clutching twigs she had torn from a nearby tree, she lashed theatrically on Dad, drawing out agonizing cries.

Though Dad left Greenville in 1961, he took Alabama's rules with him to Minnesota. When Dad showed me *Mandingo*, miscegenation was still constitutionally illegal in Alabama, a law that stood until 2000. Despite the ban's lifting, segregationist language lasted in Alabama's constitution for another twenty years. In 2019, a bill was passed for a voter decision on interracial marriage. Although approved in November 2020, 44 percent of Alabamians voted against change. However, in 2021, the Alabama Constitution of 2022 and an amendment erasing racist language were endorsed by 76.4 percent of voters.

I believe Grandma Opie's glimpse of Dad with the white girl swinging together triggered memories of the price Grandpa Ike had paid for his interracial progressivism, because when Dad committed other missteps, she wasn't as harsh. For instance, when Dad mistakenly drank from a "whites only" fountain, she scolded him loudly and whooped him; but later at the bus stop, "She laid out the entire story for me," he said.

But Dad wasn't totally spared. In 2023 Alabama was still one of seventeen states that allowed corporal punishment in schools. "We got our asses kicked every time we were late for school or misbehaved," he explained. Kids faced the school's "BOARD OF EDUCATION," an oak paddle that left a memorable imprint. "The principal would tear your butt up with that paddle!" Dad said.

This understanding clarifies why my father remained passive when Mom gave Mrs. Blumer permission to beat me, another instance of Alabama's violent legacy shaping his approach to disciplining us.

However, the punishments Dad endured at school were milder than those Papa Lum administered to his older children. Mirroring the end-of-day whippings I read about on plantations and experienced at home, Papa Lum treated middle-of-the-night beatings as a family tradition, whipping his children with a switch made from braided tree branches.

"He would wait until we were in bed and then wake us up one by one. Even if only one of us did something wrong, we would all get a beating for it," Aunt Toopie said.

As the girls hit their teens, Grandma Opie made Papa Lum mellow out. But he punched the boys like men, even drawing blood. "They were really bitter," Dad reminisced. "I heard Bud tell my dad, 'You won't beat me anymore, old man,' ready to pummel Papa back."

Like me, Dad gradually learned to traverse the traps. "If you were walking, you couldn't get close to white people. You had to stay out of their way. And if the cops were on the street, you had to just walk by them, real easy," he said.

The son of the family's insurance agent would bump into him on the way to school, but Dad held back. "We could have kicked his ass, but they probably would have hung our asses," he said. "It wouldn't have been just kids getting in fights. It would have been, 'These niggers touched this white boy.' That reality was always there, as long as you were in Alabama."

At five, after a long day in the cotton fields, Dad found a dollar on a bus. Without prompting, he handed it to a white man, saying, "Hey, you dropped a dollar." Dad reflected, "I just thought because he was white that I was supposed to give it to him. My family never told me anything like that."

He continued: "Those are the kinds of things that haunt me, man, even to this day." During elementary school, my father was a paperboy and cleared tables at the pool hall downtown. "When we delivered papers to the white neighborhoods, we used to ride by their houses and throw the papers, hitting the screen doors. We had to be good throwers, and we were. Those white kids would sic their dogs on us. I had a three-speed Schwinn, and my friend had an old, big, fast bike," he said. "We were faster than those dogs, sometimes even German shepherds. They would yell, 'Nigger, nigger, nigger, get outta here!'"

Dad's mastery of newspaper-throwing, developed amidst the looming threat of being chased by German shepherds, revealed an inherited fear of dogs that I sought help for from "Dog Whisperer" Cesar Millan for a 2012 YouTube episode. At the time, I didn't know that the fear can be traced back to European colonists using dogs as weapons of intimidation against Indigenous people. The practice took a more racialized turn during chattel enslavement when, amid slave rebellions in the eighteenth and nineteenth centuries, the Cuban bloodhound breed was used to terrorize the enslaved—especially escapees.

Dad's observations over the years made it clear that in Alabama, distinctions between Jim Crow and Uncle Sam blurred. By 1930, Birmingham had enacted laws that were revealing: it was illegal for people of different races to even play checkers or dominoes together, and racial segregation was mandated in all bus facilities. Alabama law was even more explicit. No person or corporation could require any white female nurse to work in hospital rooms or wards, public or private, "in which negro men were placed." Because Dad kept his head down, spoke only when spoken to, and did what he was told, he survived.

"White people and Blacks lived together," Dad noted, recalling his father's white acquaintances from tree-cutting and lawn-mowing, "but they just coexisted," with peace maintained as long as Black folks knew their place.

51

Whispered Prayers: The Quiet Battles of Grandma Opie

The nights in Greenville were filled with a symphony of country sounds—crickets chirping, frogs croaking. Lying awake between his parents, my father would sometimes hear his mother murmuring her heartfelt pleas to God. Grandma Opie was often unwell, her body ravaged by years of repeated childbirth and compromised kidneys. She had endured the heart-wrenching loss of three children at birth, while raising and nurturing fourteen others who had survived. It was no wonder that she grew weary and worn, seeking strength and protection in her unwavering faith.

There were also prayers for the soul of Dad's eldest sister, Ruby, who had died unexpectedly at age twenty (reportedly from a tooth infection), and for Uncle Tonk, who left Greenville abruptly in 1938 when he was sixteen. Grandma Opie's prayers became a spiritual fortress against the slings and arrows that life sent her way. She beseeched God for the gift of more years, a desperate plea to remain with her maturing family for as long as possible. She bore her illness for six long years, starting when my father was around five.

Aunt Toopie, my father's senior by almost seven years, was intimately involved in Grandma Opie's care. Her health dramatically worsened in 1957, when she suffered complications from what may have been a blood clot in her leg—a moment scorched in my father's memory. He'd been told that a spring from their worn-out mattress had broken through the fabric, piercing a critical vein in his mother's leg and bringing on a rush of blood. "She damn near bled to death,"

Dad said, his voice still trembling years later. He was terrified to see his mother in that vulnerable state. It was a pivotal moment—his realization of how seriously she was deteriorating. She recovered from that incident but never regained her previous vitality.

This story helped me understand his aversion to blood, evident in the way he would grind his teeth during the bloody boxing matches we watched together. This childhood memory profoundly affected him, leading him to never use a closed fist on me or Tiffany, which can cause bloody noses. Belts and boots cause pain, but they do not draw blood.

When Dad told this story, Aunt Toopie chimed in with an unexpected revelation that rocked both Dad and me. She said that the cut on Grandma Opie's leg had in fact occurred about a year earlier during a heated early-morning conversation between Grandma Opie and Papa Lum. The two of them had gone outside and huddled together under a tree, so their children couldn't hear them argue. But when Grandma Opie rushed back into the house, her leg bleeding profusely, it was clear something had gone terribly wrong during that clandestine exchange. But Grandma Opie never discussed whatever had caused the bleeding.

The mystery of Grandma Opie's leg wound persisted all the way up to Dad's final interview. Regardless of how it had occurred, one thing remained clear: the remnants of that injury plagued her in the form of three distinctive, puffy, and bluish bruises on the inner part of her leg, just below her knee. They served as a constant reminder of a hidden battle fought within her own body. As time went on, Grandma Opie's movements grew slower, her voice softer, and each breath was harder to draw.

52

Unmasking the Cycle: Anger and Abuse in a Segregated Society

t's probably no surprise that, given the physical violence that defined their lives and the frustrations of living in a rigidly unjust society, some of the men around Dad ended up taking out their anger on the women in their lives.

My cousin, Rev. Eli Thigpen, said Black men living in the Jim Crow South often found their voices at home: "When you're a Black man in a white man's world, you're a boy, you're an uncle, but you're never called a man," he said. "You walk on eggshells when you're out there in the world, on the job. But when you come home, that's your castle. And you let all your frustrations out. You want to be in charge."

Eli's words resonated with me: in all the years of my childhood, I recall my father directing his rage toward a white man rather than me only a few times. One time I saw Dad seemingly ready to hit a white man during a pickup basketball game at the YMCA. I was a teenager, and a much older man who was guarding me got mad when I spun around him. Dad charged over, slammed him down, raised his fist in the air, but then backed off. Looking back, I think his fierce reaction was amplified because I was still healing from my neck surgery.

From what I know of Dad's childhood, my hunch is that his nightmares involved flickering flashbacks of the dozens of times he saw his mother intervene when his brothers were beating their wives. The younger siblings, including my dad, the baby, were powerless to protect their horrified mother from getting hit as she strove to protect her daughters-in-law. I'm not sure whether Grandma Opie's sons ever accidentally hit her, but the possibility tormented my father his entire life.

He always believed that the major peace disruptor in the Hawkins household was the illicit corn whiskey brew known as white lightning. The potent drink turned men all over Greenville upside down. "They would be all happy and the next thing you know they would try to kill the world, but especially their wives," Dad recalled. "I saw that violence. And I saw my mom refereeing, trying to keep these dudes from hitting their wives. And that was a hard thing, man." Today, the Adverse Childhood Experiences (ACE) Study, conducted by Dr. Vincent Felitti and Dr. Robert Anda in collaboration with the Centers for Disease Control and Prevention (CDC) and Kaiser Permanente, has found that witnessing physical violence as a child can impact a child as significantly as being a direct target of that violence.

"I was in a family of wife beaters," Dad concluded sadly, then added, "I never saw my dad hit my mom, but I wouldn't put it past him." Dad was aware that some of his sisters also suffered from abuse, and although horrified by it, he intuited even from an early age that it was a symptom, a coping mechanism on the part of disempowered men to exert control over something or someone in their lives. One brother-in-law, Dad recalled, "used to beat my sister all the way home, but it seemed my dad was never home when they did that stuff. So, they were abusers, man. They were major abusers. Black women went through a lot."

Crossing a Hawkins woman was risky. I remember Aunt Helen telling me that she swiftly grabbed a red brick and brandished it in self-defense against her attacking boyfriend. Another aunt sliced her husband so badly that he had a few nights in the hospital to consider the wisdom of ever again mixing whiskey and spousal aggression. Still, Papa Lum must have known what was happening. In a small town like Greenville, news traveled fast. So why, I asked my dad, did this notoriously hot-tempered man never reach for his shotgun when their husbands attacked his daughters?

"If it weren't for my mom, he would have killed their asses," my father said. "She told him to stay out of it because she wanted them to stay married. If he had been younger, he would have killed them."

It is painful for me to realize that many of the men in my family accepted the centuries-long characterization of Black women as property, treating them in a way depressingly analogous to the way enslavers and overseers abused them. I see now it's just a short leap from the misogyny of their generation to the pimp books and movies I devoured in my youth, up to and including the "money, cash, hoes," mentality promoted in the music I listened to. Misogyny against Black women is an inescapable part of our American story.

Dad was most anguished by his inability to protect his mother. "I so much hated seeing my brothers do that to my momma," Dad said. He was far too young and too small to intervene. So in a twisted way, he tried to redress this grievance as an adult, with our own mother. Unfortunately, to "protect" her, he had to turn his children into villains.

Hearing Mom's declarations of "chest pains" and "I might die today," Dad transformed back into that helpless boy all over again. But now he was big enough and strong enough to act as a protector. Whenever our mother ordered our attack dog of a father to harm us, he was seizing an opportunity he never got with his own mother. In the middle of that dangerous cycle, Tiffany and I never stood a chance.

Hearing him explain this during our last interview in February 2019, my entire childhood flashed before my eyes. I transitioned from a state of confusion to one of understanding—and even gratitude that parents didn't turn us into walking filicide statistics. Until then, I had no real clue about the fragility of our situation or how vulnerable I truly was.

I often wonder whether Grandma Opie, watching from heaven, felt heartbroken seeing Tiffany or me pinned to the floor by one of our parents. Everything I've learned about my grandmother suggests she would have disapproved. Aunt Toopie described her as "the holiest woman I've ever known." Despite being a Black woman from early 1900s Alabama, she resisted the influence of the oppressive Slave and Black Codes. Her maternal kindness, her dedication to her children's well-being, including that of her daughters-in-law, was a testament against violence. My father was blessed to have experienced that caliber of maternal kindness, even if for only twelve years. Grandma Opie wanted the best for her children, yearning to provide them with a peace she herself never knew.

Grandma Opie brimmed with pride for her children's accomplishments. By the 1950s, her four elder daughters had married, relocated to cities like St. Paul and New Orleans, and begun families with their husbands. While they primarily became homemakers, some took side jobs in dry cleaning, unknowingly laying the foundation for the future businesses their children would establish.

Aunt Corene never failed to dazzle Grandma Opie. During her family's visits to Alabama, Aunt Corene would arrive draped in her signature sequin dresses, while Uncle L.C. sported sharp-brimmed fedoras, pristine shirts, and impeccable shoes. "To someone earning ten dollars a week, that meant the world," my father reminisced.

Around 1958, noticing Grandma Opie's slowing pace during a visit, Aunt Corene arranged for her to travel to Minnesota to consult with Dr. Abrams, a respected Black doctor in the Twin Cities. While medical consultation was the premise, Grandma Opie's genuine curiosity was to experience her daughter's Minnesota life.

After Dr. Abrams looked over Grandma, he came up with a plan to tackle her kidney problems. She stayed in Minnesota for about two weeks, but her heart was set on getting back to Alabama to be with her youngest kids. Dr. Abrams tried to persuade her to stay longer, knowing she'd be neglected in Alabama's segregated healthcare system. But Grandma was adamant about returning home.

My grandmother may not have had much of an education, but one of her decisions has put her brilliance on full display sixty years later. Before catching the train back, she made Aunt Corene promise something important: if anything happened to her, Aunt Corene was to take Dad and his two little sisters straight to Minnesota for good, to give them a chance at a new life away from Alabama. That was her biggest wish—to get her babies out of there.

Grandma Opie boarded that train back home, keeping her worsening health to herself. At just nine years old, Dad watched as his mom struggled more and more, her kidneys failing and her legs swelling from blood clots. Grandma was barely in her fifties, but her body was giving out—much like how I saw Dad tire out during that Badgers football game in Wisconsin. And it didn't help that she, even more than most Hawkinses, drank Coca-Cola like water, to soothe her worries.

Her health worsened, partly because of the subpar medical care she received. When Grandma Opie needed kidney surgery, she went to L.V. Stabler Memorial Hospital in Greenville. That state-of-the-art hospital mainly catered to white patients, while Black patients, if they were lucky enough to get in at all, were shuffled off to a little ten-bed white house across the street. The depth of the apartheid hit home when a cousin recounted a daunting memory: his mother, fighting complications from her thirteenth pregnancy in the mid-1950s, had been coldly turned away by a white doctor who said, "I told her not to have any more children, so I'm not doing nothin' for her." Tragically, she passed away soon after.

It became harder and harder for Grandma Opie to walk. Dark spots spread across her legs. The doctor told the family there was no point in treating her at the "colored" house; instead, he visited her at home, administering an injection with somber warning: if this didn't improve her condition, there was nothing more he could do.

Grandma was fully aware that, with five kids younger than eighteen, she had to plan for their future. Sitting with Aunt Toopie by the living-room heater one day, Grandma Opie said, "Your mama is getting sicker. I might not be around here with y'all much longer." She urged Toopie and her sisters to continue to "be good girls," to never forget God, and to take care of one another and their baby brother, Lee Roy.

Around that time, on a walk to the store, Aunt Toopie and her siblings ran into a man whom the local cab driver revealed was their long-lost brother Tonk, who had made a middle-of-the-night exit from Greenville in 1938, the same year Papa Lum was jailed. Whether these events were connected remains unclear. The hushed reasons for his departure marked a common story for many Black men in rural towns back then. Uncle Tonk survived the run but died young at age fifty-nine in 1979, a smoker with a sweet tooth.

What's clear is that Grandma Opie deeply mourned the loss of her firstborn, a grief that added weight to a body already worn from a lifetime of hardships: from seeing her father's bullet-riddled figure slumped over a mule at age eight, to the family's hasty departure from their home and land and assets, to the physical toll of so many pregnancies and births, to her final decline in health under an inadequate medical system. Reflecting on all this and more, I marvel at her endurance. Yet, Grandma Opie found solace in her unwavering faith in the Father, the Son, and the Holy Spirit, along with an innate kindness that anchored her spirit, granting her serenity.

Diving into Grandma Opie's life story, with Dad as my guide, opened up new windows into his shattered heart and the boy he was at twelve. "I knew my mother was carrying burdens," he told me. "I just didn't know what those burdens were."

Her funeral in February 1961 was "the largest I've ever seen," my father remembered, with a miles-long procession of cars and a throng of mourners overflowing from the Friendship Baptist cemetery. At her resting place, the young Lee Roy, suddenly motherless, stood with his siblings, encircled by a racially diverse crowd of mourners from across the region.

During our final interview, my father shared a lingering memory of standing beside his mother's open casket, overwhelmed by the finality of her closed eyes and yet captivated by her elegantly styled hair. He glimpsed his mother briefly before being ushered away to his older siblings, as though distance from the casket might lessen his pain. In the pews, surrounded by family, he fell asleep, his twelve-year-old way of coping.

Yet, there was a haunting detail my father never shared with me, a secret unearthed through my aunts' stories. After Grandma Opie breathed her last at home, her body was taken away in a hearse. My father, in a desperate bid to stay close to her for a few moments longer, ran after it. He chased the hearse until his breath and legs gave out, watching helplessly as it carried her away, shrinking into a speck on the horizon. He never confided this to me, but my understanding of childhood trauma tells me that it nonetheless lay buried somewhere in his heart.

When discussions about Dad's future arose, some elder siblings and relatives offered to take him, but not the four girls. Grandma Opie, however, had beseeched Aunt Corene to keep her babies together, in Minnesota. The day following the funeral, Aunt Corene kept her vow. Dad and two of his four teenage sisters, Betty and Dorothy, packed into Aunt Corene and Uncle L.C.'s 1961 Ford Fairlane 500 and headed north. As the miles unfolded, Dad felt an easing tension, his body's sweltering heat giving way to soothing coolness. The moment they crossed the Alabama border, he felt like Jim Crow's noose was loosening, and a breath of fresh hope filled his lungs.

In St. Paul, Dad, Betty, and Dorothy moved in with Aunt Corene and Uncle L.C. They planned to live there for about five months, awaiting Aunt Helen and Aunt Toopie's arrival from Alabama. Aunt Corene was their initial guardian, but when Aunt Helen, seven years older than my father, turned eighteen, she took over, and they relocated to a nearby house. Aunt Helen set strict expectations for Dad. She warned of the traps all around—arrest, dropping out of school, teenage parenthood, and bad company. She emphasized that, being only eighteen, she wouldn't be in a position to rescue him. He vowed to stay focused and contribute financially to the household.

Dad joined seventh grade at Marshall Junior High, at the time a mostly white integrated school with a smattering of Black, Indigenous and Latino students. During one of his first gym classes at school, he was thrust into a wrestling lesson. Dad was matched against a strong white boy. The match started with the white boy taking the lead. "He was competing. He was handling me for a while," my father remembers. "But something got into me once I thought *This is a white boy.*"

All at once, the animosity and rage he'd harbored toward white people in Greenville surged through him, getting channeled into this innocuous wrestling match in gym class. But for my dad, it was a long-awaited opportunity to release some of his pent-up frustration, without fear of reprisal. Suddenly, he became possessed, flipping the white boy onto his back with unnecessary force and pinning him to the ground. The teacher counted the pin, but my father didn't release his hold immediately. "I beat his ass," Dad said. "All those memories, all that animosity from Alabama, it all just came back. I remember asking myself if I was turning into my father."

Three years after Grandma Opie's death, my dad already felt like a man at age fifteen. As different as St. Paul was from Greenville, there were moments when he felt like nothing had changed. As in Greenville, he had to watch his step everywhere he went. One evening, he got a particularly rude awakening.

He was enjoying the last weeks of summer, hanging around the neighborhood with his friends after playing baseball. They passed the juke joint and the Edgar B. Ober Boys Club. A car carrying two Black men drove up slowly, stopping across the street from the boys.

"Hey fellas! Hey fellas!" one man beckoned. For a millisecond, my father's Southern-boy paranoia sounded an alarm within him, telling him not to respond to the man. One of his friends, however, bolted over to the car. The rest followed.

"Y'all live near Central, right?" the man inquired, probing each of their backgrounds.

Sensing trouble, my dad began to discreetly distance himself. "I gotta go, fellas. Need to wash dishes," he said, hoping to escape.

Before they could all make their exit, the situation escalated. The man in the car whipped out a .38. Four of Dad's friends took off running, but Dad and his friend Herman found themselves at gunpoint with a man screaming at them: "You motherfuckers better not move an inch, or I'll blow your motherfucking heads off! I know y'all stole my motherfucking car and I want it back. I'll blow your motherfucking brains into next week if you niggas don't get me my shit TONIGHT!"

Terrified, Herman and my dad denied the theft, but the man wasn't convinced. "You niggas know you did it! Now I got some motherfuckin' questions for you. Come upstairs."

He nudged them into the stairway of a nearby building, and with a gun at their backs, they were pushed up two flights into an apartment that reeked of reefer. Another dude was lying on the couch, visibly high as hell. He also had a gun, and the two boys were subjected to more questions and verbal abuse.

"You niggas are a damn lie," they were told. "Should we kill you now, or you gonna tell us where the car is?"

"We didn't do anything, man. We don't know shit about the car man, seriously. We don't."

But the men weren't convinced. "I swear, if you niggas know anything about the car and ain't sayin' nothin', I'll blow your nuts off. I ain't playing witchya."

Eventually, he and Herman were allowed to leave, but they were given a warning to take back to their friends: "We have little niggas on the streets who are just a little older than you. I'll put them on you. We watchin' all you motherfuckers. You better not tell anybody about what we just did to you. You niggas do not say a muthafuckin' word! My boys are listening out there. And if I find out that you motherfuckers did anything or know anything about my car, I'll come and blow your heads off ma damn self. I'M NOT PLAYIN WITCHYA. YOU NIGGAS HEAR ME?!"

For the next few stressful years, Dad and Herman stayed on the alert for any trace of those men and their "little niggas." "They never saw us, but we saw them," my dad recalls.

Later, Dad's friends told him that his claim of needing to wash dishes had been their cue to run—everyone knew he'd never washed a dish, thanks to his four sisters.

Twenty years later, on the streets of St. Paul, my father recognized the dude who had called them over. "He was in a wheelchair," my dad said, "with an amputated leg, with somebody pushing him."

He reflected then on his move to Minnesota in 1961. He'd thought he had managed to escape the war zone of the South, where whites were lynching Blacks, but he had unwittingly moved into the war zone of the North, where Blacks were lynching Blacks. Two places, worlds apart, with one thing in common: Blacks were being lynched.

53

"Black Elvis" vs. the KKK

During his days at Marshall Junior High, my father considered returning to Greenville for high school. Jim Crow was still in the air, yet so were his beginnings. The summer of 1964 saw him in Alabama, keen to strengthen ties with his family—especially his father and brothers—and the town he once called home.

By sixteen, he was transformed—a foot taller, with a perm "conk" hairdo, dyed reddish-golden brown, akin to the Temptations. His prowess on the basketball court had grown. I even found an old newspaper article from back then, reporting on how he'd caught fire and hit eight consecutive outside shots during a game. His fingers danced on the guitar strings with newfound grace. In younger days, he'd quietly trod in shoes passed down from his brothers. But in Minnesota, his feet flaunted an array of suede—with the blue ones catching many an eye. This, alongside his striking hair, birthed his new identity as "Black Elvis." It was only later that I understood his emotional reaction to Rev. Battle's words about his footwear. To my father, sensitive and ever-so proud, the memory of stepping out in frayed, hand-me-down shoes from his brothers was one he yearned to forget.

That summer, the local basketball coach made him a proposition: play in Greenville for two years, and a scholarship to any HBCU was likely his. Dad was considering it, but then events unfolded that reminded him of why he'd been so relieved to leave. One day that summer, my father, his father, and two of his brothers were wandering through town, the older men chugging and passing back and forth a bootlegged bottle of white lightning corn whiskey. Nonchalantly, one of them handed it to Dad in a casual rite of passage, signifying he was no longer seen as a child. Eager, yet feigning indifference, my father took a hefty swig.

Within seconds, the homemade liquor seared down his esophagus, settling heavily in his stomach. Bent over, he coughed violently amid the echoes of Papa Lum's and Uncle Mook's laughter. The sting was so sharp that words escaped him. "It felt like I drank a bottle of razor blades, which were cutting up my chest," he recalled.

In a flash, my father realized that his future did not lie in the South. *I can't stay here*, he thought. *Staying here will end up killing me.*

His decision wasn't driven solely by health risks. In 1948, the year of his birth, Alabama boasted one of the nation's highest homicide rates. He remembered all the tales of murder he used to hear as a child, even though his family tried to shield him from unpleasantries. "When I was a kid, somebody died every weekend," he said. "There were always crooked things going on."

During that summer, he played basketball in Greenville under the glowing lights of Dunbar Park, a segregated haven for "coloreds" situated next to a wooded area. One night, as darkness descended, a cacophony erupted on the field as everyone began shouting, "Klan! Klan!"

"I'd heard about the KKK my whole life, doing things to people. But I *saw* them that night," he said. "A truckload of the Klan was coming down the dirt road. They had lookouts for that."

Trucks adorned with torchlights and loaded with white men pursued the Black kids, driving them deep into the woods, until they could retreat no farther. That night, the woods became their protector.

"I wasn't afraid of the woods because there were so many of us in there. I would have never ventured into those pitch-black woods alone, but the darkness worked in our favor that night," Dad said with a chuckle. "We got through the woods, and they couldn't drive the trucks through. So, they took to chasing us on foot and they got lost in there. By the time you got out of the woods, you were in the Black neighborhood."

That encounter with the KKK might have saved my father's life, and mine, because it solidified his resolve to return to Minnesota. Had he stayed, he likely wouldn't have crossed paths with my mother, which happened when they were both thirteen. Mom was living with her grandparents in their grand home, and Dad shared a rented duplex with his sisters. They came from different worlds, but their connection was magic, especially since they'd both been rescued from traumatic situations by family.

In 2019, Mom reminisced with me about their early days. She was enthusiastic about opera, pageants, and dancing, while Dad dreamed of serenading larger audiences as a soul musician. Their first meeting was in 1961 at McCarrons Lake in the St. Paul suburb of Roseville. Dad saw her splashing friends and playfully suggested she give him swimming lessons. They flirted until Dad had to leave. They never swapped numbers, and he never revisited the lake, but over the next three years, while playing lead guitar on the local "Chitlin' Circuit," he kept an eye out for "a girl named Bobby" (Roberta).

Dad's musical debut occurred at the Hallie Q. Brown Community Center in St. Paul, where fate eventually reconnected him with Mom, igniting a romance spanning five decades and resulting in three children and four grandchildren. "We were inseparable. I practically lived at her house. After high school, it was just us," Dad said with a smile.

By 1966, as Dad was finishing high school and Mom was preparing for college, the military draft for the Vietnam War was looming. "Black men were being drafted by the thousands, much as they are sent to prison today," Dad said, "and I was getting letters every day from Uncle Sam, saying 'I Want You.'"

Dad quickly secured a job at West Publishing, which, unfortunately, also employed Elroy Stock, a white supremacist who would later target me. At night, Dad played with his band, The Xciters, sharing stages with big names like Curtis Mayfield. The Xciters, the high school group supporting The Amazers—who were managed and guided by Martin—gained popularity with singles such as "Without a Warning." A recording contract seemed within reach, but Dad faced a crucial decision.

"I had a job a week after I graduated, but I wanted to go to college. I got asked to play basketball, but I didn't have a scholarship," he shared.

He wanted to go to college, but even with frequent appearances on his high school honor roll, he harbored insecurities about his early Jim Crow education. I now realize how little I understood Dad's anxieties, which might have prevented me from using a word—"mentality"—that could evoke such emotions in him and lead to that vicious attack with his steel-toed boots.

Dad sought advice from Uncle Ronnie, an air force serviceman, who encouraged Dad to enlist. Despite negative voices from his past, Dad held a quiet confidence that he could succeed and secretly explored enlistment to stay closer to home and his soon-to-be-wife, my mom. He saw the dual opportunity of serving while performing at nightclubs on military bases.

After scoring well on the enlistment test, he opted for the air force and was bound for training in Texas. Knowing his sisters would be devastated, he waited until the day he had to leave to inform them. Indeed, when the recruitment officer came to Aunt Helen's apartment to pick him up to report for basic training, my aunts exploded, admonishing their baby brother in front of the officer, telling Dad he didn't have to go. But Dad did have to go, and he was eager to start his life's next chapter.

The day he joined, there was confusion over his name. An officer pronounced it as "Leo Ray Hawkins." Dad tried to correct him, saying his name was "Lee Roy Hawkins." But the officer pointed to his birth certificate, scribbled out by a midwife in Greenville, which read "Leo Ray." So, the officer told him that would be his new name. Again, for our family, there's so much—and so little—meaning in the name of a Black descendant of enslavement.

After basic training, Dad was assigned to Minot Air Force Base in North Dakota. He and Mom communicated daily. "We'd often fall asleep on the phone," he recalled. During a lengthy break from his military duties, my eldest sister was conceived. My parents married quietly on November 2, 1968. Mom was twenty-one, and Dad was twenty. She wore a white dress reminiscent of Jackie Kennedy, while Dad donned his air force uniform.

"I loved your mother," he told me, and of course he did. Their bond was strong, sometimes intensely so, as both feared losing the other. Soon they'd have their own child to cling to. Our little family had begun.

Despite Dad's zeal to provide for his growing family, Uncle Sam put up roadblocks. After marrying Mom, Dad immediately applied for married housing, but was denied. "I tried, in every way I could, to get answers and get housing," Dad said. "I found out that people who were the same rank as me had houses."

Fate had another plan, however. Mom, holding baby Tammi, attended a service at Mount Olivet in St. Paul, where renowned fire-and-brimstone preacher Rev. Stanley King was the pastor. King had ties to Minnesota's political royalty: Senator Walter Mondale and former Vice President Hubert H. Humphrey. Mom told Pastor King about the housing situation, and he contacted Mondale and Humphrey.

Days later, Dad's superior officer approached him with surprising news: "We got you a house, man. When can you move in?" When Dad hesitated, asking for a month, the officer's face reddened and he said, "You better get your ass in that housing, Hawkins!"

"He was mad as hell," Dad recalled. "He told me, 'All this shit we've been going through over you? You better get in there as fast as you can!'"

Hearing that story reminded me of all the national leaders who came through Mount Olivet during my childhood. In a sermon, the Chicago pastor Rev. Otis Moss II expounded on the power of the Black church:

> Never confuse position with power. Pharaoh had a position, but Moses had the power. Herod had a position, but John had the power. The cross had a position, but Jesus had the power. Lincoln had a position, but Douglass had the power. Woodrow Wilson had a position, but Ida B. Wells had the power. George Wallace had a position, but Rosa Parks had the power. Lyndon Baines Johnson had a position, but Martin Luther King had the power. We have the power. Don't you ever forget.

54

The Mysterious, Notorious Life of Lum Hawkins

Family stories can be as complex as the elders who share them. Around every warm narrative recited at family gatherings, there often sits a concealed tale, either awaiting the right moment for its disclosure or hoping it remains undiscovered. In the vast library of Dad's life experiences, one particular story remained tucked away, one he believed to be too deep for my comprehension—and perhaps, for many years, his own.

My exploration into our family history has shown me that while elders might guard challenging truths, those with steady integrity, when prompted, step forward with honesty. Some might dance around the truth, while others remain silent, but Dad was different.

Aunt Corene often remarked, "Lee Roy always tells the truth," and I agree. This understanding deepens the sting I felt when my research brought to light the unexpected sorrow that Dad's father, Papa Lum, had been murdered. I had grown up with the knowledge of his passing when I was a mere three years old, innocently assuming it was due to natural causes. Whispers from family gatherings of "Who shot Papa?" became distant memories, clouded by childhood innocence. To think of Dad holding onto such a crushing reality for more than four decades, dreading the moment we'd question him, is agonizing. For a man of such honesty, keeping such a painful secret must have been a heavy load.

Once I found out the truth, I called Dad immediately. "Your father was *murdered*?" I asked, incredulous. "What happened?"

"Aww, man," Dad said, heaving a huge sigh, perhaps relieved to finally get a forty-two-year-old secret off his chest. "Daddy messed around down there in Greenville and got killed. Runnin' the streets."

"Runnin' the streets? He would've been in his seventies," I said. "He was that old and still living in the fast lane?"

"Yeah, man. Can you believe it? Even at that age, my dad was well over six feet and still had a stomach as flat as yours. He was out there runnin' women, and he was drinkin' in the Chitlin' Circuit nightclubs and after-hours joints with my brother. And he just ended up getting killed."

From the stories I'd gathered, Papa Lum was a man of style, consistently donning crisp white shirts and suits. But between the lines of family accounts, I discerned a deeper tale. Widowed for thirteen years, Papa Lum found fleeting comfort in wild nights with casual liaisons and white lightning. Perhaps, for a while, the bite of the drink numbed his epic losses—but such escapism has its price.

I was just three years old in February 1974 when Dad got the call from Alabama about Papa Lum's death. I don't remember that call, but my first memory of life is Dad whipping me with his tongue hanging out when I was that precise age. He was twenty-six, working as a legislative assistant at the Minnesota State Capitol. Married and the father of two small children, he was focused on moving his little family to the suburbs, where he believed the schools were better. Then, Alabama came calling.

Dad led a convoy to Greenville. Although he was the youngest, being the only male family member in Minnesota brought a heavy sense of duty. That responsibility was magnified as some of his sisters quarreled over Papa Lum's life insurance, each suspecting the other of hiding funds. Dad found himself mediating, while also juggling late-night calls from Southern relatives seeking financial help, despite his own pressing needs. Given his "survivor's guilt" from leaving Alabama behind, his heart's compass pointed always toward giving. Each time he faced the choice to help someone tied to Alabama, he felt the pull of Grandma Opie's memory.

Although Dad had a million questions about his father's situation and how his brother and family were coping after his death, every word during Papa Lum's funeral was chosen carefully. A swarm of long-lost cousins and neighbors greeted him, expressing amazement at how much he had grown and changed; but when Dad tried to ask questions, he was met with silence and guarded explanations.

Many relatives would nervously launch into a series of unsolicited denials about Papa Lum's demise, all designed to let my dad know that they had no idea who had killed him. This young man who was once the baby of the family had rocketed up in height, served as a wartime soldier, and was now the head of his own family. His father had just been murdered, and some feared he wasn't just going to let it slide. They took one look at this strapping young man and assumed that he had come to Greenville to avenge his father's death.

"The whole time," Dad recalled, "I was wondering which of these folks knew who killed my dad, and whether I was going to have somebody come up and shoot me, thinking I was ready to shoot him."

But my father wasn't in Greenville to solve a murder; he was there to bury his father and then hightail it back home to Minnesota with his family as quickly as he could. "They wanted to see what I was going to say and how I was going to react. I'm down there with my family and my wife and kids and stuff, and these people are thinking I'm trying to kill somebody. There are some crazy people out there, man."

As Dad told me about the mystery surrounding Papa Lum's murder, I could see it still weighed heavily on his heart. So we decided to find out more about what happened, calling three relatives who we thought might have some information. But they seemed reluctant, nearly half a century later, to discuss the subject.

"I don't know nothin'," said one relative, who had married into the family. "I can't answer no questions."

After we concluded that phone call, Dad seemed crushed, because he knew she was lying. And she wasn't the only liar or obfuscator. Many in Greenville, including close family members, saw or knew details about the murder, but they kept them from Dad.

But eventually we pieced together the most likely account: Papa Lum was in a gambling house. An argument began—possibly about a woman's honor or a gambling dispute—compounded by white lightning courage. Even though a buddy begged him to leave with him, seventy-four-year-old Papa Lum stood his ground. His killer shot him at close range. Some say he was killed by an adult man; others claim a young boy. A theory exists suggesting that adults in these situations often use youngsters to take the fall, so the adults can avoid stiffer sentences. But in this case, no one was ever arrested.

After the shot, men in the house, including some family members, carried Papa Lum outside, where he bled to death. Amid the differing accounts, one consensus remains: confronting Papa Lum was risky—to stand against him meant either killing him or facing a severe beating.

For me, one of the most poignant aspects of his murder is my never having had the chance to meet him. The absence of a single photograph deepens that pain. I hold on to the hope that someday, someone will uncover one.

Only two years after Papa Lum was killed, a phone call from Newark, New Jersey, delivered another shock to our family. A detective informed Dad that Izaiah "Bud" Hawkins, one of his three brothers, had died after a fall into a cellar while staying in Newark with his girlfriend. "We can't prove it, but I believe your brother was murdered," the detective told my dad. Yet, with no witnesses or concrete evidence, Bud's death was officially labeled an accident. His son, Louis, faced a similarly mysterious fate two decades later.

The lack of official police attention to Black homicides is deeply troubling. The irony, however, is the fact that some Black people, often because of fear or indifference, withhold crucial information about such crimes from the victims' family and police. In my family, this selective "ignorance" regarding the murders of Papa Lum and other relatives hindered my dad's path to healing and acceptance.

While I often saw the repulsion in Dad's face when discussing Papa Lum's murder, the wound seemed even deeper for Mom. Dad's secret, which she too had protected for so long, was now out in the open. Once again, I had gone against our family's decades-long practice of repressing painful truths and storing them deep in our bodies, especially away from social clubs and church members who might judge us for murder being in our family's history.

My love for my paternal first cousins, the children of my father's siblings, is just as strong as the affection I felt for their parents. I often refer to the adult children of my dad's sisters who relocated north as the "Lost Tribe" of Greenville because, like me, they have spent a lot of time pondering why their parents were so secretive regarding their upbringings in Greenville. For the Lost Tribe, the question "What happened in Alabama?" echoes continuously. Unlike me, some of them overheard their mothers crying and asking one another, "Who shot Papa?" They yearned in their hearts to alleviate the burden of unanswered questions that perpetually undermined their mothers' spirits. Unfortunately, those questions remain unresolved, and we are still feeling their impact. The enigma of Papa Lum persists to this day.

55

"You Black Fucker"

The turmoil of Papa Lum's murder wasn't the only adversity Dad faced. Once he was home from the funeral, he returned to the edges of the corporate America he was just getting acquainted with, only ten years after the Civil Rights Act had become law. As my siblings and I were among the pioneering Black children integrating schools, Dad too was blazing a trail as a Black adult working as a telephone installer and technician for a Fortune 500 company. There, he battled the same dragons we fought in school. Often, he'd come home quietly, like a simmering fuse ready to erupt. I stayed away.

It wasn't until our conversation in February 2019 that I approached the subject. I was eager to understand his journey as a Black employee at US West. I questioned him on what it felt like being among the few Blacks in an overwhelmingly white environment.

Dad told me that during my high school years in the 1980s, he and his Black peers were frequently sent to growing St. Paul suburbs, such as Inver Grove Heights. These weren't coveted assignments because the region, blanketed in thick woods, required they string phone lines through trees, posing serious safety concerns. "They would send us into the areas the white boys didn't want to go to or couldn't handle," Dad said. "It was racist to the bone."

One incident triggered Dad's pent-up frustration. On a task that involved his climbing a pole to access a junction box serving several homes, he had to coordinate with a technician at the central office. As he relayed his needs over the phone to a white female technician, their conversation could be heard over the phone line of the family whose line the two were trying to fix. "This kid picked the phone up and heard me talking," Dad recalled. "He said, 'You Black nigger! Get off my phone you nigger, you Black fucker!'"

The white woman on the phone overheard the racist comment, gasped "Oh, Leo," and then suggested that Dad should leave and let someone else finish the job. My father, clearly agitated, responded, "Yeah, I don't want to have to do another piece of work out here."

The shocked woman promised to inform the higher-ups, especially since Dad's immediate supervisor was away. Dad realized, however, that his white supervisor would be more upset about the future logistical challenges than the blatant racism he'd encountered. "My boss was a jerk," Dad said. "He was the one who put me out there in the first place. He gave me all the shit jobs."

The decision escalated to Dad's boss's superior, who posed a simple question to Dad: "Leo, how do *you* feel?"

Dad firmly replied that he was leaving that location, to which the man responded, "You're outta there, and you'll never have to go back."

That very day, Dad was reassigned to Maplewood, close to home. "That was the job I wanted, because the cable there was mostly buried," Dad remarked. "So, I didn't have to climb poles."

However, the moment Dad's immediate supervisor returned and found out why things had been shuffled around, he exploded. "That bastard, he had a fit," Dad said.

But Dad heard through the grapevine that the woman from the control center and the manager who had made the decision argued back. "They probably told him, 'You've got to be crazy,'" Dad said. "'We're lucky this nigger isn't suing us.'"

The dangerous situations Dad and his Black colleagues faced went beyond just difficult suburban assignments or intricate wiring jobs. The crack epidemic had exploded, and the associated drug trade terrified some of Dad's white co-workers. Paralyzed by fear, the co-workers sometimes reported street-side business activities to the police.

Dad explained: "When the white boys would go up there and get in trouble with drug dealers or pimps and stuff—and they did—they sent us after them to talk to the damn people. Some of those drug dealers and pimps, they were going to put caps in those white boy's asses."

He continued: "Some of our employees were literally running out of the ghetto. There was one who reported hookers walking around on Selby Avenue, and when the pimps found out he was responsible, they had to get that dude outta there."

When such situations arose, it usually fell upon Dad or a Black co-worker to mediate the next day. "They would call one of us and say, 'I need you to go talk to this customer, because he's really angry. Go over there and cool him off.'"

But on numerous occasions, when Dad or another Black technician approached, the person they were sent to confront recognized them. One might ask, "Lee Roy? Hey brother, you work for the phone company?" And time after time, Dad or one of the other Black technicians would find ways to massage the situation—usually by showing basic respect. "So that's what we did," Dad said, "to the extent that one brother told me one day, 'Leo, you know man, they couldn't fire us if they wanted to, with all this shit we're doing. I mean, they're using the hell out of us.'"

One memorable incident involved him and a team of white colleagues. Their task was to set up a new phone system for the 3M Company. The project was overseen by a young and rising Black executive from 3M who was responsible for supervising both companies to ensure successful project completion.

Dad was proud of the young executive's professionalism and leadership. The brother had high expectations, and like any good leader, he wasn't afraid to step in and provide correction when needed.

One day, Dad walked into the office to find a group of older white colleagues, including one about to retire, talking loudly. One guy, who didn't see Dad walk in, was trashing the Black executive supervising the project. "'That Black-ass nigger doesn't know the stuff he's talking about,'" Dad recalled him saying. "He was swearing like a sailor saying, 'I can't stand that nigger,' over and over. The guy couldn't stand seeing a smart Black man. All that racism came out. Then he looked up and saw me."

Dad stood there silently, stunned. The man's colleagues immediately began pleading for Dad not to go to Human Resources and turn the man in. "They started saying, 'Leo, please forgive him. He didn't mean it. He just got out of whack.'"

Faced with a dilemma, Dad considered the potential consequences of speaking out. He thought about our family's financial responsibilities, including our mortgage, and memories and survival lessons from Greenville especially flooded his mind. In that moment, Dad chose silence, focusing on the importance of his job and providing for his family.

"With the racism, there were all kind of scrapes that I could've got into, but I didn't. I just kept going, like a 'good nigga,'" Dad said. "That might've been some of my Southern heritage. I don't know because there's a lot of things we went through, man, just to make that successful run toward retirement."

As Dad shared his stories, I began to understand the significance and lethality of the "John Henry" archetype and the struggles faced by countless professional Black men I knew. "John Henryism" was a concept introduced by Black epidemiologist Sherman James in the late 1970s and into the 1980s. This concept outlines the health disparities faced by Black Americans, especially high rates of hypertension, attributed to the stresses of enduring chronic racial discrimination. James's John Henryism Active Coping Scale highlights attributes like mental toughness and an intense work ethic. It captures the mindset of my dad and many Black people of his generation who believed they could overcome racism through superhuman efforts characterized by unmatched excellence and a willingness to shoulder extra burdens and assignments that white colleagues refused or were shielded from. He brokered treaties with pimps and drug dealers while constantly enduring the mental toll of racial slurs from customers and co-workers. Beyond these feats, he took advantage of his company's tuition reimbursement plan to earn his master's degree. However, this achievement never led to any significant promotion and, in fact, sparked more resentment and concern among some less-educated white supervisors and co-workers who possessed only a bachelor's degree or a high school diploma. The stress of living up to those standards day in and day out showed up in Dad's medical charts.

During the early 2000s, the decline of the industrial economy, with its high-paying jobs, became clear, just as Dad and Grandpa Buddy had predicted. I reported on General Motors's intention to cut twenty-five thousand jobs by the close of 2008. Simultaneously, Dad caught wind of potential buyouts at US West. By that time, he had transitioned to an office role in the company's Minneapolis headquarters, a change that spared him from climbing telephone poles in freezing Minnesota weather. When the expected buyouts materialized, Dad decided to retire and cash in on his three decades of service.

At age fifty-seven, he had recently undergone prostate surgery and was awaiting radiation treatments. He was managing his diabetes, and his doctors congratulated him on his robust heart. But I didn't know that his healthy cholesterol levels were maintained by medication. I naively believed his retirement would make it easy for Dad to improve his overall health and lose weight.

Reflecting on his work journey and healthy pension, Dad acknowledged that he had "won," but much like John Henry, at the cost of his physical and mental health. Even a decade after the incident with the loud-mouthed bigot of a co-worker, he couldn't shake off the memory, his own silence, or the weight of the truths he kept concealed.

Meanwhile, as a child on the receiving end of his worn, swinging leather belt, I had been oblivious to whatever had transpired that day at his job.

I had known my father was carrying burdens. But I hadn't known what those burdens were.

56

Names and Scars in the Blakey Bloodline

Though the term post-traumatic stress disorder wasn't coined until the twentieth century, the psychological wounds of enslavement, the after-effects of Jim Crow, and the horrors of warfare have had intergenerational consequences. Countless narratives hint at the trauma experienced by those ensnared in these atrocities. While a deeper examination of my mother's lineage awaits another project, I share a snippet here of the inspiring yet distressing journey of my mother's paternal great-grandfather, Civil War Private Isaac Blakey, to show how his reality influenced my mother and rippled to me.

In 2015, I discovered a newspaper ad from February 25, 1858, that further illuminated the meaning behind our three family surnames—Blakey, Blakely, and White. Published by slave dealer W. C. Harvey in Roanoke, Missouri, this advertisement in the *Glasgow Weekly* announced a "Public Sale of Negroes." Among the listed was a young Isaac, believed to be around nine years old and my great-great-grandfather, Isaac Blakey Sr., later known as Private Isaac Blakey.

This revelation reinforced the heartbreaking reality that many ancestors, on both my parents' sides, were painfully separated from their loved ones through enslavement transactions that often led to siblings from the same family to take different—European—last names.

Private Isaac Blakey endured sixteen years of bondage. Despite the ruse of adjusting his age to join the Civil War, the war brought more anguish. Governed for a lifetime by Slave and Black Codes, he battled kidney disease, heart disease, diabetes, neuralgia, rheumatism, and a leg injury from a Civil War bayonet until his death in 1917 at the age of seventy-two.

I regret not asking Grandpa Buddy about Private Isaac, considering seven of his siblings were born before Isaac's passing. Once again, our elders were often babysat by the last generation of our enslaved ancestors, and their lives and experiences helped shape us all.

In my research, I found an article in the *Sioux City (Iowa) Journal* with the headline "Enslavement Descendants to Have First Reunion," about the family gathering on August 28, 1971. As fate would have it, I was being born on that day, so my parents couldn't attend. At the reunions I later attended, Private Isaac was consistently described as "a runaway slave" who escaped his plantation to fight for freedom in the Civil War.

During the Second Battle of Bull Run on August 28, 1862, he engaged in combat against Confederate soldier Jasper Stinson—as we have seen, a potential great-great-grandfather of mine—who perished on the battlefield. This astonishing coincidence is a testament to history's intricate maze and the tangled web of antebellum families and relationships.

Digging deeper, I found that Private Isaac not only survived the war but also later found the siblings he was torn from during that crushing "Public Sale of Negroes." Yet, Isaac's successes as a "free" man didn't free him or his bloodline from the scarring whip.

During a 2019 conversation I had with Mom, she expressed surprise: "I didn't know he was a slave." Maybe she repressed the memory. She later advised a cousin, slated for an interview with me, to discuss only the positives, saying, "We want to look good." I don't begrudge Mom. Countless Black Americans, and indeed Americans across the spectrum (especially in Florida), have lamented the popularity of "slave movies" and revisiting America's ties to enslavement. Knowing that Mom prefers to repress or deny our painful memories, facing her great-grandfather's suffering might be agonizing, even embarrassing. Yet, however distant our enterprising landowning ancestor seemed, and despite the scant reminders of his shackles, his indomitable spirit, John Henryism, and the piercing whip permeated every corner of my childhood home.

But his influence was mostly felt by his twenty children, among whom was my great-great-grandfather, Isaac Blakey Jr. Born in 1877, he was the eldest of three legendary brothers. In 1905, they moved from Missouri to South Dakota to build their own farms. Isaac Jr. was a devout churchgoer, a successful businessman at Yankton's farmers' market, and a renowned pheasant hunting guide, counting celebrities like actor Clark Gable among his clientele. However, to his family, he presented another side: he was stern, emotionally distant, and sometimes cruel. Like Grandma Charity, he whipped Grandpa Buddy and his siblings early and often. The Black Codes taught him to embrace his illiteracy and hate books.

If he saw family members reading, he'd label them "lazy" and send them to toil in the fields. He would also rouse them in the dead of night or at dawn's first light to whip them with leather from a horse's harness, all under the guise of ensuring their productivity and "protecting" them. Seeing Mom's Blakey grandfather in the context of that parent-as-overseer role put my own middle-of-the-night whippings and theatrical punishments into perspective and helped me strive to compassionately understand that my mother's belief that fathers should be primarily responsible for disciplining the boys was likely rooted in her socialization as a grandchild of a farmer who took a similar gender-assignment approach in running his operation. Unsurprisingly, such treatment bred resentment in his eleven children. This explains why they placed such a high premium on education, leading to future generations becoming college deans, professors, lawyers, diplomats, entrepreneurs, and executives. Most of our elders fled their South Dakota farm, migrating to bustling cities like Minneapolis, Los Angeles, and Seattle.

Yet, they often returned to see their matriarch, Maggie Blakey. As the farm's CFO and behind-the-scenes pillar of strength, Maggie often subdued her voice to accommodate Isaac Jr.'s Slave Code–inspired insecurities, especially his illiteracy, since he resented her being able to read. Revered as a healer, Grandma Maggie delivered countless babies and, before her passing in 1960, battled a protruding goiter caused by the same slow thyroid that plagues Mom. This familial pattern of thyroid issues echoes broader findings, such as those in a 2013 study in the *Journal of Aggression, Maltreatment & Trauma* showing that women physically abused in childhood have a 40 percent higher risk of developing thyroid disorders than nonabused peers.

The harsh discipline Mom unleashed—predawn or midnight whippings, declarations of "don't buy us books," and biblical waterboarding—also reflected the influence of her grandfather Isaac Blakey Jr. These actions, while distressing, also hint at the deep scars left by his father's early years of enslavement and subsequent wartime experiences. God bless them. My research suggests that being the son of a man enslaved for sixteen years and later wounded in the Civil War deeply affected my great-grandfather Isaac Jr., shaping his and subsequent generations' lives.

Private Isaac not only taught his sons to farm, hunt, and fish and transition to landownership, but he also—understandably—perpetuated the Slave Codes. The oral history that most explained the impetus of my mother's disciplinary techniques came from kin who had lived on the Yankton farms where the Blakey brothers—Spencer, Henry, and Isaac Jr.—prospered.

My cousin Phyllis Blakey-Thornton, now in her seventies, had assumed as a child that the Blakey brothers, including her grandfather Spencer, had been enslaved. This belief stemmed from seeing the keloid whip scars on their backs. On a scorching day in the 1950s, as Spencer labored shirtless in his field, Phyllis took him warm water, as instructed by her grandmother, Lovey. She was transfixed by a pronounced scar on Spencer's back and asked about it. Spencer tersely said, "You have no business looking at your grandpa. That mark isn't something you need to know about." But Lovey stepped in, telling Phyllis that Spencer had been enslaved as a boy and subject to his master's whip.

"I asked, 'What's a master?' I was too young to understand the concept," Phyllis told me. "I said, 'What are you talking about, Grandma?'"

"Your grandpa used to be a slave when he was a little boy," Lovey chillingly told Phyllis. "He got whipped with a whip."

The truth, however, was that the Blakey brothers were born after emancipation. The scars were likely from beatings by white men up-holding the codes, and Private Isaac Blakey himself. They concealed the truth: it was their father, not them, who was a "slave."

I understand their reticence. How do you explain to young ones that their patriarch was enslaved and transmitted parts of that terror to the next generation? Or that they lived in a country, the United States of America, where every white man could whip or kill Black people with near impunity? Many of us naively believed that whipping ended with emancipation, oblivious to the government-sanctioned brutality against our kin for decades thereafter.

Even if my mother professed ignorance of her family's enslaved leg-acy and Private Isaac Blakey's suffering, her bones told her she needed to "protect" us with the whip, like our grandparents had been "pro-tected" from and by the whip.

57

"You're Just like My Father"

reached out to Mom a day after speaking with Dad in February 2019. She opened up about how her abusive childhood may have made her ill, being diagnosed with lymphoma at age seventy.

"I might have lymphoma from breathing in chemicals," she shared. She detailed how her stepfather, my beloved Papa Elmer, would lock her in their putrid basement, making her clean up after his hunting dogs amidst the overpowering smell of Lysol and feces.

This sparked a flash of clarity that had eluded me as a child, and that had started to become clearer when Tiffany recalled Mom locking her in the garage: to Mom, the ultimate misery was being a child locked in cold, dark, scary confined spaces, like garages, basements, and closets.

Mom's tension with Papa Elmer mirrored the resentment she held for her biological father, Grandpa Buddy. The divorce of her parents had left her feeling deserted, and Papa Elmer "was so controlling, every day it was his way or the highway," she said. "He'd tell me, 'Your dad doesn't want you. You can't go there.'"

I don't question Mom's memories. While unaware of Papa Elmer's early life, I knew he had grown up during Jim Crow and served in World War II. By then, I knew how Black male pain was often displaced on weaker targets.

Before the divorce, Mom's memories were of caring parents. In the 1940s, Grandpa Buddy left Yankton and an unkind father at the Blakey farms to seek a better life in St. Paul. Reflecting on the farm's dynamics, he thought, "If I can work like a dog for my father, I can work two jobs for myself."

After marrying in 1947, Grandpa Buddy introduced his wife to farm life in Yankton, but they eventually returned to Minnesota, settling in a well-kept duplex before Mom's birth in 1948. "I was really blessed," she said. "I had a lot of attention. A lot of attention."

By the early 1950s, the Blakeys lived in St. Paul's diverse Summit-University area. Their home was enclosed by a white picket fence with pink trim. Mom and Aunt Connie had a brief walk to school and returned for lunch to Nanny, their homemaking mother. "Family, family, family," Mom said.

Grandpa Buddy's relentless work schedule found him at Montgomery Ward in the mornings and Burlington Northern in the evenings, resting only on Sundays and Mondays. Nanny often found him asleep in the bathtub, spent from exhaustion—our real-life John Henry, with a Blakey twist.

But Grandpa Buddy's John Henryism hurt his marriage, and Mom. Her mind blocked out most memories of her early years. "I think I knew my parents were having trouble," she recalled, hesitantly. "They were arguing and fighting all the time. Mostly about . . ." Mom paused, struggling to find the words. "A lot of ladies liked Dad. Oh man, your grandpa. And they worked with him at Montgomery Ward. Their families knew about it, too, because a lot of the women were separated."

While Mom described her parents' unstable marriage and Grandpa Buddy's reputation with women, I wondered aloud whether the term "messy divorce" was fitting. She agreed and labeled Grandpa Buddy's 1950s actions, when he was in his mid-twenties, as "womanizing."

"I loved my dad, but he was gone a lot." She sighed. "It was all about him." And with that, the echoes of her screams, "You're just like my father!," came roaring back to the surface of my mind.

Her accusations that I emulated Grandpa Buddy's love for freedom had merit. His global escapades, like trips to Morocco, Nigeria, and Paris, influenced my worldview. Embracing freedom helped both of us find healing. He'd tell me, "I want you to enjoy your life as much as you can. Just keep takin' care of business and have fun, grandson. And don't apologize for it to anybody!"

All this likely planted in Mom's mind a resemblance between Grandpa Buddy and me.

Not long after I left Mom and Dad for college, Grandpa divorced again. He enjoyed every second of his life as a bachelor. Once, Mom chuckled that she saw pantyhose hanging in the bathroom of the high-rise pad he lived in. After my playful spread in *Ebony* as an "eligible bachelor" around 2003, when I joined the *Wall Street Journal*, she felt I was being "selfish." And in truth, I considered Grandpa Buddy to be a rather good role model, especially since he had a bald head through the 1970s when everyone had Afros. That made me feel unafraid to shave my head in the face of a terribly receding hairline!

Still, I felt for Mom. I finally understood her. Her memory and concern—and a very valid one—was that Grandpa Buddy had deserted her when she was a young girl, consigning her (literally) to the dogs.

58

Lysol and Coons

After prolonged conflicts, my mom's parents separated and Grandma Loretta, aka Nanny, stayed with their daughters in the family home. Then, my mother told me, Papa Elmer came "wining and dining Nanny and being the nicest man on earth to us," acting like a gentleman and bringing the girls ice cream and cookies. "He would call and say, 'Is Mother Dear home?'"

The courtship soon led to marriage, and my mother's childhood effectively ended. "He moved in, and that's when the whole thing hit the fan," she said. "He didn't want Mom to have friends. He was possessive with her, and they argued a lot." In addition to their fights, Mom remembered Papa Elmer hitting her mother, after which he would "go off for the weekend and say he was hunting."

He also hit Mom. "He spanked me a lot," she said. I asked her if Papa Elmer was the first person to whip her. "No, Grandpa Buddy started the belt thing. Everybody—all the kids in the neighborhood—were getting . . . yeah." Mom couldn't bring herself to say "beaten." She remembers Grandpa Buddy starting to strike her with a belt when she was four or five. "He would take his hand, too, and just—blam!—in the butt. But Papa Elmer was the one. He would beat us across our back, our face, everything, with the belt. And then also make me stay down with the doo-doo and all that," she said.

Papa Elmer began buying coonhounds—from blueticks, to Plotts, to redbones. He'd ship these dogs from the South and temporarily house them. "He would bring them to our basement, and I had to go down there and clean up," she said. Her slightly younger, full biological sister sometimes had to join her.

Once, Mom blurted out to Tiffany, "You're just like my sister!" It's another example of the complicated and confusing dynamics we faced as her children. Hearing Mom compare her relationship with us to her fraught ties with her sister and father left us confused. Unaware of her past traumas, we felt like unwitting stand-ins for figures from her childhood nightmares. We hoped to help her recognize us as individuals, distinct from other family members. Her path to healing lay not in casting us in roles from her unaddressed history but in confronting and mending that history herself.

And soon, the dynamics of Mom's home life got more complicated, as the family added three more kids. Mom said she was at the top of the family's pain spectrum. Compared with her full biological sister, Mom felt unloved. "I don't know, he liked her better," she told me, and he liked his three biological children even more, she added.

She remembered being out with Papa Elmer and her half-siblings and running into people they knew. "He'd say, 'This is my child, and these are Loretta's children.' Everywhere we went. He was just plain mean."

He was also very concerned about skin color. "Light skin and dark. A lot of people were like that at that time," Mom said. "His mother may have been mixed or something. There were white people in his family. They had gray eyes in the family. And if you were white, you were right; if you were Black, get back."

Furthermore, Mom was burdened with numerous household responsibilities, from babysitting to burning trash. She even took care of a hefty rabbit named Mr. Rabbit in their garage. Hearing her stories, I drew parallels with the exhaustive list of chores my sisters and I had growing up, like scrubbing toilets under the stringent aroma of Lysol. The memories of severe punishments for minor oversights also came rushing back. I wondered, if my parents hated violence and abuse when they were kids, why did she replicate that toxic environment for us?

Hearing Mom's stories gave me a new appreciation for my sister Tammi, and anyone who is the eldest of their siblings, as well as for people forced to grapple with divorcing parents at a young age. More work and more responsibility was heaped on Mom—a reality, I believe, that always drew her closer to Tammi. They had a sense of comradeship that Tiffany and I never had with Mom. I'm grateful. At least Tammi didn't have to suffer like we did. If she did, she never discussed it.

But what is clear is that, because I reminded Mom of Grandpa Buddy and Tiffany reminded her of the sister she sometimes intensely resented, we paid with our hides. My adult interview with Mom finally told the truth of our beloved mother's past as a young girl who felt abandoned and abused. Understanding more of her story, and the roles she placed us in because of it, guided us to our path of forgiveness.

Mom said that as a teenager she was often caught in the intense arguments between her mother and Papa Elmer. Just as Tiffany bravely stood up to our parents at age seventeen, Mom courageously intervened to shield her mother from her stepfather's wrath. Great-Grandpa Sam Davis also intervened on multiple occasions when Mom called him for help. "I was probably about fifteen when Grandpa witnessed the abuse," Mom told me.

On the final straw, he arrived armed with his pistol. Although small in stature, he was determined. "Oh no," he told Papa Elmer, "you're never going to do this, especially with my grandchild."

"They insisted that I move in with them," Mom said, her relief palpable after all these years. "That's when my whole life changed."

Sam and Roberta Davis—my great-grandpa Sam and great-grandmother Roberta—were pillars of kindness. If they had known of the violence in our home, they would have stepped in as they did for Mom. On my father's side, Grandma Opie would've done the same. Great-Grandpa Sam, born in 1909 to formerly enslaved people who had been freed, resisted Papa Elmer's abusive tendencies. Yet, Mom reintroduced whipping to us. Why emulate Papa Elmer when her life improved so much after escaping his clutches? Why not follow her grandparents' compassionate approach? This remains a mystery to me.

My mother seemed to be fascinated by the chivalry and protectiveness her grandfather displayed toward his wife and family. She wanted

Dad to extend to her that same brand of protectiveness. He obliged, even when it meant whipping his children.

In her 2019 interview, Mom shared family stories from the Great Depression. Great-Grandpa Sam juggled multiple jobs, including one in the meatpacking sector of the Cudahy Packing Company in St. Paul. It was a perilous industry, with high injury rates, but he was thrilled to have a job during a depression—especially as a Black man. Today, Human Rights Watch still considers meatpacking to be among the riskiest jobs in the United States.

In fact, Great-Grandpa Sam got injured on the job. "He had to come home because he couldn't even stand up," Mom said. "They said, 'You can't work here until you make sure you're okay.' They had just bought the house and had their first child. He worried he was going to lose the house."

His bosses told him he could return to his job once he recovered, but my great-grandmother Roberta "didn't know what to do," as Mom put it, with no income, so she secretly called his boss and asked whether she could work in Great-Grandpa Sam's place.

After initially dismissing the idea, his bosses offered her a job. As Mom's version of the story goes, Great-Grandpa Sam thought the conditions were too dangerous, so he told her not to go. "And she said, 'Sam, we've got to do this for our children,'" my mom told me.

Great-Grandmother Roberta was assigned to the sausage line. None of the work was automated at the time. "She was stuffing sausage, and she had to put them in this big machine, and the machine was run by big wheels then," Mom said.

About a week and a half into the job, Great-Grandmother Roberta's hand got jammed in the machine. "A man saw it. A white guy," Mom recounted. "He came and threw his body into the big wheel, and then another man threw his body in to get it to stop, but they couldn't get it to stop electrically. Her hand, above the wrist, was engulfed by that sausage machine."

Her co-workers wrapped her bleeding right hand and arm in paper and cloth. An emergency crew sped her to the hospital. Great-Grandpa Sam received word of the accident and rushed to the hospital to be by

318 | Lee Hawkins

his wife's bedside. But he was immediately overwhelmed by what he saw. "He had a breakdown," my mom said. "He was saying, 'Why did we get into this?'"

Within days, infection set in, turning the scent of medical tape and anesthetic into a pungent odor that filled the room. "Grandmother recognized the smell, and so did everyone else," Mom said. She knew amputation was an option and said she was prepared.

"I want to do the surgery now. I don't want my husband or anyone here," my mom told me she said. So, the surgery took place. When Great-Grandpa Sam arrived the next day, he was met with the sight of a massive bandage encasing her arm. "What happened?" he asked, taking in the bulging wraps and bandages. "They did surgery, and I'm going to be okay," she assured him, according to Mom. But, my mom told me, "He went into a frenzy—he was just so disappointed and upset."

After a month with her doctor's team, acquiring a prosthetic and learning to navigate life one-handed, her main worry was her infant. Her mother, Rosetta Walton, arrived in Minnesota, promising to stay as needed. Yet, upon her hospital discharge, my great-grandmother Roberta took her baby into her bedroom, changed the diaper, and told her mother she could handle everything on her own.

Throughout my life, I've heard varying tales about whether Great-Grandpa Sam was aware of Great-Grandmother Roberta's employment at the plant. Some said she took the job secretly, fearing his disapproval, while others believed he eventually consented. A few even asserted that she'd been working there well before his injury. But according to Mom, he was firmly against the idea. Perhaps Great-Grandpa Sam knew about it, but societal pressures and traditional expectations might have pushed the narrative that a man shouldn't let his wife work in such a dangerous environment.

I speculate that Great-Grandpa Sam must have known, and those who implied otherwise were most likely driven by their obsession with image. Tradition said a man should not allow his wife to work in a meatpacking plant—or even at all. Perhaps haunted by his failure to protect his wife from her devastating injury, Great-Grandpa Sam dedicated the rest of his life to serving her wholeheartedly. Besides being a painter, handyman, and landscaper, he managed the household chores, her medical needs, and her medication. Whenever I saw him, he was usually loyally serving and taking care of his wife. I frequently wondered whether he ever felt as if he hadn't protected his wife and had failed her. Had he struggled to forgive himself, even though he was blameless?

Mom witnessed his unwavering devotion and the guilt he carried, especially after moving in with her grandparents, which helped shape her empathy for the sick and her fondness for the elderly. Like us, our parents idolized the Davises, striving to emulate their bond—my parents being two wounded souls who had been pulled from the chaos of parental separation and abandonment fears by older family members. Mom and Dad clung to each other like shipwrecked survivors clinging to a lifeboat.

I observed these call-and-rescue dynamics in our household, where moments of tension—often attributed to Tiffany or me—would evoke a response of unwavering duty in Dad, reminiscent of Great-Grandpa Sam's loyalty, except great-grandpa didn't show it through violence. It was as though our father transformed into a fiercely protective force, akin to Will Smith's passion-filled slap of Chris Rock at the Oscars in 2022 after Rock commented on Smith's wife's shaved head. After the infamous altercation, Mom expressed her approval, saying, "Well, he did it because he needed to protect his wife." This wasn't merely a casual observation on her part; it was an expectation. She received that same unwavering defense from Dad. In return, he had the chance to protect our mother in ways he regretfully couldn't protect his own. This was the intergenerational cycle of our childhoods, unfolding before our eyes. And had those "chest pains" of my mother's indeed been a heart attack, Tiffany and I would have been dead meat.

59

Breaking Bread

> I have a dream that one day on the red hills of Georgia, the sons
> of former slaves and the sons of former slave owners will be able
> to sit together at the table of brotherhood.
>
> —MARTIN LUTHER KING JR.

Researching the stories of Private Isaac Blakey and my great-grandparents Sam and Roberta and how this impacted our mother was freeing, but there was one more development on Dad's side of the family that provided an opportunity to go even deeper into the 400-year archive of history about my paternal side: Reaching out to and meeting my white Pugh cousins who descend from our shared heritage with the men and women who enslaved Black families, including Grandma Charity. This marked a critical step toward confirming that enslavement marked the beginning of the belt whipping practice and opened the door for me to do more research into our family history for years to come.

Connecting with the white Pughs has started a healing process and stirred a multitude of emotions, as well as a better understanding of American history in general. Those family members have plugged me into so much history about our shared family history, and I have helped spark memories that were lost long ago. I learned that repression of traumatic memories and the denial of multicultural family identities often prevent future family members from acquiring the critical story nuggets necessary to truly discover who they are. Fortunately, on the white side of my family, there are several family members who also have a deep appreciation for genealogy, who are not so ashamed of this dark history that they refuse to acknowledge or research and study it.

I feel the same. I know they are not Jesse Pugh; they are people who share DNA with him, just like me. They should not be held responsible for the actions and sins of their forebears. Still, there's more to be done, especially in the ugly areas of the story—the parts that would spark fear and reticence within most families. But my decades as a journalist have immunized me from the affliction of feeling the need to run from stories that could be dangerous, stories that thrust a writer into unfamiliar settings and possibly open wounds and unlock mysteries so unsettling that even men and women on their deathbeds chose not to address before appearing before their maker on their own judgment day.

These unsettling mysteries: murders and lynchings, the stealing of land and property, the rape of enslaved people, the abandonment of enslaved children, secret children and affairs, and more were revealed through scientifically sound DNA and through interviews with elders who were locked in a race against time, relieved to get the chance to answer questions they were never asked before and to learn information from me.

One of the biggest breakthroughs came when Jim Pugh's name appeared on my Facebook feed after more than ten years. We had first met in Wisconsin when I was a reporter, and he was a spokesperson for a pro-business lobby. His fedoras reminded me of those my grandpa Buddy wore. But Jim was white.

I once had mentioned to him that my paternal grandmother's maiden name was Pugh. We laughed about the coincidence. Then, seeing a photo suggesting that his Pugh ancestors were from Virginia, I reached out on Facebook, as my white Pugh predecessors were Virginians, too. Jim's swift reply was, "Well, hello cousin." Further investigation confirmed our shared lineage back to Lewis Pugh, a Welshman in Virginia in 1695.

I joked, "I want my reparations, Jim. LOL." But the jest touched a deeper truth about our family history. Still, we pledged to dig into our shared past.

Jim introduced me to Lloyd Pugh, an eighty-four-year-old Civil War aficionado from Virginia and a repository of knowledge about Pugh genealogy. Jim, having explored the family's Confederate roots with Lloyd, hinted at a joint exploration but warned me of the strong Confederate pride among the Virginia Pughs and the cultural differences I might encounter.

Nonetheless, I was excited to meet Lloyd, as I saw him as a key to understanding the past and the effects of enslavement and the Civil War on my family. Lloyd invited Jim and I to his home in Virginia, where he shared volumes of family records and photos with me, and even invited his children to come meet me. They all welcomed me as family. His colonial-style house was a trove of Confederate artifacts. We discussed our common Pugh ancestry, tracing back to Jesse Pugh's father, Willoughby, from the Revolutionary War era. Lloyd's ancestors remained in Virginia, while some Pughs, including Willoughby, ventured to North Carolina and Alabama.

With Lloyd, I gained insights into my European ancestors' values and the profound impact of their white supremacist beliefs on enslaved ancestors like Grandma Charity. In his den, Lloyd shared the revelation: "My great-great-grandfather John Boyd Pugh was the overseer of Madora Plantation in Albemarle County and later the Baylor family farm in South Virginia. We were just common dirt farmers, and eventually, the farmers became overseers."

My thoughts turned to the brutal role of overseers in enforcing enslavement, and here I was, confronted with the fact I share a name with not only enslavers but white men who regulated Black people's lives with whips and guns. Lloyd noted that his great-grandfather probably didn't use a whip, since he became an overseer after emancipation. Of course, we now know the history of overseers and "able-bodied men" being required to serve "Slave Patrol." And whipping went on long beyond emancipation.

The white Pughs staunchly supported the Confederacy and its principles. Lloyd detailed John Boyd Pugh's capture and imprisonment at Point Lookout prison in Maryland. Even after the war concluded in April 1865, he resisted taking the Oath of Allegiance to America for nearly fifty days because of his unwavering Confederate loyalty. Another Pugh relative, Lloyd's uncle, showed similar defiance at Libby Prison in Richmond.

Lloyd remarked, "My dad used to say the Pughs inherited stubbornness from these ancestors," a trait he and Jim take pride in. Lloyd said he's not ashamed of his ancestors and noted that he collects Civil War memorabilia only because he wants to celebrate his southern heritage, not the enslavement of Black people. I see no separation between the two, but I recognize that Lloyd has the right to view the subject differently. What's most important is that he gave me access to mountains of photos and information that helped my research.

The Pughs of the Confederate era fought hard to keep enslavement alive, and ultimately, the bondage belief system, which today includes colorism, after-dark curfews, self-hatred and Black-on-Black murder, plantation diets, the condemnation of Blacks who have interracial friendships and relationships, mistrust of other Blacks, and the promotion of "spanking."

Other white Pugh family members helped me drill more precisely into the impact of the legacy of violence on many Pugh children descending from both sides of enslavement. When I had my first conversation with my white cousin Donna Schipani in February 2016, she was forty-seven years old. Cousin Donna is a third-great-granddaughter of Jesse Pugh. Donna now lives in Iowa with her husband, but she grew up on the Alabama side of the Florida Panhandle—where many of the Pugh family members of Roy Jones Jr. live—and considers herself an Alabaman to the core.

It was the congenial and kind Donna who helped me trace the tradition of whipping through the generations, allowing me to see that whipping also stayed alive on the white side of the family long after slavery. After posting a video on Facebook about corporal punishment in Black America, I was surprised to see that Donna commented on the post. "I had to pick my own switch and carried stripes on my backside and legs for days," she wrote.

I called her the next day, and she confirmed my longtime hunch that corporal punishment had been a key part of the white Pugh culture, and that her parents had been similarly beaten. And just as the abuse was handed down through the generations on the white side of the family, so it was handed down on the Black side. My parents simply replaced the whip with a belt.

Indeed, connecting to some of the white Pugh family members

showed me that, despite the difference in race, the two sides of the family are more alike than different, down to the brutality of the whips and belts that left the stripes on our skin. In a 2017 paper published by the American Psychological Association, writer and professor Stacey Patton made the connection between the plantation in our living rooms to those of the South.

"Historians and anthropologists have found no evidence that ritualistic forms of physical discipline of children existed in precolonial West African societies prior to the Atlantic slave trade," she wrote. "West African societies held children in much higher regard than slave societies in the Atlantic world, which placed emphasis on Black bodies as property, not as human beings."

She said that West Africans, where 82 percent of my blood can be traced to, believed that children came from the afterlife, that they were gods or reincarnated ancestors who led profoundly spiritual lives and held extraordinary mystical powers that could be harnessed through ritual practice for the good of the community. In fact, she added, it was believed that coercion and hitting a child could scare off their soul. Indigenous people of North America held similar beliefs.

"As colonization, slavery, and genocidal violence made life harsher for these groups, parenting practices also grew harsher," she said.

But despite the DNA that unites us, when it comes to how we view and interact with history, the white and Black sides of the Pugh family couldn't be any different. The legacy of slavery and Jim Crow still shape the way we view our respective experiences in America, and who we exalt and value as our heroes. And even within the same races, family members can have different perspectives, based largely on where in the United States they live.

This was clear to Cousin Jim as he sat down at a barbecue restaurant with family from the South. He lives in Wisconsin, where, according to the Wisconsin Historical Society, between 1842 and 1861, more than 100 freedom seekers were helped to freedom in Canada by Wisconsin residents.

"Then, to go to Petersburg (where Lloyd is from), which was the hotbed of the Confederacy, and have dinner with my cousins, it's a different culture," he said. "There are pictures of General Lee on every wall in the barbecue hall, because General Lee was the leader of the Virginia army . . . Yeah, it's different, but these people are my family. It was definitely a learning experience to get to spend time with everybody."

I, too, recognized that I needed to be tolerant of the differences in views that I had with family, both Black and white. In Alabama, I met my fair share of Black cousins who said Jim Crow "wasn't that bad," citing the fact that Black people had thriving communities and businesses—a fact they were proud of. Some saw integration as a major setback, some even said they would rather not know about murdered family members or ancestors who were enslaved, and some warned me that meeting white family members and doing research could get me "into trouble" with white people.

When you're chasing information about your roots, you must be open to hearing about the perspectives of everyone, and to learning the hows and whys behind those perspectives. You must understand that everybody has their own preferences and interpretation of the world. And while we may never agree on much, there's still value in tracing roots together, and accepting that family history means different things to different people.

The fact is, Jim, Lloyd and I have become good friends since we reconnected. I'm no fan of General Lee, but I would never want to see that Confederate history removed from curriculums. I also appreciate that Lloyd was kind enough to open up three full binders of information, going back four hundred years, to help me gain a better understanding of the history—albeit dark—that we share. He also introduced me to his children, as they all gathered around to hear him share his encyclopedic knowledge of the Civil War and the Pughs with me, both topics I needed to understand to better grasp the Black side of the family's American journey. I was grateful for that, and I can say that even though he's proud of the Confederate heritage and I'm ashamed of it, I have enjoyed getting to know the white Pughs, and every one of them has felt like a visit with family.

My view of them as family is partly rooted in my understanding that their willingness to open up and share family heirlooms of information, despite how difficult that can be, gave me access to records I otherwise would never have been able to find, especially with backstories. Many times, through my research process, I felt the sting of being told that a record was burned or "all of the records before 1977 have been purged." In some cases, the burning of courthouses and the purging of old records means that we can never truly connect to the ancestors we discover as we push further back into the 1700s and early 1800s. Therefore, white family members who have handed down or kept access to critical family records that can reconnect Black descendants of enslaved people can help facilitate the processes of healing and enlightenment.

One of those people is my cousin Gail Luker Allred, the woman who helped me find the Jesse Pugh will. I relate to her on a unique level, because she is mostly white but part Indigenous and has dedicated her time off as a retired teacher to helping Florida residents with Creek lineage get verified and gain formal membership into the tribe.

In one of our phone conversations, she opened up about how it felt to be approached by a cousin and descendant of "Charity, a negro girl," in Jesse Pugh's will.

"I can tell you, I cried over that because now there is an absolute connection with someone who has this in the lineage—that they lived this, and that it's on a piece of paper, as a woman," she said. "Especially in that time, you had no choice. You pretty much were chattel, and that's a hard thing for a woman of my time to embrace; to understand that. I can think about it, but to actually understand it, that's a hard thing."

And then we crossed into the territory of what Gail felt she needed to say; a point that so many descendants of enslavers who address the pain the actions of their ancestors caused reach during conversations with Black relatives.

"Someone owned another human being and had all rights to them. That is not something that I took lightly, because there were other families," she said. "I have other family ancestors that did, and one was a David Collin Mims, and he owned dozens and dozens of people and that's not something that you or I relish."

This history does haunt many of my white cousins.

My response has been to remain quiet when they discuss the ways in which it impacts them; to not make judgment, and to not immediately weigh in. There comes a time in many contacts with a white cousin where, if you speak long enough, the inevitable topic will come up. They eventually will broach or directly address slavery. It's the elephant in the room that both terrifies us and connects us.

Like me, Jim was grateful to Lloyd for sharing his almost encyclopedic knowledge about the Pugh family's role in the Civil War.

I asked him how it felt when he was sitting in Lloyd's den, looking at the wills that contained the names of the enslaved, and learning the fact that some of his ancestors were enslavers and overseers. "Did it affect you?" I asked, "or did you just realize that this is just a part of history that happened?"

"I don't think it was stunning when I saw the documentation. You couldn't have had relatives in Virginia in the 1800s and not have people who either owned enslaved people or were familiar with it," he said. "The thing that I saw that was probably most startling were the wills that articulated slaves, and who was owned, and attached dollar values to slaves, and that they were handed down through generations. And that's horrible, man, to see that firsthand documentation."

For me, seeing the documentation inspired me to feel more empathy for my parents, who, without having an opportunity to trace belt whipping back to the precise plantations where it all began, couldn't have known how wrong the widely held belief that belt whipping was "a Black custom" actually was. While it might seem natural to condemn my parents for the violence they manifested, understanding the larger historical context is crucial. Indeed, the violence that plagued our family wasn't a mere personal failing but was also a reflection of the traditions of the white overseers whose blood runs through us. Though driven by a protective instinct to shield our children from a hostile world, our methods were entrenched in a dark legacy. But hope remains. It's time we recognize that every child, irrespective of color, deserves a life of dignity and freedom, especially from violence and fear.

60

Breaking Every Chain

Exploring the rich historical context was eye-opening, but the real depth of emotion emerged during my final interview with Dad. To this day, I don't know why in that last, uninterrupted three-hour interview I did with my father in February 2019 he chose to tell me so many things he had held back his entire life. That interview proved to be revelatory. Dad dug deep to recall memories from his time in Alabama that he had suppressed for decades, disclosing information that he had never shared in hundreds of conversation-filled meals, car rides, trips to the barbershop, or bull sessions at the kitchen table.

Whatever his reasons, my father blessed me that day with an abundance of thoughtful and insightful answers to all my questions about our family's complicated past. Those final revelations provided crucial missing pieces that helped me make sense of the chaotic and oppressive puzzle of my childhood.

I started by asking him perhaps the most fundamental question of all: Why did he beat me and Tiffany when, as the cherished baby of his family, he had rarely been beaten by his own parents?

Dad was taken aback by my question, but not offended. He knew that the biggest predictor of any sort of domestic abuse is the abuser's having been abused—and that situation didn't apply in his case. He thought for a few minutes before answering.

"I really can't say, because I didn't see a lot of things," he said, referring to all the stories his older brothers had told him about the violence that his father, Papa Lum, had inflicted on them before my dad was even born. "I don't know, man. It was just some kind of a stress that I had, evidently. That's a hard one."

"Was Mom also telling you to do that?" I asked carefully. "To beat me?"

"Well, sometimes. You *know* that. And I felt guilty about that part. Really, I did."

We both fell silent. I stayed quiet and he eventually continued: "There was right or wrong for me, and when I felt that one of you did something wrong, that's when the discipline started."

But then he surprised me, conceding that with many of the beatings, he was taking out his stress on us. In those instances, he said ruefully, "I figure that I probably wouldn't have given much of a damn whether it was right or wrong."

My mind conjured an image of my father as that quintessential young brother from the seventies: in a mod turtleneck, crisp "slacks," a neat Afro, and sideburns. Only now do I recognize the enormity of the challenges he faced. My parents were only twenty years old when they had Tammi. Everyone I've spoken to from that time emphasizes how madly in love they were when they married in that traditional military wedding. There was my father, a Southern young man without a college degree, stationed in the icy depths of a Vietnam War–era air force base in Minot, North Dakota, with a baby imminent. The pressure to not merely survive, but to thrive, must have been stressful.

Shortly after, I was born. Then, he was hit with the news of his father's death in Alabama. And just a few years following that, his brother Bud died in that ambiguous "accident" in Newark, New Jersey—where he'd relocated in search of a "better life."

"People were dying, and there was a lot of responsibility for me," Dad said. "I had people asking for money and stuff like that."

The stress he felt, he said, arose from being a young husband and father, as well as from "all of the things that I had seen my mom go through—and that was hardcore."

Dad sighed heavily before continuing. "And so, if I thought you guys did something, that was when I would get out of control like I did. Because it *was* out of control. I don't give a damn how you put it."

I figured that story was the last piece of information I needed to get a definitive understanding of "what happened in Alabama." Then he gave me more, including the incident of his mother's bleeding leg and its mysterious cause. Knowing intuitively that being exposed to all that violence against women put him at risk for committing it himself, he vowed not to turn into one of the men he grew up around who hit women.

Even the thought of witnessing his mother's bleeding that day deeply unsettled him. Yet, he never voiced even a hint of a suspicion that Papa Lum might have been the cause. Just like the day he pressed his foot on my neck, I suppose the mere mention was too much to comprehend, bear, or utter.

"When people have pains like that, man, it bothers the hell out of me, when I think about physical abuse to anybody, especially women," he said. "To deal with things like that is so critical, because I ended up being that way in a sense myself when it came to women. Because I saw it in the males around me. And I had to fight like hell to try to get that right. And I did get it right, that I wouldn't do that. I saw it from them, and I saw what I was heading to. And I made it up in my mind, That's it, I have to find a way to go through this without violence."

Even now, his words underscore a stark truth: while society, including my father, recognized and approved of the need to shield our mother and other women from violence, this same understanding wasn't extended to children. Children, smaller and far more vulnerable, all too often don't receive the protection they need from the very adults responsible for their safety. It's baffling to me that while my parents could never tolerate the idea of any woman, especially my mother, facing physical abuse, they still subjected Tiffany, a girl, to welts from a swinging belt and even a law enforcement–style hold. It remains incomprehensible how society can value the safety of adults—and even dogs—over children, ignoring the fact that hitting the young is a form of domestic violence. Sadly, children often find the least protection from such harm in the very places they should feel safest: their homes and schools.

Nevertheless, our father recognized, and I agree, that his violence could have been even worse. "One thing that worked in my favor was that I wasn't a heavy drinker who would go crazy or anything," Dad said.

But he easily could have been. The Adverse Childhood Experiences research has found that children who witness violence involving their mother are at a higher risk during adolescence of facing drug and alcohol abuse and depression.

Greenville held countless stories like this. Dad recalled some of the intelligent and talented Black boys he used to know who ended up lost to liquid lightning and violence. Some had no shot at realizing their potential. We both thanked God that he and Mom avoided that trap. They drank little and never touched drugs. I shudder to think what would have happened to Tiffany and me if they had.

The cumulative effect of everything Dad went through in Greenville was that he had been traumatized without knowing he was traumatized. The ghost of Greenville lurked in every room, every hallway, every closet of our house. It took us, as father and son, almost thirty-five years to finally begin to escape it.

Another realization is that there are millions of adults out there just like my dad—survivors of Jim Crow, a system and crime against humanity that manifested in various forms across the United States, including twenty-one states and the District of Columbia. Contrary to widely held public perception, discriminatory practices akin to Jim Crow laws were not exclusive to the South and occurred in the North as well, particularly during the era of enslavement. However, it was the South that became infamous for the most severe and violent institutional horrors, such as whipping, lynching, and murdering Black people. States like Alabama, among the most notorious enforcers of the Jim Crow system, have yet to offer reparations or fully acknowledge the depth of the state-sanctioned violence and murder inflicted upon seventeen generations of Black families impacted by slavery and Jim Crow. Instead, millions of survivors like my father have been, and continue to be, expected to bury their memories and stay silent. I hold unwaveringly—and this book stands as my testament to that belief—that breaking this silence is the only way forward.

Regarding my family, it became clear that despite our apparent positive strides in education and finance, some of us carried Slave Code violence forward. This, I suspect, is largely because we lacked knowledge of

332 | Lee Hawkins

our country's and families' history, blinding us to the destructive patterns we inherited. Dad once reflected on the violence. "If it was up to me and the way I felt about things, I wouldn't have ever done anything like that," he said. "I don't know how I got out of control like that. Something was back there in my life that did that to me, and I know it."

I was determined to search out what was "back there" in Dad's life, and fortunately, my father joined me in that quest. He talked candidly with me about his past because he had figured out that the more light we can shed on our forebears, the better positioned we are for healing.

Of course, Dad's post-Alabama life in Minnesota carried its fair share of racism, too. When our conversation shifted to the 1980s, he told me about the stress of his job and his experiences as a Black man working for corporate America that I related. I was appalled by the pressures he faced.

"Those were rough days," he admitted. "Yeah, that could've been when I had my issues. Boy, I'm just so sorry I didn't have more control on that situation, because yeah, I could imagine I never was under control."

"Yeah, but you were young too," I said, acknowledging how much he had evolved over that nearly forty-year period. "You were only in your thirties."

"Yeah, the pressure of life was there, man. We wanted things and we thought we had to do that, but the fault wasn't on y'all kids. It was just me."

Dad's obvious regret and his willingness to take responsibility was therapeutic for both of us. We laughed a lot during that interview. My father always had an uncanny ability to take the most dire circumstances and find humor or inspiration in them. He was the only person I ever knew of, besides Richard Pryor or Redd Foxx, who could tell a story about having a gun pulled on him, staring down its barrel, and being saved only by the grace of God—and make it hilarious.

I was deeply moved by how beautifully my dad expressed his feelings, detailing how his past experiences influenced both his worldview and approach to parenting. Through love for his children and the eager pursuit of self-reflection and more formal education, he identified the root causes of his anger and the abuse I faced during my childhood. Without reservation, he condemned our culture of corporal punishment as an obstacle to Black progress. And he embraced my encouragement to recognize himself—and those he left in Alabama—as what they truly are: survivors of Jim Crow apartheid. This conversation unveiled layers of my father I'd never seen. As we ended it, my heart swelled with a renewed respect and depth of feeling for him.

Feeling the buzz from my interview of Dad on that crisp February day, everything felt in place for the phone interview Mom had lined up for the next day. I was bubbling with anticipation. My conversation with her began on a high, meandering through tales of her younger days, her dreams, how she met Dad, and surprisingly, the reflections on Papa Elmer and Grandpa Buddy that I shared. She had never been so open, and I appreciated it. I assumed it was difficult for her.

About two hours in, she asked why I'd asked about trauma. I explained that I believed that childhood trauma is at the heart of so many of our societal challenges, and that I wanted to learn about her struggles so I could understand my own and help others. I said I was writing about the whippings we experienced as children, how gravely they had impacted me, and the confrontation and family therapy that evolved from them. My goal, I said, was partly to use my own childhood to help spur a sea change of peace and nonviolence across Black America—in our homes and in our communities—so that our children can finally be free of violence and the shackles of white supremacy and the legacy of enslavement.

My mom was livid. She grew angrier when I told her that my earliest memory was getting hit as a three-year-old in the duplex in Rondo, but that my research had revealed that Papa Lum was murdered around that time, so I understood what Dad must have been going through. She insisted that my memory was wrong. And I surmise she felt I was "embarrassing the family" by any mention that dad's father had been murdered.

The tension was thick, even over the phone. Her reaction solidified an assumption I'd carried for a while—that she would deflect the blame for her past actions onto me. As Alice Miller wrote in *Thou Shalt Not*

334 | Lee Hawkins

Be Aware: Society's Betrayal of the Child: "The victimization of children is nowhere forbidden; what is forbidden is to write about it."

Mom snapped and screamed at me. Deep down, I felt that her earlier nods to counseling and (feeble) apologies were less about true remorse and more about keeping up appearances. Instead of discussing the violence she had brought down on us, she lied and said she had never hit us with a belt. In her eyes, it wasn't her moments of unchecked anger that were the issue, but the audacity Tiffany and I exhibited by talking about it.

As Mom continued to rant, she reverted to a former version of herself, but without the cocky "Do you want us to kiss your ass?" bravado from 2003. This time, her attack was all about the horror of people knowing what she and Dad had done to us, even though she denied ever whipping us with a belt.

"You want revenge! This is cruel, Lee," she shrieked. "Your poor father!" She then launched into yet another gaslighting episode, spouting a mix of wild claims. She argued that I should "talk to other African American people" about whipping being intrinsic to our culture and insisted, "We didn't beat you—we spanked you on your bottom." Finally, she questioned, "Do you really think you're going to help people with this?" It was the verbal equivalent to frantically shutting every window in the house.

I hung up.

That night, I left back-to-back voicemails for Dad. I apologized for upsetting Mom but asserted that I wouldn't alter my book on the basis of her concerns about her social standing. I declared that she had a choice: to be upset or to be proud of the bravery of her children.

Days slipped by. By the third day, I started reconciling with the possibility of never hearing from my parents again. I'd proceed with my book and pray that they might eventually come around. Doubts hovered: Was Dad angry now too? Would he revert to the childhood patterns, call, and threaten my life because Mom was upset, believing she could shut down the book's publication and distribution in the name of maintaining appearances at church? It wasn't the first time someone had tried to use pressure tactics to try to kill a story.

Revisiting my father's final interview, it became clear that each of his revelations acted as an essential building block in what I've named FUTURE: Family Unity Through Understanding Roots and Experiences. This process involves in-depth research into family origins and analysis of that research. FUTURE is designed to help individuals navigate and reconcile with the challenging aspects of their family history, tracing how these elements have influenced their lives. It's a method I've developed to systematically confront and understand how a person's ancestral past has affected their present, facilitating a journey of discovery and connection across racial divides and generations. We are not responsible for the sins of our forebears, but we can break toxic cycles, and break every chain, in the present to help shape a better FUTURE.

I held out hope that this structure and promise of FUTURE wouldn't come crashing down, that my dad wouldn't regress to his 1980s self, fly into an irrational rage, and tell me that exploring the traumatic effects of our history was "disrespecting your momma!"

But as I revisited each of his confidences, I genuinely doubted he'd turn against me this time. Over our four-year collaboration, he'd shared too much and grown too much.

In the weeks leading up to my unsettling conversation with Mom, Dad and I had plans to record songs together, reminiscent of a cover we had done in 2015 of "Do You Hear What I Hear?" My worries of Dad distancing himself were always undercut by a comforting certainty: he loved making music. Whenever we spoke, he was always eager for the studio.

The four years of interviews both weighed on him and freed him. Throughout those years, he had bottled up his pain, avoiding confronting the past. Whenever he vaguely mentioned "when Daddy died," without saying "when Daddy was murdered," I sensed the turmoil brewing within him more deeply. I also grasped the impact of Aunt Helen's death in 2013. Her significance lay not only in being the teenager who had raised him but in being one of the rare souls who understood the nightmares rooted in Greenville and her little brother's journey beyond them.

In time, I became that person for him; and he, for me. The journey was both a comforting embrace and a clarifying light.

Another day passed, and all I could do was hope that my father would remember all this and call me. I was sitting at my desk at work on the afternoon of February 21 when Dad's number popped up on my cell. Without saying hello, I blurted, "Did you get my messages Dad?"

"Hey son, I did. I got the messages, and everything is cool, man. How are you doing out there?"

Stunned by the normalcy of his tone, I needed an update. I asked whether Mom was still upset, and he said she was but had gone shopping with a friend. This was his first chance since the day I'd spoken to her to be alone to call me.

"Aw man," I said, "I didn't know what to think. I thought you were gonna go MIA on me." He laughed and then launched into one of his trademark motivational talks, one that I especially needed to hear after Mom had torn into me nine days earlier. Since I knew Mom had undoubtedly chewed him out, too, for his cooperation with this book, I expected him to be shaken, unsure, and maybe even confrontational. Instead, he was calm, peaceful, and proud.

He told me I had always been a leader, and as a journalist, I had a responsibility to write the story as I remembered it, not to please others. He explained Mom had trouble seeing me as a journalist with an obligation to tell the story objectively, because—understandably—she's my mom.

The journey to forgive my mother has been complex, underpinned by undying love. I realized that the pressures she faced as a fearful and concerned Black mother, and her actions in the face of those pressures, were shaped by the legacies of slavery and Jim Crow. Through my process of "genealogical resolution," I recognized that curiosity is the highest form of love a child can extend to a parent and to a bloodline whose actions they did not always understand. No one is perfect—especially me. I cherish the interviews she gave and the kindness she extends to her grandchildren and learned long ago to value our relationship for what it is, understanding that love transcends our past limitations. My relationship with my mother, now closer and unique, has taught me to meet people where they are, embracing the complexity of relationships. I am grateful for her; she gave me life and has significantly influenced who I am today.

In our conversation, Dad and I talked about and understood that my mother has always been fearful of my exercising free speech as an adult, especially when advancing opinions and work that delve into controversial areas. This includes addressing accountability-pushing topics like exposing the origins of child abuse and internalized stereotypes within the Black community. "Let me handle your momma," he told me, "and you just keep writing, son. I know that she's gonna come around to supporting this and supporting you."

He told me that whipping culture is "crazy," and that Black families finally need to see how the past relates to the future and how our history still haunts us so we can retire the belt and all the enslavement-inspired beliefs that accompany it. And then, he rendered the ultimate support: "Is there anything else you need?"

It meant everything to hear him say that, because he definitely understood, like never before, even as he was standing ground against tremendous pressure at home.

And then I thought about Aunt Corene's words: "Lee Roy always tells the truth." Despite my father's imperfections, his honesty never wavered. Even when I confronted him about the violence in my childhood, he never denied or downplayed it. He openly admitted to whipping us, acknowledged that it was wrong, expressed remorse, and apologized—many times. Dad never tried to shift blame onto us or minimize the severity of the abuse. Instead, he faced the consequences head-on, fully accepting responsibility for his actions. That kind of character defined him.

Tiffany and I were able to forgive our father for the painful episodes of the past because of his genuine love for his children, which he demonstrated in many ways, but especially by actively participating in our healing process. He dedicated himself to personal growth and improving his relationship with his adult children. I know that Grandma Opie's spirit felt pride in watching Dad's evolution toward restraint and love, watching him finally stand up against the generational waves of violence that she died trying to end.

I told him again how much I admired the depth it took for him to brave those four years of interviews, and that listening again to the interview about his whole life from three years old on made me so proud of him, of his evolution, and of how much he'd accomplished, especially relative to where he had come from. He had become a strong father, husband, and grandfather who showed us so much love over more than four decades, so much more than the dark moments that we all regretted. I was grateful that he willingly fielded an onslaught of tough, probing questions that once would have thrown him into a fury.

"You're a deep man, Dad," I said just before we hung up. "A deep man."

61

Chest Pains, Part Two

On February 23, 2019, two days after that last phone conversation, a Sunday, my dad played guitar for the church choir in a black suit and a Kente Kufi—an orange, green, and black hat symbolic of West African heritage. This ensemble mirrored our fascination with West African culture and the traditional American style passed down to me.

Although he had felt unwell for a week, he remained devoted to Mount Olivet and attended that Sunday service. Afterward, he planned a two-hour rest before a concert date at Mystic Lake Casino that evening with Mom. Dad wasn't particularly fond of concerts, preferring to perform himself. However, he made exceptions for icons like B. B. King and Aretha Franklin. Having recently celebrated his and Mom's fiftieth wedding anniversary, he was particularly excited about this concert with Buddy Guy and the Staple Singers. Their track "Will the Circle Be Unbroken?," about a family mourning their mother, always resonated with us.

The trek from the parking area to the concert hall was grueling. Dad's inadequately rehabbed knee, under the pressure of his weight, forced him to hobble and take frequent breaks, with Mom waiting patiently.

Arriving just in time, they took their seats. Mom noticed Dad was breathless. Under dim theater lights, he requested a stage photo. She obliged, but when she turned to him, he had slumped over. Pulseless.

Six strangers helped carry him out of the theater while casino staff scrambled to find a defibrillator. His heart was briefly revived, sustaining him until he was airlifted to Memorial Hospital in St. Louis Park. During the flight, they had to jump-start his heart once more.

That Sunday, I was at home in my apartment near New York City, working to hit my draft deadline. By 10 p.m., I saw several missed calls from Tiffany. She said Dad had "passed out" at the Buddy Guy concert and was being airlifted to the hospital.

Given Dad's history of type-2 diabetes causing dizziness, we weren't overly alarmed. We assumed that Mom, with her medical knowledge, had ensured he was taken to the hospital. Our parents were always going to hospitals. Mom conquered the years of chest pains, a pulmonary embolism, and lymphoma, with Dad faithfully attending her treatments. Dad had all his medical issues, too, but since they always seemed to rally and end up fine, we didn't imagine it could be as serious as it was. All the years of emergency room visits and family prayers about health tests had programmed us to think that Dad could overcome any challenge.

Yet, the fact that a helicopter was involved forced me to wonder whether God was calling him home. Was his resilience reaching its end?

I reached out to Tammi, who was en route to the hospital and similarly in the dark. We started praying, harder and harder. Writing became impossible. Just before midnight, Tiffany called once more. "The doctor wants to talk with you," she said.

He told me that Dad had had "a cardiac event." Just three years earlier, Grandpa Buddy's doctor had told us, "There's nothing we can do." I felt a jolt of fear I couldn't suppress.

The doctor told me in a clipped accent: "We found a 95 percent blockage in one artery and an 80 percent blockage in another artery. We cleared those arteries and put in stents. He is now resting."

The doctor told us that he had seen this many times before, and that he had worked with plenty of people who had stents placed and then walked out of the hospital and managed to lose enormous amounts of weight under his supervision. Finally, I thought, this would be the wake-up call Dad needed to turn his health around.

My mind raced back to seeing Dad ambling slowly after that football game, the same man who played basketball well into his fifties, long after I had quit. A surge of anger took hold. In that heartfelt conversation just two days before, Dad mentioned he had felt unwell all week. He'd gone to the clinic three times. Yet, his doctors had dismissed this obese, diabetic, seventy-year-old Black man's concerns without testing his heart. Proper tests might have revealed those blockages, but they hadn't bothered to run them.

Seething, I bought a ticket to Minnesota and packed the clothes I thought I'd need for perhaps a week there. My hand paused over my freshly dry-cleaned black suit. I refused to pack it.

On my flight, I replayed the interview I'd had with Dad for this book. I homed in on the segment where he recounted Grandma Opie's words, spoken shortly before she died: "She talked to me a lot before she died. She was just telling me, 'I'm not gonna be here much longer.' It was hard for me to get that into my head. I couldn't even fathom it. I denied that all the way."

In the past few years, my dad had often reminded us all of how immensely proud he was of us. And whenever he'd get so sentimental, my sister Tiffany and I would ask him why he kept telling us that. "Because I want you to know that, because I may not be here much longer," he'd say.

We always shrugged that comment off with, "Oh, Dad," and laughs. Our parents, we believed, were always morbid and overly dramatic about the possibility of tragic events unfolding. "You still have so much more to do. God's not through with you yet," was my common refrain. But who was I to tell my dad what God's plan was? Clearly, denial ran in the family.

I closed my eyes and said another silent prayer, asking God to give my dad at least one more chance. "And here I am, coming to you again, God, asking for yet another miracle," I said, feeling the guilt amid my desperation. "I know that you are a miracle worker, but you've done it so many times. And I want to thank you. Please, Lord, do it again."

My faith told me that Dad could emerge even stronger from this.

Arriving in Minneapolis, I bypassed the rental car delays and opted for a cab to the ICU. The room, reminiscent of a small college dorm, accommodated about six visitors. It had a curtain entrance and a window overlooking the hospital's main entrance. As I neared, I glimpsed Dad amidst a web of tubes. I smiled briefly and hugged one of my mom's sisters, but my focus was immediately drawn to Dad. A tube extended from his mouth, another from his nose, and monitors were all around him, displaying his vitals. The rhythmic sound of oxygen stressed the gravity of the situation. His perfectly styled hair and vibrant, youthful skin offered a fleeting hope, but it was soon overshadowed by crushing apprehension.

Seeing all those contraptions, I knew that this could be it. I left the room and sought solitude in a corner, where I could let my tears flow without anyone seeing or hearing me. I prayed and prayed.

When I reentered the room, I gave Mom a long, love-affirming hug. I thought of the panic she must have felt seeing her teenage love unconscious in that theater seat and the frantic moments when the casino staff searched for a defibrillator.

By the second day, the hospital was carrying out procedures to regulate Dad's body temperature. Outside his room, family and friends filled the waiting area, furnished like a homey living room, with a TV softly playing in the background. Yet, our focus remained on Dad as we comforted the steadily growing flow of visitors. Our guests—a sea of Black faces—flowed in. And Nurse Zoe, originally from West Africa, prayed with us. Right there, with Mount Olivet's pastor, we held our Baptist vigil, filled with expectancy, hope, constant prayers—and a lingering skepticism.

My father's sentiments toward healthcare were complicated, mainly because of his memory of Grandma Opie being sent home to die, with the doctor maintaining there was no point in her going to that small white house that served Black patients across the street from the hospital. I might not know every detail of Grandma Opie's last moments, but the centuries of injustices Black Americans have historically faced in healthcare are well-documented. As Jason Silverstein has highlighted in the 2018 *VICE* article "Jim Crow Laws Are Gone But They're Still Making Black People Sick": Jim Crow's detrimental health effects were vast: all the way up to at least 1964, white nurses could legally decline helping Black patients; integrated mental health rooms were forbidden. In 1929, only six Mississippi hospitals served Black patients. It is no wonder that by 1946, fewer than 10 percent of all births of Black children in Mississippi took place in a hospital compared with nearly 70 percent of white births, Silverstein wrote.

W. E. B. Du Bois lost his two-year-old son to a treatable infection because "no White physicians [were] willing to treat a Black child," a story that he recounts in his 1903 classic *The Souls of Black Folk*. Even in cases of child rape, many white doctors refused to examine Black girls.

Intuitively knowing this as a survivor, Dad was adamant about not being removed from life support, fearing that potential racial biases might lead to his premature end. He similarly resisted organ donation, concerned that doctors might value his organs over his life. This is a notion echoed by organ donation statistics: Blacks constitute more than 25 percent of waitlists but fewer than 15 percent of donors.

Were his fears unfounded?

Observing my father's hospital experience added more layers to this narrative. His second day was tumultuous, with varying doctor outlooks. Yet, the constant visitor flow moved the nursing staff. Nurse Zoe, originally from West Africa, prayed with us, while another white nurse, from a different floor, came to check on Dad when she wasn't on the clock.

By the third day of his hospitalization, two young white doctors shared concerning updates. His organs were faltering, requiring kidney dialysis, which carried significant risks. I told them we wanted to go for it, we wanted every measure taken, knowing it was my father's wish.

"He's a very sick man," one doctor responded.

My mom shifted nervously in her chair. "If this were your father, what would you do?" she asked him.

"I wouldn't even have to question it. I would let him go," he said. We were going to find more difference of opinion ahead of us.

Later that day, I told a friend that I had been praying for God's will to be done. "Why pray for God's will?" he asked. "Why don't you pray for what you want? You want more time with your dad, right? Then pray for that."

The family gathered around, and we held hands and asked God to bless my father while they wheeled him away for dialysis. Prayer had worked for us before during other illnesses. I waited in a chair outside his room until one of the doctors came and told me, "He made it through. It looks good."

But at about 3:30 a.m., Tiffany awakened me in my hotel room and told me that the nightshift doctor—not the ones who had met with us the previous afternoon—wanted to talk to the entire family about Dad's decline.

A dialysis machine had been moved to my dad's room. As we waited for the doctor, a white nurse came in to change a filter in it, looking annoyed. She complained to my sister about how Dad's low blood pressure was making his blood thicken, so she had to change the filter more often than usual.

After she left the room, Tiffany told me that the same nurse earlier had been griping under her breath about the family's choice to pursue dialysis. In front of Nurse Zoe and my mom and sisters, she even kicked my father's bed and blurted out, "What's the use?!," making sure everyone could hear her. "You're just putting a Band-Aid on a very deep wound and prolonging the inevitable."

I later made it clear to her what the family's desire was and told her, "Your job is to execute it, not to give us your opinion." She bolted from the room.

When the nightshift doctor—a foreign born man—arrived, he told us, as the earlier doctor had, "Your father is a very sick man. His lungs aren't clearing up. He's on dialysis; without it, he'll stop functioning in two hours. His organs are shutting down." We thanked him and reiterated our hope for a miracle, clarifying the family's choice to continue dialysis unless his heart ceased beating on its own.

"We believe in prayer," I told him. We yearned for a peaceful moment with our father and our devastated Mom, but the doctor pressed on with his opinion. "Well, I'm spiritual. But if God is going to pull a miracle, he doesn't need me," he asserted. I tried to convey our faith in divine intervention through any medium, even through him.

He departed briefly but returned a few minutes later, pressing his case further.

Having heard my sisters' stance previously, I firmly reiterated our view. I drew parallels between halting dialysis and physician-assisted suicide to stress our feeling, trying to quell his eagerness by telling him, "This isn't a Dr. Kevorkian thing."

Sir," he tried to intervene.

"No, listen, you've spoken. We're clear about our stance," I responded.

He continued to elaborate on the technical challenges, defending the nurse's complaints about the dialysis machine. The back-and-forth intensified as we tried to maintain our ground, explaining our beliefs and perspectives, requesting time with our father.

Then, he turned to me, and kept talking. This time, he started telling me that "stopping all the things that we're doing is by no one's definition in the medical community, physician-assisted suicide.

"That's a very polarizing thing to say, and it's actually a little on the offensive side to say to a physician. So please don't say that."

He was upset and wanting to argue with me about that, but not the least bit concerned or sincerely apologetic about the nurse kicking Dad's bed.

I was stunned that the doctor kept arguing with us after many declarations of our position. I told him that I didn't make the statement to offend him, but that I said that to illustrate to him how his badgering was making us feel; that he seemed to want to force the end of our father's life, and I couldn't understand the urgency. Did he really care about what was best for the patient and family? Or did he want a resolution before his shift was over? Or did he need the room for another patient? I didn't get it.

Throughout, the doctor emphasized the severity of Dad's condition. It felt like a cyclical conversation: we understood him, but he refused to respect our opinion and my father's patient rights, almost as if he resented us for daring to exercise those rights. The interaction became so heated that my mother felt compelled to mention our father's excellent insurance coverage, thinking the doctor might be questioning our ability to pay.

Reflecting on the confrontation, I pondered how Black people without our resources or knowledge fare in these situations. Do they relent under pressure?

I felt compelled to explain why it was that we felt the need to fight so hard for Dad. "This man is a Vietnam-era veteran. He wasn't born with voting rights," I told him. "So, we're going to honor him. That's the situation with him. He's a Jim Crow survivor. That's what you're dealing with right now. He's our concern right now," I said, continuing:

"Everybody in this room is a beneficiary of him, except for maybe her," I said, pointing to a white nurse in the corner. "So, we're respecting him, and we appreciate you. And thank you for coming."

"We are just needing time with him for grieving," Mom added. "We just want peace. Peace."

The doctor finally backed off and told us, "We'll try to get him started again."

Nurse Zoe stood tearfully in the doorway. "This is not right," she whispered. It comforted us, especially my mother.

I hugged Mom and kissed her cheek as snapshots of her life with Dad no doubt flickered across her mind: their wedding, children, grandchildren, anniversaries, retirements—all of it. Despite misconceptions some people hold—including some doctors who think Black people can withstand more pain than whites—we bleed and hurt like anyone else. Our ancestors and John Henryism toughened us, but that doesn't make us immune to pain. We are resilient, often seen as superhuman, but it doesn't mean we're numb.

By 7 a.m., things began to shift. The kidney doctor, noticing the dialysis equipment wasn't set as he had instructed, was infuriated. "Why isn't this machine turned up?" he demanded. "Everybody, get out!"

I left my phone playing dad's favorite—Curtis Mayfield and "God Can" by the Mighty Clouds of Joy. Later, the doctor approached, revealing that he'd listened to our Gospel music. "Maybe there can be a miracle," he mused. "I'll try something unconventional. I'm going to connect your dad to two dialysis machines." Gratefully, I thanked him as he hurried away.

But then, a "Code Blue" alert sounded. Hospital staff, including Nurse Zoe, dashed to my father's side.

I ran to the family room with a defeated feeling and told Mom and everybody else, "You need to come now!" We all ran back, and just as we approached to go in, my father's heart stopped.

He died February 28, 2019, at 8:28 a.m., by Tiffany's estimation, though the time is noted as 8:30 a.m. on his death certificate.

62

Came a Long Way

The memories of my father's funeral on March 9, 2019, still float hazily in my mind. In the grip of a winter storm, the ceremony took place at Mount Olivet, where he'd spent forty-six years as a musician. The sanctuary, adorned in red carpeting, took on a horseshoe shape around the central pulpit, with choirs flanking each side of the altar. The pews were filled. I was seated snugly between my mother and my father's two remaining sisters, Aunt Corene and Aunt Toopie.

The service was overwhelming—the vast number of mourners, the prolonged speeches, and the tearful adults expressing their appreciation for my father's profound influence in their lives. As a music teacher, coach, uncle, and role model for people across races in the Twin Cities and beyond, his legacy was clear. Through the moving speeches and gospel tributes, I promised myself not to let tears stain my eulogy. It wasn't easy, but I kept that promise.

An older cousin remarked to me, "You're Lee Sr. now. If the family needs something, they'll turn to you." His statement hit me hard, and I knew I couldn't take that on, as the stress would kill me, too.

My father had an inexhaustible heart. More than his material generosity—like giving money or gifting guitars to kids—he acted as a chauffeur, trusted friend, artist, guide, and steady pillar, especially attuned to my mother's worries about her health. But in his eagerness to be there for others, he often overlooked his own health, brushing off my suggestions to be more active and eat better. Instead of frequenting a gym or opting for healthier meals, his enthusiasm for meeting new folks drew him to the regular company of the staff at our local Red Lobster, particularly after Sunday services. As I saw his health decline, he'd caution me, "Don't end up like me, son." I told him I would try not to, knowing, however, that I battle food and sugar addiction, too.

My frustration with his weight struggles simmered, but I let it go, for I knew he spent his twilight years doing what he loved: spending quality time with his wife, our kin, friends, and his grandkids, and being ever-present for us all. The irony wasn't lost on me when, during the days after the funeral, our home was filled with the very foods that ultimately had killed him—pies, cakes, cookies—and so much more. "It's like bringing cocaine, meth, speed, and heroin to the home of somebody who just OD'd," I grumbled. I was that perturbed.

Yet, that anger eased when our house overflowed with the love of about thirty loved ones, all joining hands in prayer. Sister Ballard, a cherished church friend, spearheaded a moving prayer, repeating "Thank you, Jesus" more than twenty-five times. Right there, I committed to spending the rest of my life continuing the journey of emancipation that Dad and I had started together.

And I'd fight to stave off type-2 diabetes and heart disease, fulfilling his adamant wish that I avoid them. The journey of emancipation for Black people includes recognizing that more than 150 years after the Emancipation Proclamation, the deadliest vestiges of the enslaved food diet still bring smiles to our faces, and are just as deadly.

Dad's Alabama childhood was a blend of love and despair, marked by challenges such as his mother's death, the resulting move and separation from his father, and threats from the KKK in Greenville. The Adverse Childhood Experiences (ACE) research links childhood trauma to chronic diseases like heart disease, cancer, and diabetes—all of which my father battled. People with high ACE scores often face significantly shorter lifespans.

The effects of racism also impact Black Americans' life expectancy, which was 71.8 years in 2020, nearly 6 years fewer than that of white Americans. Mary Bassett, at Harvard's T. H. Chan School of Public Health, says, "There's never been a time, not a single year, where the [US] population of African descent hasn't been sicker or died younger than whites."

The increased likelihood of ACE-related early death has hovered over my family for generations, and the cycle of trauma, without intervention, can continue to perpetuate shorter lifespans in the Black community.

But not every remnant of enslavement and Jim Crow saddled Dad. His life, similar to all the Black ancestors and elders in this book, is not a story of intergenerational trauma but one of intergenerational resilience and evolution, as he and my family managed to rise above many of the obstacles placed before us. As I was finalizing funeral arrangements, I ventured into his closet, looking for a black tie to complement the black suit I'd hastily bought. Inside, the walls were lined with meticulously gleaming shoes. Clearly, Dad, down to his shoes, strived to reject every part of Alabama that reflected the social and economic injustices that tried to thwart his progress. The immaculate shine of his black and brown wingtips reminded me that, long ago, my father had risen above. In many ways, those shoes reflected his determination to outshine the constraints of Jim Crow. Regrettably, the internalization of the reckless diet that was forced on our ancestors was the lone remnant of enslavement he couldn't overcome, but I laid him to rest with deep respect, recognizing his long-standing battle against it.

The funeral spanned one full day, encompassing a family viewing, public viewing, and the service. Then, at Fort Snelling National Cemetery, my father was buried with full military honors, complete with a gun salute and a solemn presentation of the American flag to my mother by a uniformed veteran.

In my eulogy at his funeral, I tried to contextualize the cardiac arrest he had suffered within the broader framework of the long-standing history of racism in the United States. I stressed that Dad was, in essence, a "Jim Crow apartheid survivor." That era of racial segregation is often mistakenly perceived as a "separate but equal" system, merely delineating separate communities for Blacks and whites in the South. But I felt it crucial for my family and friends to reflect on a frequently overlooked truth: Jim Crow, characterized by lynching, unchecked violence, rape, and terror was a crime against humanity that the United States has thus far failed to define and acknowledge as such.

Our family's disagreements with doctors and nurses concerning the use of dialysis for my dad felt like another form of injustice, a battle for his dignity, his honor, and his right to be treated with respect and equality.

Ultimately, my daddy, Lee Roy Hawkins Sr., departed from this world as he entered it—a Black child of Jim Crow—and his life bore witness to the triumphs and tragedies of that era. Even as he saw unprecedented progress, including the tenure of a Black president of the United States of America, he left with his family having to fight for him to be counted.

ACKNOWLEDGMENTS

My heartfelt thanks extend to everyone who contributed to the creation of this book. While it's impossible to name all, I must acknowledge those who provided substantial editorial, research, financial, and professional support: Tracy Sherrod and Patrik Henry Bass, Gary Morris, David Bordelon, Ezell Kendrick, Adrian Nicole LeBlanc, Michelle Erpenbach, Matthew Deighton, Tiffany Hawkins-Morrison, Dave Umhoefer, John Bussey, Duchesne Drew, Dr. Lee Jenkins, Donald Downs, Allan Sloan, Johnnie Roberts, Julie Wolf, Constance Rosenblum, John Geoghegan, Jane Fleming Fransson, Betti Van Epps-Taylor, Beth Kujawski, Marv Balousek, Jacqueline Mitchard, Francesca Walker, Jennair Rennie, Dr. Ian Smith, Heather Johnson, Jessica Williams, Tamika Thomas, Jennifer Hudson, Keysha McNeil, Michelle Williams, Alvina Alston, Lisa Dixon, Terranya McDaniels, Sarah Jones, Christina Hendricks, Bakari Sellers, Michelle Levander, Josh Friedman, Martha Shirk, Michael Connolly, Neal Scarborough, David Brancaccio, Joanne Griffith, Doug Belkin, William Julius Wilson, Dr. Alvin Poussaint, Daymond John, Robert Thomson, Antoinette Harrell, Betti Van Epps, Susan Blakely, Katharyn Haas, and Stephanie Capparell. Special gratitude goes to the USC Annenberg Center for Health Journalism's Fund for Journalism on Child Well-Being, Mayo Clinic, Kaiser Permanente, the Alicia Patterson Foundation, Julie Fluno and the Fluno family, the McGraw Fellowship for Business Journalism, the National Association of Black Journalists (NABJ), Nat and Simon Olson and the Olson family, the Logan Nonfiction Program fellowship, the Harlem Family Institute, the Rosalynn Carter Fellowship for Mental Health Journalism at the Carter Center, the O'Brien Fellowship in Public Service Journalism at Marquette University, Ancestry.com, Mapping Prejudice, American Public Media, the "What Happened in Alabama?" and "Marketplace" teams, and the *Wall Street Journal*. My appreciation also extends to the additional editors, interviewees, experts, readers, mentors, and organizations that have supported this and my other works. I extend my heartfelt gratitude to cherished mentors who, though no longer with us, continue to inspire me from beyond: the late Jeff Zaslow, Cathy Panagoulias, Lucette Lagnado, William F. Buckley, Nat Hentoff, and Jim Brown.

A profound thank you to my Lord and Savior, Jesus Christ. Also, the cherished inner circle in my private life—my dearest, closest loved ones, my beloved family members (especially those who gave of their time and sat for interviews), friends, and colleagues. Your belief in me and unwavering support, always offered from the shadows of discretion, fortify me daily. It's within this sanctuary of mutual respect, privacy, and protection that I find my strength. Without your encouragement and faithful presence, thriving would be beyond my reach.

LEE HAWKINS is a distinguished journalist, musician, and series creator who was a finalist for the Pulitzer Prize in 2022. His most recent work documents the lives of Black American descendants of slavery and Jim Crow survivors, exploring the intergenerational impact of racial violence and racism on their families. His reporting delves into the effects of adverse childhood experiences and trauma, highlighting long-term impacts on health and life expectancy.

Hawkins also covers various aspects of entrepreneurship and corporate and investment worlds, focusing on the generational effects of economic discrimination, including racial covenants, land theft, and economically motivated historical homicides affecting families of color.

For nineteen years, he was a reporter at the *Wall Street Journal*, where he was a lead reporter on a series about the Tulsa Massacre of 1921, making him a Pulitzer Prize finalist in 2022. His work has been supported by numerous academic institutions and nonprofit organizations, including the Carter Center's Rosalynn Carter Fellowship for Mental Health Journalism, the Alicia Patterson Foundation Journalism Fellowship, the McGraw Fellowship for Business Journalism, the Logan Nonfiction Fellowship, the O'Brien Fellowship for Public Service Journalism, and the USC Annenberg Center for Health Journalism National Fellowship for reporting on child well-being.

Hawkins is a five-time winner of the National Association of Black Journalists' Salute to Excellence Award. He was the creator, executive producer, and host of the series *What Happened in Alabama?* in collaboration with American Public Media, where he also serves as a special correspondent to *Marketplace*, focusing primarily on business topics.

He resides in New York City.